RETURN
TO
EARTH

RETURN TO EARTH

Colonel Edwin E. "Buzz" Aldrin, Jr., 1930-
with Wayne Warga

Random House, New York

To Charlie, Sam and Joan

Whose place I took
Who took my place
While she stood by me
always . . .

RETURN
TO
EARTH

There was a jolt as the small drogue chutes opened, rather like a rough landing on a bumpy runway. I took a quick look out the window, then settled back to wait. Minutes later, three bright orange-and-white-striped main chutes opened, jerking us like puppets against our couches, and we slowed down considerably. We were, it seemed, in a state of suspended slow motion.

We floated down through a bank of stratocumulus clouds as big and lush as the ocean they covered. The change was impressive. I had become so accustomed to seeing the starkness of space, where there is no haze and where delineations are quite sharp, that the sensation of looking out on a hazy early morning on earth was a welcome change. I could see the ocean below, and as I looked at it, I sniffed to smell it. Not yet.

The sensation caused by the change of scenery pales beside the sensation of getting used to the fact of weight. For a number of minutes, movement is an effort. Arms, which had floated before, now hung heavily and had to be willed to movement. Legs, which are about as necessary to space travel as an appendix is to a body, stirred to activity by threatening not to function at all.

We landed with all the grace of an old freight elevator. Air Boss had announced to us that the wave height was between three and four feet, but it looked more like thirteen or fourteen. And it felt like it too. Our chutes, tilting in the wind, brought us in at one angle, and the moon, governor of the tides, sent a wave our way from an opposing angle. With an enormous thwack, as jarring as it was noisy, we landed. Before the impact, my hand rested on circuit breakers which, when pushed in, would enable Mike to jettison our chutes. After impact, my hand was jammed painfully down beside me. All of us grunted in distress; I grabbed the circuit breakers and Mike jettisoned the chutes.

The *Apollo* spacecraft is a marvel of engineering. It is totally life-supporting, a miniplanet containing all facilities necessary for maintaining life. It also floats, whether right side up or upside down. There is no way to determine which way you'll end up after landing, especially in a good wind and a delayed chute jettison.

It brings a smile now, but at the time, it wasn't quite so amusing. There we were, officially taking our position in the history books of mankind, floating upside down in the Pacific Ocean. It was July 24, 1969. The water was dark green and unfriendly, but its mist seeping in smelled good.

We bobbed around for seven minutes, the amount of time it takes the floatbag motors to pump air into the floatbags—three little balloons—which would turn us upright.

"Air Boss, *Apollo 11*. Everyone okay inside. Our checklist is complete. Awaiting swimmers," Neil radioed.

Air Boss came right on and told us three swimmers were already in the water, and our flotation collar would be attached in less than two minutes.

It was over. No exclamations, no slaps on the back. No handshakes. All that would come later, at least the handshakes. We sat in silence, three men alone together with their private thoughts. The reverie seemed to last much longer than it actually did. I spent most of it convincing myself not to be seasick, and so, it turned out later, did Mike and Neil. It was one thing to land upside down (we got ourselves upright before the world watched us on television), it would be quite another to scramble out of the spacecraft tossing our cookies all over the place.

The flotation collar was fit into place, the hatch flew open and three gray-green biological isolation garments were thrown in. They came from one of the water rescue team men: a navy frogman, also wearing an isolation garment topped by a face mask with a filter on the side of it. He looked weird, right out of Jules Verne. But he still looked like a human being.

The isolation suits were like rubberized flying suits except that the zipper ran diagonally from lower left to upper right. A hood was attached, with a visor and a filter for breathing. You could talk, but the sound was muffled, and you could hear, but the information was garbled. As soon as we had our suits on, we put on Mae West life preservers and crawled out of the spacecraft into the rubber raft bobbing alongside the flotation collar. The suits were supposedly tested and airtight, yet minutes later moisture was seeping in and it was sticky and uncomfortable.

One of the frogmen helped us to stumble into the raft and another was right there with us from then on. Waves started rolling and splashing us, causing the hatch to slam into the head of one of the frogmen. He weaved for a moment as we all moved to catch him, but he recovered quickly and motioned us back down. Another handed us scrubbing cloths and detergent with which we had to thoroughly douse ourselves twice—once with one cleansing substance, the second with another, all to counteract any contamination we might have brought from the moon. One by one we finished and were motioned to the other end of the raft, where we sat down and waited. The cloths we had used to scrub ourselves were tied to weights and dropped into the ocean. It was all conducted as a solemn ritual, as if it had been done through the ages. There were virtually no words spoken, partly because it was difficult to speak and understand through the suits but mostly because four helicopters hovered noisily above us.

I had begun to feel queasy inside the spacecraft, and bobbing around in the raft caused more rumblings in my stomach. I breathed deep; the cool air felt good, even though filtered. I looked about the raft for anything I could, if necessary, improvise into a motion-sickness bag. I had forgotten about the special plastic bag in my pocket. Activity is a great cure for incipient seasickness—I was still looking when I realized I now felt fine. We sat there for what seemed to be an eternity. It was only fifteen minutes, but being idle was distinctly foreign, and I kept glancing up, waiting for the helicopter to start down to pick us up. We communicated by a kind of improvised sign language, and I, for one, wondered how many people were watching us. The aircraft carrier USS *Hornet* was now in view, less than a quarter of a mile away, and I developed a sudden craving for a razor, shaving cream, and hot water. I wanted to feel presentable even though nobody could tell whether I was or not because of the isolation garment. The president of the United States and a lot of television cameras were waiting on the *Hornet*.

A Billy Pugh basket appeared from one of the helicopters and began dropping down in our direction. The Billy Pugh basket, named for its inventor, is a practical plastic and metal scooplike object which can literally scoop people right out of the water. I was second up in it, and during the ride, which lasted about two minutes, I had a peculiar feeling of loss. It wasn't until I glanced down that I could understand the feeling. Down in the water was *Columbia*, our spacecraft: small, compact, and a virtual extension of each of us. Now we were leaving. It had done its work and we had no more use for it. We had shed it, discarded our cocoon. It seemed small and helpless, yet minutes before it had represented safety and security.

I scrambled into the helicopter and the first person I saw was Bill Carpentier, a short, wiry, and humorous doctor from Canada who was a paramedic. If one of us had been injured, he would have jumped directly from the helicopter into the water to treat us. Instead, he was standing in the

4

door smiling, his hand extended in greeting, the first recognizable face from what I would hereafter refer to as "before." We shook hands and he helped me out of the bulky Mae West.

Mike was walking around the inside of the helicopter, stopping now and then to do a deep knee bend and I started around behind him. We were both unsteady, trying to make legs that felt like rubber function on a floor slick with salt water. Neil scrambled in next and grinned when he saw us pacing and bending around. He took a few unsteady steps and sat down, fastening his seat belt. He shot us a glance, a communication which we understood without his speaking. He was giving us Neil Armstrong's rumored philosophy about exercise: "I am allotted just so many heartbeats in a lifetime and I'm not going to use any more than necessary at any time." Since Mike and I were frequent and enthusiastic exercisers, Neil was advising us that we were using up valuable heartbeats.

But I wanted to get my legs working and steady. After all, in a few minutes I would be stepping out of the helicopter to be greeted by the president and I preferred, if at all possible, not to fall on my ass in the process. It seemed a rather undignified possibility.

On the flight to the carrier we continued to exercise. The ride lasted about fifteen minutes and at the end I still felt unsteady, though much improved. We fastened our seat belts to land, and once we touched down on the flight deck and waited for the elevator to take the helicopter below deck, we paced and bent some more.

Just before we left the helicopter we ripped the *Apollo 11* insignias off the isolation garments and handed them to the helicopter crew. It was spontaneous and a way of saying thanks.

The helicopter door opened and, with Neil leading, we walked down the ramp. I noticed that Neil instantly gripped the handrail on the stairs and the next thing I knew I was hanging on too.

There was a lack of reality about everything, a kind of euphoric strangeness to all that was going on. The plastic face mask was such that I had no peripheral vision and it tended to fog up slightly. I could hear music from the band but it was somehow delayed.

There was only one opportunity to do anything as we left the helicopter and I suddenly realized that nothing had been planned, nothing rehearsed or discussed as just about every other thing had been. I wanted somehow to convey a greeting and convince whoever was looking on that though we probably looked absurd, we felt just fine, thanks. We waved and walked the short distance along a red carpet to what was officially called the Mobile Quarantine Facility (which was a big mobile home purchased at a trailer show and refitted for our use). John Hirasaki, the engineer in charge of the trailer and the second familiar face from before, held the door. John, Bill Carpentier, and the three of us would remain together in the quarantine trailer until we were in permanent quarters back in Houston.

The first thing we did on board the *Hornet* in our trailer was lock the doors, close the draw curtains on the windows, and take off the isolation garments. One by one we lined up for a rather hurried set of medical measurements: blood pressure, temperature, respiration, and heart rate. It took just a few minutes and then we headed for the showers. Or rather shower. There was only one, a condition causing momentary dismay, but after eight days, five more minutes didn't hurt much and I waited for my turn.

I did, however, become irritated when I started to dress and found a pair of baggy boxer shorts instead of the jockey shorts I had requested; I had anticipated returning to the amenities of earthbound living and now there was the slight irritation because it wasn't right. Before Bill Carpentier had been deployed for the recovery some ten days before the launch, we had given him the personal items we wanted on board, along with a list of supplies (booze, mostly).

Once shaved and dressed in a loose and comfortable flying suit—with sneakers, not the customary boots—I quickly explored the quarantine home. There was lots of blond wood and the upholstery was predominantly blue. Double-deck bunks lined either side of the long hallway, and there was a pullman kitchen and conversation area with a table that could be used for eating or work, but opened out into an area for physical examinations. In the bathroom, which was located in the front of the trailer and to one side, there was a window. While Mike and Neil finished dressing, I pulled back the drapery enough to see what was going on outside. I could see that they were constructing a plastic tunnel leading to a larger enclosed area which before long would contain the spacecraft. We were in the *Hornet's* cavernous hangar bay.

The next order of business was a conversation with President Nixon, who had flown halfway around the world for the splashdown. A microphone was rigged up just outside the trailer, close by the main window, and we took our places behind the window and had our first encounter with the priorities of protocol, the president, and the odd construction of trailers. We couldn't look out the window unless we were kneeling or seated, but we figured that the president would understand. We didn't know that the national anthem would be played at the start of the ceremonies and that three astronauts would stand up and present three crotches to the world. Since the zippers could be opened from either end, we had only to glance down to check our flies; this was fortunate because using our hands for a quick check would have been observed by a good part of the television audience. We sat down as soon as possible, checking to be sure we were correctly zipped up.

President Nixon was clearly enthusiastic. He danced a kind of jig when he greeted us through the window and then went on to announce that our safe return concluded the greatest week since creation. It was only a matter of time before he would be reminded that there once was a fellow named Jesus Christ—reminded by editorial writers and cartoonists around the world. Because of my state of mind those first several hours back on earth, I didn't realize what he had said until I read it in a newspaper several days later.

For our part, we had had no time to prepare any remarks; so we kept up a steady flow of "Yes, sir" and "Thank you, sir."

The president also remarked about Mike's mustache, something about its having grown under rather unusual circumstances. The subject of promotions came up, as it invariably and obliquely does after every space flight. Neil was a civilian and I was already a full colonel; so I deferred to Lieutenant Colonel Mike Collins, who not many days later became Colonel Mike Collins.

When it was my turn to speak, I requested a moment of silence to pay tribute to Gus Grissom, Roger Chaffee, and Ed White, who had become to us symbols of the sacrifice put into space travel. They had given their lives in a flash fire in the first *Apollo* spacecraft two years earlier. The moment was observed and the president, after telling us he'd be seeing us soon at the White House, was gone.

There were more medical examinations, one of which was not the most restful activity for guys as tired as we were. One by one we were checked on an ergometer, which looks like an exercycle except that it gets progressively harder to pedal during the eighteen minutes we each rode it with our noses clipped shut and a breathing device in our mouths. The ergometer provides a fairly thorough check of your physical condition at any given moment; it gives a vital clue of the extent of deterioration during a period of weightlessness. The check was repeated twenty-four hours later and the results were that our deterioration was typical and our bodies were returning to normal.

By the time our exams were completed, the president was in the air on his way home and the USS *Hornet* plus three was steaming toward Honolulu. And John Hirasaki was on his way to the kitchen, reappearing a few minutes later with a tray of glasses and ice, offering us a choice of Scotch, bourbon, or gin. Scotch, with ice and water applied as one applies vermouth to a martini, was what I had. Dinner a few hours later was steak with more of the same liquid refreshment. Nobody drank too much, but everyone slept very well indeed.

Before we had gone to bed for the night, Bill Carpentier had helped us compute a schedule for waking and sleeping. In space we remained on the same time schedule as Houston, and the decision was that the six hours lost by traveling east from Honolulu back to Houston could keep us on schedule—provided we didn't start sleeping late. The next morning we did sleep late and kept right on taking our leisure until we were totally off schedule but more and more rested.

The spacecraft *Columbia*, looking somewhat the worse for wear with its scars from the heat of reentry and a good dunking, was at our side. After breakfast we left the trailer and went through the plastic tunnel to the spacecraft where, more because of training than necessity at this point, we began straightening things up. We took the boxes of lunar rocks out of the back wall of the spacecraft, and John placed them in a special sterilization mechanism. From there they were put on a plane and flown to Houston.

More than anything, I wanted the pleasure of doing nothing for a while, a desire shared by both Mike and Neil. We played hearts, read a little, and eventually Mike and Neil began a marathon gin rummy game, which would endure through the weeks of isolation. I played some solitaire but mostly tried to think about nothing in particular. The enormity of it all was beginning to occur to me. I had often thought of it before, and Neil and I had talked about it off

9

and on during training. But there was something different about it now: the trip was over, the goal accomplished, and so much time and effort had been put into it. Before, thoughts had been focused on the technical achievement ahead of us. All that precise work was now done and behind us. It would take a couple of years for it to become clear to me, but that day on the USS *Hornet* was actually the start of the trip to the unknown. I had known what to expect on the unknown moon more than I did on the familiar earth.

That afternoon there were ceremonies officially welcoming us aboard the *Hornet*. The captain and the chaplain officiated and we were presented with plaques and a set of mugs. Earlier we had been given hats with our names, flight, and carrier embossed on them. The chaplain conducted a service of thanksgiving. We then officiated from our trailer at the reenlistment of four *Hornet* crew members, giving them their oath and congratulating them. I signed their orders as the reenlistment officer. There was also a large cake especially decorated for the occasion and the traditional sword for cutting it. Because of quarantine precautions, we weren't allowed any cake, although food was sent in through the air lock sterilizer. Neil acted as our spokesman and thanked the crew for their excellent recovery work. When it was all over, somebody in the mobile quarantine— I don't remember who it was and we never did agree on who said it first—innocently remarked, "And now it begins."

We were on the *Hornet* two nights. On the morning of the third day, we steamed into Pearl Harbor for our first solid ground in more than a week. And our first ceremony on solid ground.

Just after we were hoisted from the carrier, Admiral John S. McCain, Jr., commander of the Pacific forces, stopped for a chat through the rear window. He is a short, wiry man who has a reputation for being a bit salty and always going directly to the subject at hand. He looked at us, smiled, and said, "You lucky sons of bitches. I'd have given anything to go with you." Admiral McCain is also as honest as he is direct.

The quarantine trailer was by now on a flatbed truck which backed directly up to a platform containing a somewhat more subdued Admiral McCain, various dignitaries, press, and a crowd of some two thousand people. From one of the windows of the trailer I could see a broomstick flying from the mast of the *Hornet*, the symbol of a mission well done.

With the perspective of hundreds of ceremonies and a number of years, the ceremonies that day in Honolulu have become a pleasant memory. The enthusiasm was genuine, the elation was real on both sides of the trailer window; and there we were, three goldfish maybe, but we were safe goldfish.

From Pearl Harbor we traveled on the truck bed to Hickam Field. It was a long trip because we hardly exceeded ten miles an hour all the way. Mike and I couldn't understand why we traveled so slowly and though we asked a number of times, no one could tell us why with any degree of certainty. Somebody somewhere had made the decision and that was that. Along the way there were crowds at various places, and all the way to Hickam a young boy, who we were told had at one time had polio or some other crippling disease, ran along beside the truck. His name and address were communicated to the trailer and John Hirasaki put his name on the autographing list. Quiet, efficient John kept the list of names to whom we'd send pictures. We autographed pictures and first-day covers whenever we had spare time. It became a kind of escape, a way of not thinking too much about the long isolation and debriefing ahead or about the unknowns beyond that. To be sure, there were many people to thank. So many that I am still signing pictures, even though we signed what seemed like thousands during the first few weeks.

Once inside Hickam, we moved quickly and efficiently to a C-141 starlifter, a giant transport jet. The isolation trailer rolled into its belly and then we were in the air on our way to Houston. Inside the spacecraft we had not felt particularly cramped, but the trailer was confining and the feeling was increased by its being enclosed in the starlifter. We could barely see out the trailer windows to the plane windows. There was space around the trailer for three or four people to stand. Some of the rescue crew was on board the plane along with some of the NASA recovery team. Our watches were set on Houston time, the time schedule for the entire trip. But by now time made no sense. In Houston it was the cocktail hour; so we obliged most agreeably. We were supposed to arrive at roughly midnight Houston time.

We touched down in Houston, sat back, and waited to roll onto another flatbed truck. We waited and waited and waited. If the loading at Hickam Field had been smooth and quick, the off-loading at Ellington Air Force Base was anything but. First one method of getting onto the truck bed failed, then another wouldn't work, and finally, on the third try in more than an hour, we bumped and swayed down onto the truck bed and were driven slowly into a brightly lit area and backed up window-first to another platform. Bill Carpentier couldn't resist: "They can send men safely to the moon and back, but they can't get the men off their airplane." We smiled.

Louis Welch, mayor of Houston, was there along with several thousand other people. Robert Gilruth, the stately director of the Manned Spacecraft Center, spoke in his characteristic halting way about his genuine pleasure. There were television cameras everywhere.

Four other important people were there, although I had to do a bit of looking to find them. Joan, with Mike, Jan, and Andy, thirteen, eleven, and ten at the time, had steered off to the side, since they had spent the last many days in the glare of television lights and the peering gaze of many people. They looked ill at ease and no wonder. They had been given several arrival times and, once finally advised and reassured, had come to Ellington only to arrive two hours ahead of me. After that they spent better than an hour watching us being unloaded.

Small red telephones were hooked up to the trailer during the ceremonies and we were allowed to speak to our families. It was a nervous, hesitant series of conversations and not at all private, but as private as could be in such circumstances. I don't remember any revelations in the short talks with my kids, but I do remember asking my youngest son how he was doing in school only to be told, "Daddy, it's summer vacation." Jan and Mike spoke with me briefly, Mike's agony somewhat more evident because his voice was starting to change. And then came the first words with my wife: "Joan, would you bring me some jockey shorts tomorrow morning?"

"Oh, thank God," she said and started crying. After that we just looked at each other for a minute.

By 1:30 A.M., we were moving slowly along NASA Road 1 on our way to the Manned Spacecraft Center and there were still people in the street waving to us. It was nearly 2:30 A.M. when we arrived at the Lunar Receiving Laboratory and it took a while for the trailer to be sealed to the side of the lab before the door opened and we entered our new quarters.

The quarantines have since been discontinued, but for this first experience various scientific organizations had gotten together and set down various rules. It was extremely remote that any germs could survive the lunar environment, but it was generally considered that if there were any germs, they might thrive fairly well in the earth's fertile environment. There was also interest in testing to see if any toxic properties had somehow made their way back with us. The air-conditioning system inside the laboratory maintained a pressure lower than outside so that air was always coming in and none of it escaped without traveling through a number of filters and pumps before reentering the outside world. All of the precautions were explained to us so that we wouldn't think it was just a bunch of Mickey Mouse thinking, but whenever the opportunity arose, one or the other of us would poke fun at the NASA engineers who supervised the quarantine. They met their sealed-off Waterloo several days later when a stream of red ants appeared in the kitchen and proceeded to grow steadily in numbers. We happily kept them well informed about our visitors.

In the Lunar Receiving Laboratory our number grew: two cooks, a photographer, a NASA public relations man, another doctor who was a lab specialist, and a man who took care of the janitorial duties. After that, the number continued to grow whenever there was the possibility of somebody being contaminated. One man came in because his glove ripped while he was holding a moon rock, and a photo technician accidentally put his hand on one of the film magazines with lunar dust on it. After he had his picture taken showing his dusty finger, he came to live with us. Each new arrival was required to wear a sterile mask for the first day.

We were an all-male group until just before Neil's birthday on August 5, when a young woman assistant in some of the rock analyses was involved in a spill, put on her mask, and joined us. It caused quite a stir in the press at the time and became somewhat of a joke within the lab—especially when she was assigned to the room adjoining Mike's. It turned out after her arrival that there was, well, something questionable about her contamination. The quarantined area had a special phone for families to call in and our lady arrival had not so much as entered when she got a telephone call from her boyfriend. We were all suspicious, but remained cordial and made no comment on the matter. Yet we couldn't help speculating: How did he get the number?

Did she give it to him? Had she expected to be contaminated in advance?

Since we fell into this humorous little intrigue as though Sherlock Holmes would soon be helping, it must be clear that the three weeks of quarantine became increasingly boring and confining.

The lab had dormitory bedrooms for the people working there, plus separate private rooms for the three of us and the doctors. There was a kitchen, dining area, and a large living room recreation area where we could watch television and, in the evenings, show movies. Two pictures that evoked considerable audience response, mostly negative, were one starring Raquel Welch as a man-eating Spanish revolutionary and another in which three sex-starved women imprison a virile young man in their attic and then proceed to wear him out.

The major project was our debriefing. It was divided into two parts, the written and the taped. The taped sessions were conducted with the three of us sitting in a room that resembled a control booth in a television studio. Outside the angled glass wall sat various people, all with questions to ask and information needs to be fulfilled. Our crew trainer would be there one day, the men on the next Apollo mission another, then all of the astronauts. We always knew well in advance what subject was going to be covered; so it was relatively easy to prepare for the sessions and, for me, much more pleasurable than the written reports. We hunkered into easy chairs around a rectangular table and our conversation came through a loudspeaker in the next room.

For the written section I labored long and mightily, as is customary with me. Mike handled most of the command module stuff and Neil the earth lift-off, while I specialized in the rendezvous exercises. Neil and I worked at length and in considerable detail on the lunar surface activities.

We were also under constant medical observation, and

of the three of us I was the most carefully watched. The day after we had started our isolation my temperature had risen and remained at one or two degrees above normal. No reason could be found, and by the end of the three weeks isolation there was some discussion that I stay on after the others had left. I set out to convince Bill Carpentier this wasn't necessary and that I wasn't bothered by it at all. Finally I got on the phone to the star-struck Chuck Berry, "the astronauts' physician," and convinced him I was feeling swell. Actually, I wasn't bothered at all, but I was puzzled and suspected it was connected with the pervading apprehension of being confined and unsure of what was yet to come. I decided exercise would help; so after the debriefing ended in the afternoon, Mike and I would jog around the halls. My temperature still didn't go down and, in fact, remained above average for the next several months, through our cross-country tour and throughout the round-the-world trip. By the time it started down, I was going along with it. When my personal odyssey was over, the temperature returned to normal and has stayed there.

Joan has since told me that she too was quite concerned about my temperature and also by the fact that I was constantly complaining about having too little to do. About this time, priorities began to mix themselves. The jogging became an excuse for not working on my written report, and nights I'd spend mostly awake, tossing and turning. I began to notice that I was well off my normal speed. No one else noticed, or if they did, it was never mentioned to me. I have a picture taken during one of the debriefing sessions which to me is an accurate representation of how I felt at the time. Everyone else appears relaxed and there I am—eyes wide and looking frightened.

As we had been doing since we were in the trailer, the three of us spent a portion of each day signing pictures and autographing envelopes with commemorative mention of space flights. This was long before first-day covers became a controversy abruptly jolting a few careers. Telegrams and bags of mail arrived daily and after we looked at it we piled it in various places. There was a great deal of tedium to our activities by this time, but we tried to be good-natured about it.

As was expected of each of us, I dutifully filled out an expense account for the trip. "From Houston, Tex., to Cape Kennedy, Fla., to the Moon, to the Pacific Ocean to Hawaii and return to Houston, Tex.," was how it read. How we traveled was by "Government Aircraft, Government Spacecraft, USN Hornet, USAF Plane." Total expense reimbursement: $33.31. This amount took care of mileage in and around Cape Kennedy during the time immediately prior to lift-off. The expense account is one of my most treasured souvenirs of the trip and sits framed in a place of honor in my study.

Early in the debriefing we dealt with more routine matters such as food. In a word, nit-picking. We had a slight problem on our flight which others had had, but the food advisers felt it had been rectified. Not quite. As we prepared our food we had to put a special filter on the end of our water gun before mixing water with the food. The filter was supposed to lessen the amount of hydrogen we consumed by releasing it into the cabin air instead of into our food. Instead, the hydrogen went directly into us and, naturally, did what hydrogen does to anybody: it caused flatulence and, in our cramped quarters, considerable fragrance.

These debriefings were transcribed and circulated to all people involved in the mission. Naturally, the food people would tend to read the food debriefing while, say, the radiation people would tend to ignore it. At the time, I was unaware that anything was ignored. I thought everyone read it all.

As I labored my way through the food debriefing, I remembered being hungry for a snack one night while I was nestled in my hammock. And then I remembered something I thought important. I recalled seeing light flashes not unlike sparkles during several nights of the trip. I discussed the phenomenon briefly. I thought the experience unique. It sure as hell turned out to be unique.

Within two days I was sitting around wondering why nobody came back to ask additional questions. I knew it was a weird subject, but it wasn't *that* weird. Finally, I decided to call the radiation people. The radiation people were traveling and weren't expected back for a week. The next day at a management debriefing I brought the flashes up again. Management was definitely interested and work began that afternoon.

I had first seen the flashes during two of the nights on the way to the moon. When we slept, the spacecraft was quite dark and the windows were shaded. I thought nothing of the flashes the first night, and the second, I sleepily wondered if they were of any importance. The first time was somewhat like an animated cartoon where someone gets hit on the head and little stars appear in their vision. There would be a brief flash, then nothing. Occasionally there was a streak, not unlike a tiny meteor streak, and another time there was a double flash.

On another night, en route to earth, I saw them again and it jogged my memory. In fact, I had all but forgotten my earlier sightings. I had been thinking then of the moon, and now that part of the trip was over. I wondered if either Neil or Mike had seen anything like it, but they had not mentioned it.

"Hey, you guys seen anything peculiar? Like little flashes at night when all the lights are down and the covers are on the windows?"

Both looked at me blankly.

"Well, look, this is the last night before reentry. Why don't you take a look to see if you see any of these things."

Next morning not a word was said. I finally asked Mike if he had seen anything. He had not. I asked Neil.

"Yeah. Saw about a hundred of them."

"What do you suppose they were?"

"I dunno."

At the debriefing I said that at night I could open my eyes and wait and eventually there would be a little flash. Eventually, I'd go back to sleep. My immediate analysis was that tiny particles of some sort were penetrating the spacecraft and I was seeing the ionization caused by the atmosphere of the spacecraft. I next tried to figure out whether the phenomena had any orientation with the position of the sun, and could find none.

Eventually a great deal of speculation was going on. I questioned the *Apollo* 8 crew, Frank Borman, Jim Lovell, and Bill Anders, because they had made exactly the same trip as we had but without a moon landing. They had seen nothing.

It turns out that the phenomenon of "flicker-flash," as it is now called, is rather subjective. Some people have a tendency to see them and others don't, and what little research there is indicates that seeing them has to do with the desire to see them.

At the time I saw them, I had naturally believed I had to open my eyes to see them. The crew of *Apollo* 12 returned and all three said they had not only seen them, they had seen them with their eyes shut. What's more, they could tell whether they were seeing them through either the left eye or the right.

It turned out these particles not only penetrated in and out of the spacecraft, but they penetrated through our helmets and our heads as well. It is still unknown if what we see is a secondary emission—a high energy particle imparting energy to something else—or if it is the actual flash caused when the particle penetrates our retinas. Whichever it is, the particle travels through the head, exits, and continues on through the helmet and out of the spacecraft. There is no physical sensation connected with it at all; it is strictly a visual impression.

Some scientists announced recently that in the future flicker-flash might cause blindness during long space flights. They claim that the flashes not only destroy a brain cell or two but also make it impossible for other cells not destroyed to function properly. They surmise that the blindness, if it occurred, would not appear for quite a few years after a long-duration flight to a place as far away as Mars.

The particles themselves do not go through the Van Allen belts surrounding the earth. The Van Allen belts are magnetic belts reaching down to about two hundred and fifty miles above the South Atlantic and extending to about thirty-five thousand miles above the earth. Because they are magnetic, they trap nearly all of the cosmic radiation coming toward the earth.

If there was a totally engrossing part of the debriefing, this was it. It began with a casual observation buried in the food report and continued to grow. It is still growing—I often see in the newspapers articles discussing the results of further research.

During the debriefings, particularly when the controversy over flicker-flashes continued to grow, Neil began to look doubtful and annoyed whenever the flashes were discussed. I had always envied his facility with words and his ability to give a speech, but now I sensed he was annoyed by my discussions about this phenomenon. I suspect it was an inevitable thing, but I'm certain it was nothing either of us had ever contemplated. We had been the back-up crew on *Apollo 8* and had become drinking buddies. Our friendship was casual and respectful and, as friends often have, we had something going for us: a total and enthusiastic immersion in our work. When the feeling finally became apparent to me in the Lunar Receiving Lab, I quickly suppressed it. It struck me as an emotional and unscientific thing to feel, and human feelings weren't in keeping with the image we had as scientists and astronauts. In addition, Neil, being the flight commander, often functioned as our spokesman. Whenever it would expedite matters or save time, instead of the three of us giving speeches, Neil would speak for all of us, and that was fine with me.

This kind of tension simmered for the next few weeks but never surfaced. Mike, though he was undoubtedly aware of what was happening, remained his amiable and somewhat easygoing self. Although it was never stated officially, it went without saying that rivalries or arguments within the astronaut corps were not discussed in public because it would tarnish both our image as individuals and the image of the space program.

While we were in the Lunar Receiving Laboratory, another decision was formulated by the three of us. We had by now concluded that we would be together continually for at least six months and possibly a year. A cross-country trip was scheduled and we had been told a world tour was being negotiated. The requests for appearances and award ceremonies had grown to epidemic proportions. Obviously, it would be some time before we would be back in what we had come to call the "astronaut business."

Deke Slayton, who was then chief of the astronauts, appeared one day and suggested we give some thought to whether or not we wanted to return to the program or be taken off space-flying status. Deke had to start processing new crews; at that time there were missions scheduled up to *Apollo* 20 and the three of us could possibly have been available for one of the last two, but we would also have to serve as a back-up crew once again—a requirement. Then would come the years of Skylab.

It occurred to me that for several months prior to any flight on which I might serve as either a prime crew member or a back-up crew member, I would be taken off all speaking tours or public appearances. It was a routine procedure and certainly one I agreed with. In fact, I liked it. But was it worth it? The training for back-up is no different than for prime and it would be long and arduous. Besides, I had been on the first lunar landing and what could I possible do to improve on that?

There were other considerations as well. Other men were in training and naturally wanted a chance to fly. Although it seemed to me at the time that there were already too many astronauts for the various flights, no one agreed with me. The corps has since thinned out noticeably and yet there is still a problem of plenty.

Concern for others waiting to travel in space may sound slightly altruistic and overly noble, but it seemed a genuine concern at the time. The goal of every astronaut had always been to fly, and now the goal was enlarged to include going to the moon. There were also selfish motives involved and I admit to them. A major one was that I wanted to command. I had never been a commander in space and if I was to go again, I wanted to go as a commander. Any other capacity would be a disappointment to me.

The three of us discussed our future infrequently in the laboratory and one by one we reached our decisions. Mike reached his first: from the time he had been assigned to the *Apollo 11* crew he had intended to complete his mission and then quit flying, and possibly even leave the space program.

If my nights had been fairly sleepless before, they were now even more so. It is my nature to deliberate long and in detail before making any decision—large or small. It can even be said that I can and do think myself into a corner on occasion. This was nearly one of those times. So intense had been my motivation and our training that for years it seemed that I had been immersed in just one project: going to the moon. I had often given casual thought about what to do next, but the involvement with what was still ahead was simply too consuming. It was quite obvious what lay ahead in the immediate future, but I was only thirty-nine and had a lifetime still before me.

The tilt finally seemed in favor of no more space trips. How could I catch up once I managed to get myself off the banquet and speaking circuit? For the past eight years, first at MIT and later at NASA, I had been totally immersed in astronautics.

It was never actually stated by anyone, but it was becoming obvious that what was expected of us was public visibility and not a return to the immersions of training. The great coup had been completed, the space program was once again the delight of nearly all Americans, and we had an experience to share with millions of people, all of whom appeared very curious indeed. We had, in effect, a duty to perform, a duty for both our government and NASA. We were to become public relations men for space exploration—in a sense, salesmen. Though the word made me terribly uncomfortable and self-conscious when it was first used—and whether or not it was true—we were said to be heroes of the greatest technological achievement yet accomplished by man. The final implication was obvious: heroes have duties. They are public property, however reluctant they might feel.

I kept one prerogative to myself. I decided not to communicate it officially until after I had had a taste of public life. If it was unbearable, I would have the choice to reenter the program, and I said so at the time, since reentering would give me valuable time: time to disappear from the public view.

All deliberations subsequently proved unnecessary. Life changed dramatically and irreversibly. It would be nearly three years later, when, as a patient at the Lackland Air Force Base Hospital in San Antonio, Texas, I found myself standing one night looking at a ripe full moon presiding over a clear cool sky, that the experience could come full circle to a new beginning. What I said to myself was simple enough: "You've been to the moon. You did it. First. It cannot be done again, not by you, not by anyone else. Now get the hell out of here and live the kind of life you want." But getting to that moment proved to be one long and torturous journey.

On Sunday, August 10, 1969, the quarantine ended at 9:00 P.M., somewhat earlier than announced, so that we could have a private evening with our families.

Mike, Neil, and I separated for what seemed like the first time in an eternity. We were each driven home separately in the back seat of a NASA staff car. As soon as we pulled out of the headquarters gate, a television crew pulled up behind us. Still another crew, along with reporters and photographers, waited on the front lawn of 18622 Carriage Court, Nassau Bay, Texas.

I ran for the door, which flew open at exactly the right moment, and slammed shut the instant I was inside. Joan stepped out from behind it and threw her arms around me. "Not here! They can see!" We stepped into the living room and there, standing silently, were our three offspring. They looked frightened and apprehensive. We all were.

2

Home felt good because it was home and it was unchanged.

The main order of business for that first Monday was to buy me a new suit. The cross-country tour was to be Wednesday and I needed a new suit. We got up, ate a large breakfast, read the papers, and got dressed. Then the Italian invasion started.

As a matter of courtesy, the members of the press who had been occupying the front lawns of our homes for the past weeks had agreed to depart until we set out on the trip. We were grateful and sufficiently innocent to believe that everybody would indeed be gone. The Italian *paparazzi,* those famous fellows who make life all but impossible for celebrities in Rome, had no intention of leaving.

"Daddy, there's a car parked out in front. There are men in it," my daughter announced in her most conspiratorial voice.

"Just ignore them, they'll go away."

"That's what you think," she replied.

Minutes later the doorbell rang. The Italian gentlemen wanted to take some pictures and talk briefly. I explained politely that this was impossible and that all requests for interviews had to be cleared with NASA. I was so polite that I said National Aeronautics and Space Administration instead of the acronym NASA. They went back to their car.

"Daddy, they're still there."

"That's okay. We'll ignore them."

"That's what you think," Joan parroted.

Joan and I hopped into the car for the drive into Houston and a new suit. Joan was going to pick up the suits she had ordered for the boys because they would be going on the trip too. She had already bought a new dress for Jan.

Sure enough, the Italians hopped into their car and took off behind us. I started thinking of what a fiasco this was going to be—me getting fitted in a new suit and these guys taking pictures. I had visions of pointing my arm at them and saying, "Out!" as my pants slid down to my ankles. And, naturally, a crowd would gather and then we'd really be in trouble.

Bright idea. Instead of getting on the freeway for Houston, we'll slip into Ellington Air Force Base. The guard at the gate will stop them and we'll sneak out the back gate. I whipped into Ellington and asked the guard to keep them from coming in.

"Gee, sir, it's an open base and we can't restrict anyone. I'll have to get special permission."

"Well, can you just slow them up?"

"I'll do the best I can, Colonel Aldrin."

He did. He managed to hold them just long enough for me to break a few speeding rules on government property and get out the back gate of Ellington. Ten minutes later we were zipping down the highway past the main entrance to Ellington and there were our *paparazzi* friends standing by their car near the gate.

"That's what you think!" I shouted at Joan.

The experience seems amusing now, but at the time it was disturbing—how long would this go on? We found out later that Mike also decided he needed a new suit and had been chased through Ellington. Neil, who didn't need a new suit, went out to sit by his pool and discovered three Japanese photographers climbing over his backyard fence.

The rest of the day I spent sitting by my pool doing something at which I excel: stewing about the speeches I had to give, in this case one each in New York, Chicago, and Los

Angeles. I felt it incumbent on me to be profound. I had no doubt of my sincerity, but I felt my qualities at public speaking left something to be desired. I scribbled endless notes on three-by-five cards, filling at least one wastebasket in the process. I was drenched with sweat.

Public speaking takes practice and I was about to get plenty. Practice, in my case, may not have made me perfect, but at least I'm bearable. I'm even used to it and, on occasion, find it stimulating, but it's still not a case of step-on-my-foot-and-my-mouth-will-open.

On Tuesday I went to my office in the astronauts' office building to survey the damage. It was considerable. The outer office, where my shared secretary worked, was piled deep with mail bags. So was my office. Many letters, of course, did not call for a response, but I wanted to respond anyway. I never did get them all answered, even though we prepared a standard acknowledgment card and NASA arranged for some of the mailroom girls to help us. For at least the next two years there was a large pile of correspondence, which my secretary felt I should personally see if not acknowledge, on my desk and spilling over to the visitor's chair.

That first day I surveyed the damage and left. I went to a briefing for our cross-country trip. One suit for the day, but bring a change of shirts if you'd like. The state banquet in Los Angeles would be black-tie. The trip would last one very long day and we would go back to Houston the following morning. Babysitters would be furnished for the children during the banquet, and security agents would watch out for them in the three parades. I went home for still another attempt at speechwriting.

Late that afternoon we held our first press conference. It was conducted in the big auditorium at the Manned Spacecraft Center, and if I have any memories of it at all, they have nothing to do with what was said or done there. They are recollections of nervousness and discomfort. I knew it would last one hour and I only remember staring at the clock whenever I wasn't answering a question.

Over dinner Joan and I conducted a bit of diplomacy. We were delighted when the children had been included in the cross-country trip. It would be a long day, but it would be memorable. There was a ride in the presidential jet, not to mention parades, confetti, helicopters, all you could eat, and who could tell what else. The problem was the departure time from Houston. The Aldrin children have always been late sleepers and grumpy risers. They weren't enthusiastic about the trip because anything that began at 5:00 A.M. couldn't possibly be worth it. We convinced them it was.

At 5:00 A.M., Wednesday, August 13, on what would become a hot and humid day in Houston, New York, Chicago, and hot but not humid in Los Angeles, we boarded the presidential plane *Air Force II*. In the front of the plane were five Aldrins, five Collinses, four Armstrongs, assorted NASA public affairs and protocol poeple. In the rear was the press.

First stop, New York. I spent most of the flight to New York working on my short speech and was relieved to see that Mike and Neil were doing the same thing. None of us was prepared for what would happen. We landed at LaGuardia and were greeted by Mayor and Mrs. Lindsay. Then we boarded helicopters and flew to a pier near Wall Street. Mike, Neil, and I were put in an open convertible and a security car fell in behind us. Next came our wives, followed by another security car, a car full of children, and another security car.

Fireboats on the tip of Manhattan and up the East River were spraying the traditional water salute as we approached Wall Street and a ticker tape parade. We stopped briefly as more security men joined us to walk alongside our cars. We were advised not to reach out to shake hands because we could be pulled from the cars and couldn't be rescued easily.

And then it started. I know of no other way to describe it except to say that what came next was an immense sonic boom of emotion. Confetti flew, people screamed and waved, and we waved back. I couldn't believe it. I remember at one point tears came to my eyes. I had seen a troop of Boy Scouts, all carrying American flags, and I experienced a powerful wave of patriotism, the most patriotic feeling I had ever had in a lifetime of service to my country. I felt like saying, "Don't thank me, let me thank you."

We proceeded through the endless crowds—the parade lasted about an hour and a half—to City Hall. We were given a welcoming speech by John Lindsay and, in an order that would become a custom, we responded: first Neil, then Mike, then me. My theme for the three speeches I would give that day was that the footprints we had left on the moon were not ours but rather belonged to all mankind. This may sound like a cliché, but it is something I profoundly believed. The same message was delivered three times that day, in three different ways. Following the speeches, we were presented with keys to the city and we responded by presenting a photograph taken on the moon.

Leaving City Hall, I glanced back to see if Joan was still with us. She was. She was trying to get away from a man who had his back to me and was trying to kiss her. She looked horrified. I found out later he was one of those people all astronauts have come to loathe but endure. We met this particular man, whom I shall call Jerome Exploit-a-Buck, in Acapulco and he wanted to involve me in some business somewhere. Regardless of what the business was—I was rather inexperienced in these things at the time—upon investigation I discovered that for delivering me, a famous name that they could use in some way, he in turn would collect money or stock options.

During my entire time in the space program these people

abounded. Some astronauts became involved and prospered. Others lost money on suggested investments. A few became involved in some rather dubious ventures, more out of innocence than venality. A lucky few have ended up rich but uncomfortably beholden.

Joan could eventually sniff these people a mile away, but I was usually much slower on the uptake. This man she had loathed from the start. The security men were going to arrest him, but Joan told me later that she had said, "No, don't arrest him, but keep him away. I know him, I just don't like him."

From City Hall we drove to the United Nations, where a brief ceremony took place on the plaza. Neil gave a short speech and we were each presented with a book of stamps, commemorative stamps to the United Nations from member countries. We gave our customary photograph.

We clambered back into helicopters for the return ride to LaGuardia. This time I was with Joan. We sat down, fastened our seat belts, and when the helicopter lifted off, she was rigid. A few hours earlier she had had her first helicopter ride and had appeared to like it. I asked what was the matter, and she motioned for silence. I was starting to look around for something to use in case she was going to be sick when she grabbed my arm and through clenched teeth said: "Buzz, they forgot to shut the door. The damn helicopter door is open."

I patiently explained that a good many helicopters fly with their doors open. We were safely strapped in, weren't at all likely to fall out, and besides it was much cooler this way. I calmed her but for the rest of that day Joan sat in the far rear of whatever helicopter we were in.

The flight to Chicago consisted of lunch and more work on my speech. At one point we all agreed that the Lindsays were not only good hosts but also they were immensely likable people who excelled at putting others at their ease. No easy feat. His job was not easy either, but he was first and foremost a politician. His relations with the city police department were less than cordial, yet he waved and nodded his thanks to each of New York's finest as we drove past them.

I felt the peak had come in New York and that Chicago might be anticlimactic. We were met by police and security people and hustled immediately into a motorcade. The mayor later joined us in the city, before the parade started. The parade down Michigan Avenue and State Street was even more overwhelming than the experience on Wall Street several hours earlier. Perhaps because of its "second city" complex and the subsequent rivalry with New York or perhaps because the people of Chicago are less reserved and more demonstrative than their eastern counterparts, Chicago went wild. The city is also more open, not so many windows are sealed for air conditioning as they are in New York. Whatever it was, by the time we arrived at the massive new Civic Center, with its gigantic Picasso sculpture in the forecourt, we were covered with confetti and streamers and perspiring so much that they were glued to us. We were deaf from the shouting, and jaws ached from smiling.

We were shown into the mayor's office in City Hall, which is directly across the street from Civic Center, and had our first conversation with Richard Daley since he had greeted us as we raced to begin the parade. Daley was memorable for two reasons: How could a man do what he has done, be the mayor of a major city, and still have such rough mannerisms? When he made his first gaffe, we all looked momentarily surprised, but we soon recovered. And he was brusque. "You, over here," is how he had his official pictures taken with us.

Then came the public ceremonies, with keys to the city and the speeches. I felt I did fairly well my second time out. When the ceremonies ended, we were presented with large sterling silver punch bowls, each engraved to us personally from Mayor Daley and the citizens of Chicago. We were

31

told they would be shipped to us. Months later someone asked if they had arrived and they hadn't. The mayor's office was finally called and it turned out that the bowls had vanished. Eventually duplicates were sent.

We were scheduled to go directly back to the airport from City Hall. However, it was decided by someone—no one ever figured out who—that we would go up to Lincoln Park where there was a large gathering of students. The security people at first said they expected there might be a confrontation of some sort, and then abruptly changed their opinion. I scribbled furiously, hoping that in a few minutes before we arrived I could formulate some kind of speech. Mike and Neil spoke without notes and I marveled at this. Standing there clutching my notes, I spoke at last. The students were receptive and polite. It was a false alarm.

The flight to Los Angeles lasted three and a half hours and I cannot believe I spent nearly the entire trip working on my speech, but that's what I did. Joan and the children have since confirmed it. This speech would be really important—it was to be given at a state banquet sponsored by the president. It seems impossible that I would spend that much time on a three-minute speech with several days' work done on it already, but I did. I was that insecure about speechmaking.

We all ate heartily, forgetting that in a few hours we would be having a banquet in Los Angeles. We didn't forget, we just didn't think. We had no control over anything that was going on, and when food was put in front of us, we obliged.

My son Andy has always been inexorably—and usually expensively—attracted to things mechanical, particularly motorcycles. On the plane to Los Angeles, he went exploring and found an intriguing and mechanical-looking console up near the cockpit. He asked what it was and one of the crew attendants said it was a telephone and wouldn't Andy like to telephone a friend.

Andy would indeed. The call was made to his friend Phillip Goldberg, and, with everybody watching, the conversation went something like this:

"Hello, Phillip? This is Andy."

Long pause.

"Nothing much. I'm on an airplane."

Long pause.

"Okay. Bye."

Several other children lined up for similar calls and we all laughed a good deal at the tongue-tied conversations.

At Los Angeles we were welcomed by Mayor Sam Yorty and in an airport ceremony keys to the city were presented along with bouquets for the wives. Helicopters took us to the Century Plaza Hotel.

Waiting in our suite were an affable couple who, when we arrived, were moving the furniture around in the living room and laying on a spread of malts, cheeseburgers, and french fries for the children's dinner. They were arranging the furniture so that dinner would be in front of the television set. Mike, Jan, and Andy, who were not invited to the state banquet, would nevertheless share the experience. It was a thoughtful gesture from two people we had not known before and might not see again but we would never forget. The kids, by this time in full swing with the excitement, started running up and down the long halls of the suite. Joan and I had exactly forty-five minutes to shower and pull on our formal outfits to join the president for cocktails.

We were all a bit late, but eventually we reached the presidential suite. All the Nixons were there, the president, Mrs. Nixon, Julie, and Tricia. It could have been formidable, but it turned into a pleasant hour. We had drinks, and once we all fell into conversations, the president invited us into another room. There, sitting on the bar, were three identically sculpted Boehm ceramic statues consisting of *Columbia* in the form of a delicate woman bearing a shield containing a symbol of the moon and a NASA emblem. Beside her an eagle perched, wings spread gracefully. They were inscribed to each of us from President and Mrs. Nixon. There was, I remember, much oohing and aahing and at one point I noticed Joan and Pat Collins staring at the statues incredulously.

Later, when our statue arrived in Houston, we kept it briefly, then packed it off to the Smithsonian. There would be many crates going there.

At the appropriate time the suite filled with officials of various sorts, and we were all herded to a ready room adjacent to the cavernous ballroom where several thousand people were waiting to begin the official state banquet. We were lined up in marching order and one by one made our entrance, walking to a table which seemed to stretch into infinity.

And my seat was at the far end of that infinity, next to Pat Collins. Joan was at the other end of the table seated next to Mike Collins. Official greetings and introductions were made and dinner was served.

The entire dinner was televised live, and from the dais I could see all of the television cameras. By this time I had mastered the secret of the red light. Months earlier, whenever a camera was aimed in my direction, I was under the impression it was going out over the airwaves. At a press conference one day before the flight, I realized that only the camera with a red light on—the light was located either beside the lens or on top of the camera—was actually broadcasting. At the banquet, whenever the red light wasn't on me, I had my head down, reading and reworking the notes on my lap. Poor Pat Collins. Her dinner partner said virtually nothing. I don't even remember what we ate, except that I didn't eat much of it.

During dessert, Vice-President Agnew gathered the three of us together and took us down to visit several tables in front of the dais.

The president spoke eloquently and enthusiastically—but not *too* enthusiastically this time—and, at the conclusion of his speech, presented each of us with the Medal of Freedom. I was not told this was going to happen—I don't think any of us were—and there came that moment when I realized, "My God, he's talking about me."

The three of us received our medals and so did Steve Bales, a guy who symbolized to me, and obviously to the president as well, the kind of concerted effort involved in space travel. Steve was a flight controller in charge of looking at the data from our computer on board the lunar lander *Eagle*. His devotion to his work and his knowledge of computers made it possible for us to land even though our on-board computer had overloaded and wasn't working properly. Steve knew why and how. Because of this the mission succeeded instead of perhaps prematurely aborting.

I gave my spiel. When I was done, I acknowledged the applause, headed back to my seat, and slugged down a glass of wine. Now I could enjoy myself. The last speech had been made and now the fun began. I turned to Pat Collins and started talking. She was startled by my sudden burst of conversation.

When the banquet ended, we were taken to still another room to pose for pictures with the president and his party. I had always been under the impression that the president would have a staff people-arranger, someone who would line up various combinations of people for pictures. Not so. President Nixon did his own people-arranging with great ease. Mrs. Nixon, however, kept the rather tight-lipped smile and aloof manner she had maintained from the moment we entered the banquet room. It struck me that she was not having an especially good time. We would meet a different Pat Nixon when we returned from the world tour.

We said our good-nights and headed for our respective suites. Mine was filled with relatives and family. My father, my two sisters, assorted aunts and uncles, and three very tired children who had now been going strong for twenty-two hours. They were dispatched to bed and for the next two hours we all sat and talked, subsisting on adrenalin and Scotch. It was the best part of the evening and I relished it.

The next morning, after a monumental struggle to rouse three exhausted children, we gathered in the lobby of the hotel. The change was abrupt but welcome. As we stood waiting in the lobby, no one applauded, waved, or even said hello. Unhurried, we got into a helicopter to fly to the airport for the trip back to Houston. I felt almost as if all that had preceded that morning never happened.

Mike, Jan, and Andy had had the day of their lives and were only too happy to say so. Yet, within a matter of weeks their reaction to anything vaguely official would be one of silence. They have never been easily impressed, and in time would develop a defense against any kind of fame. They would react with silence, as though through silence they could keep their lives as they had been once before. Even today, they seldom if ever volunteer information about those days or introduce it into a conversation.

Joan, too, had loved every minute of it. Before we were married Joan had finished earning her master's degree in dramatic arts from Columbia and was working as an actress. Performers love acclaim and Joan was only too willing to admit it. Her brief entry in her diary is, "It is a sparkly, shiny new adventure, and it was a glorious day. I loved all of those people." Flip ahead just three short months and her diary contains a very different notation, and it isn't at all cryptic: "The tinsel is tarnished. Buzz, who was never comfortable with all this, pushes loyally on. I cooperate, but I am tired and unhappy."

No rest in Houston. We taped "Meet the Press," and when they played it back, there were Neil and Mike looking at their ease and me making notes. After the taping both Mike and Neil said they felt I had given the best answers. It was a needed boost of self-confidence.

Saturday, August 16, was Houston's day to celebrate our return and it was Jan's twelfth birthday. For her birthday she got to ride in a parade in Houston, eat lunch at the venerable, once regal Rice Hotel and listen to her father give his prerecorded message. That night there was the Astrodome Bonanza Show held in our honor. It was intended to be an entertainment; so our speeches were kept remarkably and comfortably brief. Bill Dana, Nancy Ames, and Flip Wilson entertained. The master of ceremonies and star attraction was Frank Sinatra. After the show he invited us to dinner at the Royal Coach Inn and it was our turn to be agog. I remembered listening to his music in junior high school and wishing somehow to get across the Hudson River and into New York where he was causing a major sensation at the Paramount Theatre. And now here he was, honoring us.

When a soldier is sent out of a war zone or any other area of hazardous duty, it is called, in military parlance, R and R leave. R and R stands for Rest and Recuperation. Usually, there is an officer in charge to ensure a proper amount of both. Frank Brandstetter is such a man to the astronauts. He is the man who adds most of the magnificence to a hotel in Acapulco called Las Brisas. The next week we, along with several friends, could be found resting and relaxing at Las Brisas. It rained nearly all week, but that didn't decrease our pleasure. We swam, rode donkeys, went on a safari, watched a lot of movies of football games, and, in the tradition of all vacations, ate and drank too much. The rest was so welcome that Acapulco and Frank Brandstetter have become our special personal therapy. Ever since, usually the week between Christmas and New Year, we go to Acapulco.

Two events were scheduled for the first weeks of our return. There were dozens of others, plus the massive amount of mail still to be handled, but these two events were particularly significant. One was my homecoming for a parade and banquet, something I looked forward to, and our address to the Congress of the United States of America, which, whenever I thought of it, caused me to quake.

Montclair, New Jersey, is my home town. When I left at the age of sixteen, the population was 43,000 and it hasn't grown much since. The town, too, is quite unchanged, and it is a touchstone in my life as well as Joan's. Her home town of Ho-Ho-Kus is nearby. There is a pervading sense of "before" about Montclair, and it has become more and more comforting over the years. Its importance to me doubtlessly is increased by the fact that most of my life has been spent in the service, and consequently I have seldom lived anywhere long enough to develop a strong sense of belonging. Montclair fills that need.

Neil had much the same attachment to his home town in Wapakoneta, Ohio, and at the time I went back to Montclair, similar celebrations were underway in Wapakoneta. Mike, on the other hand, was a genuine service brat. He had been born in Genoa, Italy. Reluctantly, he allowed himself to be adopted by New Orelans, saying, "Well, it's close to Houston, the restaurants are good, and I can always disown them if I don't like it." Later, while we were on our around-the-world trip, Mike made a side trip to Genoa to be made an honorary citizen.

On September 6, 1969, I went home. The NASA *Gulfstream*, a reliable old turboprop that has shuttled astronauts here and there with consistent ease, flew us to Newark. We stopped at the new YWCA building which had been built since my first flight homecoming two years earlier. I had served as honorary chairman of the building committee and had made a donation. I gave them the YWCA pin I had carried to the moon in their honor, and toured the building.

There was a brief press conference in the library of Montclair State College for the local press and television. I remember the word "enormous"—I said something to the effect that my feelings and loyalty to my home town were enormous. Directly to my right I heard a newspaperman, in a disdainful but audible whisper, say to the guy next to him, "Here comes the tearjerker routine." I didn't know which I wanted to do more: step over and address the idiot with my fist or pretend that it never happened. I was furious, but I ignored him.

Then came the parade, past the maple trees and all the familiar sights. There were a great many people and, of course, some of them I had known for years. I rode in a convertible, through a drizzly rain which dampened nothing as far as I was concerned. Joan sat beside me. Mike and Jan rode in another car behind us. Andy, who had become the first touring casualty, had stayed behind in Houston to play with his fellow seventh graders on their football team. I spotted the Italian delicatessen where I used to buy spicy salami and, in front of it, the old man who had sold it to me. I got out of the car and shook his hand. We passed the drugstore where I had held my first job.

From there we went to the stadium of Montclair High School, which was as decorated and crowded as it is for the big Thanksgiving weekend football game. There on the reviewing stand I looked out over the small sea of faces and one of the first I saw was Charlie Hamilton. Charlie ran the summer camp I attended for seven straight summers from the time I was nine years old.

The parade consisted of the Montclair drill team, a marching band, and several cars—one of them containing three elderly people and the sign WE TAUGHT BUZZ. Three people from long ago who had encouraged me to study when I was at an impressionable age. I hoped that my success had somehow touched them and that they shared in it. A picture of them riding in the parade sits on the bookcase behind my desk, next to a model of the *Apollo* spacecraft.

The mayor of Montclair at that time was Matthew Carter, an affable man who is popular in the community. His wife is one of the driving forces behind the various community activities. Her special interest is working with blind youngsters. Weeks later, among the hundreds of mementos sent to me from various parts of the world, was a complete report in braille of our flight, including the individual NASA press releases, constructed by a group of blind students. I remembered Mrs. Carter's work and sent the report to her.

Also at the ceremonies was Governor Hughes, who announced that a scholarship had been funded in my name. It is for students who have the desire but not the money and I was delighted to be the cause of it.

When it was my turn to talk, I gave the first speech in which I felt I went below the veneer of my own emotions of the moment to speak of the enormity of my feelings for my home town, my friends, and how their influences had shaped my life.

I was no sooner speaking than I became aware of a peculiar occurrence. Each word I spoke stopped in midair for a moment, then reappeared through the stadium speakers. My first instinct was to stop to wait for the words to catch up. I stopped, they caught up, and then silence. I started again, this time going right on. It worked. One of the other speakers that afternoon was so confounded by this peculiarity of stadium public-address systems and echos that he said one word, waited to hear it, then said another. The result was arresting. Everything simply stopped and he had to be told to speak on.

After it was over, I must have looked satisfied because Joan accused me of actually enjoying myself in front of a microphone.

There was a banquet that night for 700 in the cafeteria dining room of Montclair State College. As it often does after a summer rain, the night turned hot and humid and the beef Wellington turned soggy too. Before long, coats began going over the backs of chairs and from then on the evening was as informal and friendly as any gathering of so many people can be. Only Jan, who was understandably bored and uncomfortable, complained.

The main speaker was former United States Senator Albert W. Hawkes, whose politics, which were not at all dissimilar to his name, eventually cost him one final election. The senator, who died recently at ninety-two, was at that time a great gray eminence with a cane he was prone to thump against anything or anyone to make his point. He had tenaciously maintained his beliefs in spite of popular opinion. I did not agree with all his views but I admired his tenacity. He was a person to whom I felt a strong loyalty for the simple reason that he had chosen me, when I was sixteen years old, to be his candidate for an appointment to West Point, and I got it.

That night, he told about my first interview with him, which, in the dim haze of times past, I still remember. He had sternly warned me that military men are often asked to risk their lives for their country. "Sir, I can't think of a more noble purpose for my life than to serve my country," was what he said I said at the time, and as I remember it, the quote was accurate, though obviously idealistic. But it was what he said at the end of his speech, a theme he would repeat in speeches during the remaining years of his life, which gave me a personal surge of accomplishment.

"In all my years as a senator, in all the many votes and suggestions I have made, I shall remember that, to me, the most significant decision I made was to nominate a young man from Montclair, New Jersey, as a cadet at West Point. His accomplishments exceeded my wildest dreams."

Several minutes elapsed before I was able to stand up and go to him.

There was to be still another emotional jolt coming my way that evening. Clary Anderson was my football coach, friend, and counselor when I was in high school and, as some friendships do, ours had endured. We had remained in contact over the years and I saw him whenever I went home. Before the launch of my flight I invited him to come to Cape Kennedy as my guest for the event. While there, he made notes about his impressions. He then composed them into a short speech which he hoped one day to make, and this was that day.

The speech was the sensation of the evening and it received a standing ovation. It was simple, forceful, and short; it conveyed the emotion of one man watching men depart for the moon and it gave a deeper meaning to what we had done than anything I've heard before or since.

I then introduced my father, Colonel Edwin E. Aldrin, as "the man who propelled me into the astronaut business," which is a bit of an understatement. An understatement that paled beside the dreams and goals Edwin Eugene Aldrin set for his lastborn child and only son.

Not long afterward, I watched Dad as he was interviewed on television and he made a remark about me that I consider revealing about him. He was being questioned about my years at West Point and he said, "Buzz was first in his class in both athletics and scholarship his first year at West Point." True, and I shall never forget his pleasure when it happened. But he seldom mentions the fact that when I graduated three years later, I was third in a class of 435. Third place doesn't hold quite the appeal to him that first place does.

As a final gesture of the evening, I was presented with my high school football jersey and the number 28 was thereupon retired.

The following day, Joan and I were back in Houston and deep in the throes of a gigantic attack of parental guilt. When we had left, the football season was half over and Andy's seventh grade team hadn't won one game. The day we were gone, his team had won twelve to seven, and Andy had scored both touchdowns. His moment of victory was tarnished considerably because the two people he wanted most to be there were off at a homecoming parade. He was deeply hurt, and there seemed no way to make up for his unhappiness. We heard about it too, because Andy, for the first time, realized that his parents weren't infallible as far as he was concerned. We were becoming human beings and the first chink he spotted in our armor looked to him to be very big indeed. By the time we had been home two hours Joan was in the bathroom crying and I was in my study erasing from my datebook everything scheduled on any Saturday for the remainder of the season and writing in his football games. The team never won again, but eventually we all recovered.

The next speech was the most important of any I had given, or ever would give. All three of us where scheduled to speak before the United States Congress, a collective body that, more than any other organization, controlled the destiny of the space program, and, of course, much much more.

The possible subjects for my speech seemed endless, and that itself became a problem. At first I thought about speaking briefly of how I felt, as a West Point graduate, to have spent my life in the service of my country. No, that wasn't right. I then tried to find a consensus of what people thought about men going to the moon. I spent hours poring over the mail I received and finally found myself making copious notes from a large notebook containing all the editorial cartoons published after our landing. In the middle of one sleepless night, I shook Joan awake to exclaim, "That's not right! Every cartoonist, every person, has his own impression. I'll give mine. My impression is different. I was there!" The next night I awoke her accidentally by my pacing around the bedroom. As diplomatically as possible, she suggested I allow NASA to prepare my speech.

No astronauts were required to write their own speeches, and many did not. NASA employed a speechwriter. She had been on the staff since the beginning of the program, when she had only seven men to provide with speeches. The number had become massively larger and she was overworked, to say the least. She was also short of brilliant innovations, as well she might be by this time. Any mention of traveling in the heavens sent her rushing to her Bible, which had long since been worn thin. Speechwriting also took time. First, she would squeeze my own ideas about what I wanted to say out of me, then she would go to work and deliver me a speech. After all that, I would go to work rewriting it. I finally decided if I was going to change most of what she wrote, I might as well do the whole speech myself. She is still there, working long and honorably, and when I see her now on infrequent visits, I secretly think she's glad that the three of us seldom availed ourselves of her services.

While I spent sleepless nights writing my speech, Slodey, our Russian wolfhound, romped enthusiastically, happy to have company. Sometimes seeing Slodey would take my mind off my task and I would smile as I remembered how he joined our animal population. Our monkey, Popo, had been dead several months and the animals at our house consisted only of two Siamese cats and Missy, a mongrel much indulged and loved. She was sick with a heart murmur when we got her, yet Missy lives on in spite of all odds and still collects the newspaper every morning, though now we have to help her. While I was in space, Mike, my older son, had announced he would like to have a baby boa constrictor. Mike is attracted to animals much the same way his younger brother is attracted to mechanical objects. Joan asked him to wait until I was back, but the request somehow got printed in the newspapers. Senator Mark Hatfield, whose son had just such a snake over Mrs. Hatfield's strenuous objections, had his secretary telephone me and offer his snake. I accepted, and told Joan that afternoon. She rolled her eyes heavenward and said she had bought Mike a snake that morning and had already given it to him for his birthday. I telephoned Senator Hatfield's secretary who had a grand time telling me how Mrs. Hatfield had already taken the snake to the airport. We had two boa constrictors. They proved to be listless and uninteresting additions and we all cringed when we had to feed them live mice. Joan and I also cringed at the mice bill. Mike soon began making noises about getting a show dog and we agreed instantly when he offered to get rid of the snakes for the dog.

A letter arrived while I was preparing my speech offering a choice of a litter of Russian wolfhounds, or borzoi, to be presented as a gift to us from a group of French breeders. The kennel was less than an hour's drive away, and we went the next day. Mike was captivated and spent several hours making his decision. His choice was named Slodey Onegovitch de Morton Hall. Slodey went on to win a number of ribbons and a rather dubious fame. At first the dog amused us, but then he became rather a problem as Slodey developed his own unique way of introducing himself to people. He simply saunters up behind strangers and gooses them enthusiastically with his nose. Slodey is lovable, but not very bright. He has a habit of having encounters with anything from moving cars to foxtails and several veterinarians have become wealthy extracting him from his crises.

The day before our speech to Congress, Neil, Mike, and I attended the unveiling at the Washington post office building of a stamp commemorating the first lunar landing. It was, I thought, a rather well executed drawing of Neil stepping down onto the lunar surface. Lord knows what prompted the caption under the stamp, but it caused me to feel rather useless and it positively infuriated my father. I have no idea what was behind the decision or even who made it, but the caption says, "First Man on the Moon." "Men" would have been more accurate, and I must confess, my feelings were hurt. Nevertheless, we signed a large number of first-day issue sheets and presented the post office department with an envelope we had canceled on the lunar flight and later signed. Much has been written about the astronauts and their philatelic activities. What struck me that day in Washington was that the post office itself was generating extra income and encouraging this whole stamp business by having us sign a stack of first-day issues which, in turn, the post office sold to the highest bidders.

What the post office didn't know then, and what has never before been publicly stated, though it is known around NASA, is that the envelope we presented them with that day is not exactly one of a kind. There are roughly 250 more envelopes which flew on Apollo 11. We all took them along in our personal preference kits, and they were on the lists of personal belongings we submitted to NASA prior to stowing them on the spacecraft. I have 104 of the covers safely stored in a safe deposit vault, and there they will remain. Neil and Mike have the rest. At present I have no intention of distributing them in any way until I am convinced of the most ethical thing to be done.

Service widows with children to raise and educate inevitably find themselves at one point or another falling on hard times. The three of us, prior to lift-off, bought ourselves some insurance for our families in the extremely remote possibility that we might not return. Several days before lift-off we all signed commemorative envelopes which were canceled upon lift-off and given to a trusted emissary to be delivered to our wives if the necessity arose. Those envelopes are also stored away.

We signed the envelopes during the final days before our flight while we were living in the crew quarters at Cape Kennedy. As we signed the envelopes, we stacked them in boxes inside Mike's room. We took no security precautions whatever because only NASA officials and functionaries were permitted in our quarters and, to us, they were beyond suspicion. On the last day before lift-off Mike told us that one of the boxes was missing. We said nothing, but the theft disappointed and discouraged us.

On Tuesday, September 16, 1969, promptly at 11:00 A.M., we arrived to make our speeches. Our wives were shown to seats in the gallery and we were taken to the Senate cloakroom to await our introduction.

One of the first things we did was confess to one another our extreme apprehension. The second thing we did was decide one and all to go to the bathroom so we wouldn't have to go at a more crucial time. The three of us trooped off to the nearest bathroom and we were all lined up at the urinals when into our midst marched a slightly unsteady Congressman Mendel Rivers, chairman of the Armed Services Committee and clearly an important man as far as the space program was concerned. I guess the good Congressman took a drink now and then, and this apparently was one of his now days. He had seen us going to the bathroom and had decided to get his first-day covers signed, which he whipped out along with a pen. We, in turn, zipped up, lined up, signed our sincerest greetings, and returned to the cloakroom. Neil looked annoyed, Mike's face was red with embarrassment, and I was shaking my head in disbelief. The House was called to order promptly at noon.

The doorkeeper announced the vice-president and members of the Senate as they entered the House of Representatives. He then announced the ambassadors, ministers, and chargés d'affaires of foreign governments who thereupon entered and took the seats reserved for them. I hadn't known foreign dignitaries were coming and this did little to allay my discomfort. Then the doorkeeper announced the members of the cabinet, who entered to sit in special seats in front of the Speaker's rostrum. We were then announced, and a group of previously appointed senators led us to our positions standing at the Clerk's desk. Neil spoke first and I went next. This is the speech I gave.

Distinguished ladies and gentlemen, it is with a great sense of pride as an American and with humility as a human being that I say to you today what no men have been privileged to say before: "We walked on the moon." But the footprints at Tranquillity Base belong to more than the crew of *Apollo 11*. They were put there by hundreds of thousands of people across this country, people in government, industry, and universities, the teams and crews that preceded us, all who strived throughout the years with *Mercury*, *Gemini*, and *Apollo*. Those footprints belong to the American people and you, their representatives, who accepted and supported the inevitable challenge of the moon. And, since we came in peace for all mankind those footprints belong also to all people of the world. As the moon shines impartially on all those looking up from our spinning earth so do we hope the benefits of space exploration will be spread equally with a harmonizing influence to all mankind.

Scientific exploration implies investigating the unknown. The result can never be wholly anticipated. Charles Lindbergh said, "Scientific accomplishment is a path, not an end; a path leading to and disappearing in mystery."

Our steps in space have been a symbol of this country's way of life as we open our doors and windows to the world to view our successes and failures and as we share with all nations our discovery. The *Saturn*, *Columbia*, and *Eagle*, and the extravehicular mobility unit have proved to Neil, Mike, and me that this nation can produce equipment of the highest quality and dependability. This should give all of us hope and inspiration to overcome some of the more difficult problems here on earth. The *Apollo* lesson is that national goals can be met where there is a strong enough will to do so.

The first step on the moon was a step toward our sister planets and ultimately toward the stars. "A small step for a man," was a statement of fact, "a giant leap for mankind," is a hope for the future.

What this country does with the lessons of *Apollo* applied to domestic problems, and what we do in further space exploration programs will determine just how giant a leap we have taken.

Three hundred and eighty-five words each produced, it seemed, at the rate of one an hour. The ovation when I finished was reassuring, and with an enormous sense of relief, I enthusiastically joined in the applause when Mike ended his speech.

A sense of elation took over and I was as high after the speech as I had been low before. It may have been one of the greatest moments any man can have in a lifetime, but it was comforting to know it was behind me.

We were escorted from the congressional floor into a room for what I presumed would be some semiofficial gathering. Instead, one by one, we were introduced to a Japanese photographer and were asked to pose in the center of a contraption which appeared to be straight out of a *Popular Science* magazine. I was asked to sit in a fixed position and hold as still as possible. I sat in a semicircle bounded by a strip of tubing at roughly my shoulders and another just above my head. Between the pieces of tubing were strings, and behind the strings were seven cameras and a series of lights. The strings cast shadows on my face as each camera and its lights simultaneously took a picture. The result was to be an accurate three-dimensional portrait of each of us which would then be sent to Japan to be converted into statues. We were presented with the results when we reached Tokyo eight weeks later.

After we were through posing we were informed that we were being taken to an auditorium where we would brief the wives and families of the congressmen. No one had previously mentioned this to any of us. My reaction was tempered by my elation of the moment, but both Mike and Neil were justifiably furious. We did the routine presentation we were preparing for our round-the-world trip. While a short film of the voyage was shown, we took turns narrating. Afterward, we answered questions. As we left the stage the first thing we noticed was that we had been abandoned by our escorts and most of the other NASA people. The three of us were instantly surrounded and for the next hour we gave autographs and shook hands. We were finally rescued and as soon as we were out of the auditorium and back at our hotel we raised hell.

Collectively, we informed NASA that whenever any of us attended public functions in the future we would need someone to extract us from a crowd, someone who could say, "He can't sign any more autographs just now, but thanks for asking." We simply could not say it ourselves. Our work as speakers in behalf of space exploration could be ruined if we refused to give autographs. The alternative was standing for hours on end signing our names. Our objections were at first greeted with surprise and then agreement.

We then made it known to NASA that it was to their benefit as well as ours that hereafter we be informed well in advance of any public appearances we were to make.

It became quite obvious in the next months that whenever any senator or congressman on any committee of any importance to the space program, or any congressman or senator whose vote might be swayed by our appearance, asked for our presence, we went. The same rules, unspoken but clearly understood, applied to appearances requested by the NASA hierarchy.

The process then divided and diffused. If a major officer of, say, a major NASA subcontractor happened to be on the board of directors of an important or powerful educational or civic organization, one of us would be in attendance if possible. In the two years following our flight I did not refuse any appearance I felt NASA expected me to attend. The manner of the extension of the invitation generally gave the clue. If we were told, "You are invited to speak at the graduation of the class of 1970 of Slipperyrock College," and no details were given, we could accept or refuse on our own. But if we were told the nature of the invitation and the involvement of the sponsor in any detail, it was an invitation to accept if at all possible. I have since cut back considerably on the number of invitations I accept no matter who is involved. I still feel many obligations to give speeches, but the decision is made by me alone since I am no longer employed by the National Aeronautics and Space Administration and I am retired from the Air Force.

The following morning we went to the State Department for a detailed briefing on our world trip. What appeared to be a strictly routine meeting would, in fact, prove to be a most uneasy gathering.

3

Bright and early the three of us with our wives reported to the State Department for a briefing on our world tour, which was scheduled to begin in less than two weeks. The prospect of such a trip—not to mention the logistics—boggled me.

The briefing was conducted by Julian Scheer, the NASA director of public affairs, known for his dedication, thoroughness, and insecurity. Julian first introduced us to various members of what he called the "support team," consisting roughly of a man from the United States Information Agency, a representative of the White House, two secretaries, a doctor, two security men, a baggage man, and the various people from the space agency who would accompany us. Hereafter, Neil, Mike, and I would become known as the "principals," while Jan, Pat, and Joan would remain the "wives" on all official schedules. Our number on the world trip fluctuated between eighteen and twenty-five.

We were then escorted into an office where the six of us were invited to sit down. Julian shuffled papers nervously and finally sat down too. He then delivered a short speech. This is something we really didn't have to do and nobody should feel obligated, he explained, even though it would look . . . well, kind of strange if one of us pulled out. Nevertheless, he continued, we weren't forced to go on the trip and any one of us was free to bow out.

It was, in effect, a rather backhanded way of letting us all know once again that we were expected to go on the tour and to attend all of the functions. I was certain by now that my hesitation over public appearances was obvious. I felt his comments were aimed at me.

We assured him that we understood all this benevolence but that we would all be on hand for the trip. Afterward, nobody could decide what the hell he was talking about. The decision was a foregone conclusion and his additional comments had been most gratuitous and unnecessary. Neil even proposed we telephone Julian one by one and beg off, just to rattle his cage.

On the plane back to Houston we all read through the books we had been given about the cities and customs of the world and looked rather incredulously at the scheduled itinerary. It wasn't yet complete because some of the diplomatic negotiations had hit snags. We were scheduled for Israel, but if we went to Israel we should also go to Egypt. Egypt wasn't considered safe, so eventually the stops in Cairo and Tel Aviv were canceled.

It finally boiled down to twenty-three countries in forty-five days or as Joan noted in surprise, "Three kings in two days! Do you believe it?" No, we didn't.

Nor did we believe the itinerary: Mexico, Colombia, Brazil, Spain, France, Belgium, the Netherlands, Norway, Germany, England, Italy, the Vatican, Yugoslavia, Turkey, the then Democratic Republic of the Congo, Iran, India, East Pakistan, Thailand, Australia, Korea, Japan, Canada —some countries with two stops—plus assorted rest stops. I had no way of knowing at the time that there would also be an unexpected sidetrip to New Jersey.

We also noticed that there was nothing constant on the itinerary. The rule for the trip was that we would attend any official or state luncheon or dinner but not two on any given day—the State Department accurately felt that two a day would be an impossibility. There were motorcades and press conferences nearly every day as well, and on most of the free afternoons or evenings an embassy reception was scheduled. We caught on simply by reading the schedule: there would be two a day after all.

Our impression of the trip was that its purpose was to share our experiences with the people of the world and not simply to visit the American embassies anxious to score social coups. The three of us discussed this and informed both NASA and the State Department that we were going on the trip to demonstrate goodwill to all the people in the world and to stress that what we had done was for all mankind. We would take care of Americans in America. We suggested that nearly all embassy receptions be canceled, and proposed going instead to local universities. This, we thought, was a better idea, but it was one which subsequently turned out to be a bit naïve.

Frank and Sue Borman stepped in to help. Frank had flown on *Apollo 8*, the first flight to orbit the moon, and had done the first extensive astronaut tour when he returned. He eventually asked to be taken off flying status and became President Nixon's astronaut spokesman.

Frank, a wide-faced and smiling man, was known for his expertise at playing the maneuvering game. He was a born politician and cast himself in the role of astronaut adviser. We came to call him Father Borman. One evening at a dinner at his house, Father Borman quite literally stunned the three of us by confiding that we had it licked. If we played our cards right, we'd never have another worry. "All things," and he hesitated for a moment and said, "er . . . I mean . . . all material things," would be ours.

"Gee, thanks, Frank," Neil said respectfully while Mike and I drew blanks. It was one of the awful moments one encounters in life. A good bit later I would howl with laughter at the absurdity of the remark.

For the forty-five days we would be gone we secured the services of a kind, efficient, and firm lady named Mrs. Gilder to live with the children. She had stayed with them during a couple of our previous trips and it had worked out well. We also knew our neighbors would be looking in.

On September 29, 1969, Joan and her ten pieces of luggage and me with my eight arrived at Ellington Air Force Base where the president's plane was waiting. A head count was made and when all were present and accounted for we took off at 8:00 A.M.

First stop, Mexico City. If the impact of the parades and people had been overwhelming in New York and Chicago, they paled beside the emotional enthusiasm of the Latins. We were literally caught in a press of people from the moment we stepped off the airplane until we reboarded the next morning.

Quite honestly, I was terrified. So was Joan, who got separated from the other wives on the steps of City Hall and was paralyzed with fear until Julian Scheer got behind her and half-carried, half-pushed her back to her position. She later told me that when she was ten years old her dad took her, her mother, and grandmother to Times Square on New Year's Eve. She and her father became separated from the others and she had been certain she was going to be crushed to death. She had completely forgotten that experience until Mexico City.

At City Hall we were presented with decorations and keys to the city. We went to lunch with President Gustavo Díaz Ordaz and his wife. The president was solemn and serious, while Mrs. Díaz was a lively enthusiastic woman full of Latin warmth and she provided the light moments. They were needed, because lunch began at 1:00 P.M. and ended promptly at 5:30.

From there Neil, Mike, and I went off to do our first press conference. We had prepared what we thought was a good road show and we had diligently rehearsed. We brought along a film of our trip—several copies of it just to be on the safe side—and as it was shown we each had a section to moderate. The film lasted less than twenty minutes. Following it, we answered questions, the part I liked least. None of us really liked it. We didn't know what to expect, the translations proved long and tedious, and it finally came to the point where our answers deviated considerably from what was called for by the questions. We knew what we wanted to say and somehow we got it said, regardless of the questions asked.

The job of our security men was to get us out of the press conference with the absolute minimum of autograph-signing. There were only two of them on the trip, one assigned to us and the other to our wives. They did their best but we continually ran into problems. Eventually they became experts at getting the cooperation of the police in the various countries.

We had fulfilled our one state-official function of the day, so that night we were free. Frank Brandstetter, our good friend from Las Brisas in Acapulco, flew up for dinner and brought along a friend named Gina Lollobrigida. Gina exuded what she is famous for.

"I thought Gina was interesting," I said when we got back to the hotel room.

"You did? I didn't notice." Joan responded with dirty looks at me.

"Gina is giving us a party in Rome. I accepted."

"You did? Well, tell her I don't want the gory details of her car accident again. And I don't want to see her scars in the ladies' room again."

"You got to see her what?"

"Her s–c–a–r–s."

September 30, Bogotá: There were fewer people here than in Mexico City and they were equally effusive. After we gave our customary airport speeches, we got in jeeps for the motorcade into Bogotá. The jeeps drove away one by one and before we were even out of the airport the jeep the three of us were riding in broke down. The police held back the crowds a few minutes, then gave up. Suddenly people were crawling all over us. I was overcome by nausea and dizziness. One by one we broke loose and ran for the replacement jeep.

The motorcade was chaotic and frightening for all of us. But the presidential palace, where we were to have lunch, was a welcome relief, even with its attendant press, waiters, and the children and grandchildren the president invited. President Carlos Restrepo had done something we all liked. Instead of a large number of Colombian state officials, he had invited only a few and asked them all to bring their children. The result was quite a crowd, but a happy one. Gifts were exchanged, awards bestowed, and we were off to the press conference.

After the press conference, as we went to rendezvous with our wives and stop for one hour at an embassy reception, I got an important message. The prospect had been discussed before, but I had nearly forgotten it. I received confirmation via the White House that I would leave the tour in Bogotá and fly to Atlantic City where I would address the AFL-CIO convention, then return to the tour when it reached a brief rest stop in the Canary Islands.

It was something I definitely didn't want to do, but nevertheless I felt obligated. I had become associated with the AFL-CIO in spite of reservations I had about George Meany. The request came from the president. I had been warned it might happen but had conveniently forgotten the matter.

I must have looked terribly distressed at the news because Bill Carpentier, who had been our faithful and likable physician during the long postflight isolation, and was our physician on the tour, took me aside early that evening to ask if I was all right.

"I don't think so, Bill. I think I'm overwhelmed."

He smiled and said, "I think you all are." He prescribed some pills which he said would slightly decrease my anxiety. I continued to take them until Thailand, where I gave them up. I felt I could control things myself and besides it was difficult to give speeches because the pills caused a dryness of the mouth and throat.

The next morning the president's plane took off for Brazil, with Joan filling in for me at the various official functions. Bill Der Bing from NASA and I waited at the airport for three hours to catch a delayed plane for New York.

Bill is an ingratiating, soft-spoken, and thorough man who served NASA in a variety of capacities involved with protocol. We first heard of him because of his popularity with other astronaut families, and when my *Apollo* flight was announced, we asked for him specifically. During the entire *Apollo* flight he stayed close by our house and helped Joan a great deal. We were all delighted when we learned he would be going on the tour where he functioned as a protocol consultant and had the unenviable responsibility for the luggage of all of the principals and wives. This last chore earned him the sobriquet, "Poor Bill."

Since the request to go to the convention came from the White House, we all assumed that the White House owed George Meany a favor.

After my flight on *Gemini 12*, the International Association of Machinists and Aerospace Workers, known as the IAM, and a part of the massive AFL-CIO, held a convention. NASA was asked to supply an astronaut for the occasion and I was chosen because of the manual-labor experiments I had performed during my space walk. I was made the official representative in space of the workers of America and, in the process, an honorary member of the AFL-CIO machinists union.

The unions and their various publications made a good deal out of this affiliation. There was little doubt of their support of the space program because it represented many jobs, but it occasionally proved troublesome. During appearances I would always stress the term *workers of America,* but it invariably appeared in publications as *union workers of America.*

59

We were met by a most nonunion and undemocratic-looking Cadillac limousine complete with television set and telephone. Bill grinned when he saw it and said, "Workers of the world, arise to pay your union dues."

I was similarly impressed with the arrangements the union had made for my arrival at the hotel. A wedge of about seven security men plowed through the assembled members and remained constantly at my side. I found the whole thing terribly elite as opposed to the impression I had always had of union conventions.

As was becoming standard operating procedure I brought along a movie to narrate and a short speech to give. The speech had been written by NASA and it was one of their better efforts. I had checked it carefully and had made one change, a change I felt sufficiently important to also transfer onto the two carbon copies I had.

As it was written, there was mention of the superiority of the materials we used in space flight that had stamps saying they were union-made. I deleted this phrase with, I thought, good reason. I was in favor of much that the union movement represented, but a union stamp did not automatically represent superiority. The several thousand employees of the Grumman Corporation, manufacturers of the lunar landing vehicle *Eagle*, might take exception. The Grumman Corporation had no unions at the time and their product was as superior as any I had known. If I was going to represent the working man in space, I would represent all of the working men, union and nonunion.

George Meany introduced me as his best friend and I gave my speech and showed my film. Afterward there was a luncheon which seemed as formal and official as some of the events I had just left in South America. A union executive approached and asked for a copy of my speech so that it might be released to the press and reprinted for the general membership. I provided him with a copy and specifically pointed out the deletion.

The following morning as we were leaving for the Canary Islands I picked up a copy of a newspaper and saw the headline ALDRIN SPONSORS UNION-MADE PRODUCTS, with the subhead CLAIMS THEIR LABEL MEANS SUPERIORITY. The story quoting the speech contained the remark I had deleted. I was really pissed when I saw the newspaper. I went directly to a telephone to call Deke Slayton to get him to extricate me from what looked like an ongoing mess. The ever-helpful Bill Der Bing was on the telephone next to me calling his office. Deke promised to do his best, as did the public affairs office.

On the plane to the Canary Islands I continued to fume, but I comforted myself with the knowledge that two days of rest lay ahead.

(It was just a matter of time. A month later, the official union magazine arrived with the same great pronouncements followed quite closely by a letter from the employees committee at the Grumman Corporation taking issue with my remarks. A month after that I made my second appearance at the Grumman factory to give a speech of thanks and appeasement.)

Giant Step was the name of our tour. It was after 10:00 P.M. when Joan arrived in the Canary Islands. We had a sandwich while I read the diary she kept for the days I had missed.

October 2—Wheels up for Argentina at 9:00 A.M. The long flight is doubly long because we cannot yet fly over Bolivia because the U.S. has not recognized the week-old government. Detour over Brazil with fuel stop at Brasília. One hour bus tour of Brasília. Beautiful architecture. Most of us stood on the bus to give our weary rears a rest. Stood at the bar at the back of the bus and drank. When we got off the bus to shake hands at the foreign office I discovered I not only had a run in my left stocking but I had worn the heel out and it was unraveling. Problem: how to hide a foot while standing on it. Answer: impossible.

Help! We're behind schedule for the motorcade and reception in Buenos Aires. All hands change clothes on the plane to make up time. Five people, three tiny bathrooms. Unbelievable mess, but we're all good sports about it. Reception at the American embassy hosted by Ambassador and Mrs. Lodge. Reception line long and tiring. Bill Carpentier rescued me. Mike and Pat Collins have adopted me and, as usual, are fun to be with. We were all going to take in the show at the hotel tonight but I ran out of steam. Had soup in my room and went to bed.

In the morning, ladies press conference followed by luncheon with the ambassador's wife, Mrs. Lodge, who turns out to be a tizz. Lunch and conversation were regulated by the alarm on her wristwatch. Was it Victorian manners that said you spoke to the person on your left for fifteen minutes, then turned to the person on your right? Mrs. Lodge is a Victorian with an alarm. I barely got through my fifteen minutes and am visibly relieved when the alarm rings. Pat is next and is speechless, mouth agape, and trying hard not to laugh.

October 3—Copacabana Palace Hotel, Rio de Janeiro. Accepted three decorations for Buzz this A.M. No one is quite sure where to pin or drape them when presenting them. Official luncheon a bore with people pressing and pushing for autographs. Toured Guanabara Bay and saw Sugar Loaf in the rain. I hum the song, "What Do You Do on a Rainy Nite in Rio?"—without a husband? Dinner show at the hotel with Bill Carpentier, Chuck McGuire, and the Armstrongs and Collinses. Next day we get up at 7:00 A.M. for the eight-hour trip to the Canaries. Rest!

First thing that morning in the Canaries we decided to go swimming. Second thing that morning I found I forgot to pack swimming trunks. Third thing, we opened the drapes and there, politely lining the walk outside our suite, are tourists and photographers. A hotel shopkeeper brought several bathing suits to our room and I selected one. We swam, scuba-dived, and generally relaxed whenever we could get away from the small crowds that were constantly forming. The natives in particular kept asking for my picture and I couldn't figure out why. Finally Neil figured it out. The Canary Islands are Spanish possessions. He pointed at my yellow-and-red-striped trunks.

"You're wearing the flag of Spain," he pointed out.

Late in the afternoon, October 6, we left for Spain. Because of the time change we would arrive just in time for a motorcade and state banquet. I discovered what Joan meant about changing clothes on a plane. By the time we landed in Madrid the plane was a mass of cummerbunds, ties, cuff links, earrings, and velvet bows.

The motorcade went smoothly, the crowds once again were large. The state banquet that night was presided over by one of the ministers. The next morning we all met the Spanish heir apparent, Juan Carlos, an informal and friendly man. He was also well informed about the space program and had even visited Houston to tour our facilities.

That afternoon we were received by Franco. We were all curious to meet the dictator who had fought the civil war in the thirties and had ruled Spain with an iron hand and high taxes ever since. He was not at all what I had expected but, instead, was a short, fragile, and almost timid man with a weak handshake.

October 8, Paris: The greeting during the motorcade was most polite but what really impressed me was Prime Minister Chaban-Delmas. His precision and beautiful command of the situation were one thing, but his eloquence was in a class by itself. Without notes, but obviously after great thought, he extolled our activities, thanked us on behalf of the French people, and quite simply delivered a memorable speech. As a former pilot and Free French fighter, he paid tribute to the United States and its service organizations.

Next we went to visit President Georges Pompidou, a hangover it turned out, from De Gaulle's dreams of glory. Pompidou spoke of the greatness of France, its partnership with the United States, and never once looked at us from under his heavy eyebrows. Only when we posed for pictures did he try to become a warm, love-the-people-president.

Before going to bed, Joan checked her list of what to wear and when, a list we were given roughly two days before various events. We were going to Amsterdam and Brussels in one day. Queen Fabiola preferred bright colors to the usual stately black, and Queen Juliana had sent word to wear whatever we would be wearing in Brussels for Amsterdam too. Good thing, because there was only a forty-five-minute flight between the two cities. Joan laid out a pink dress, and the luggage went back to the plane before we went to bed.

October 9: Up early. Things instantly went wrong. Under our door was a telex from the American embassy in the Netherlands saying, "Queen Juliana insists, repeat, insists it is imperative women wear black for audience."

All through breakfast Joan referred to her as "a mean old biddy" and plans were laid about how to find a black dress in one of the hanging bags on board the plane without making a mess of everything and who would change where during the forty-five-minute flight.

Joan and Jan Armstrong were visibly upset and it took a good hour before any of us noticed Pat Collins wasn't bothered at all. I accused her of falsifying international telegraph forms and Neil joined in. She insisted she did not, but none of us were convinced. She just kept smiling.

She never has admitted it, but she must have stayed up half the night attending to her practical joke. We knew it was a joke when she stubbornly refused to change clothes.

Neither, then, did Joan or Jan. We knew for sure when we met Queen Juliana who is an extremely likable and unpretentious lady who wouldn't have cared if I showed up in my Spanish-flag swimming trunks.

In Amsterdam our motorcade was held in the canals and was a pleasant change. The water was dirty and the crowds were sincere. As we rode along and waved, an attractive lady, who was on board with us, walked up to me and asked how I liked Amsterdam. When I started to speak she shoved the bouquet of flowers she had in her hand directly under my nose. When she asked another question she pulled it in her direction then shoved it back for my answer.

I thought this was kind of odd, but I didn't think much of it until I saw her doing the same with Mike. By the time she got to Neil I was ready for her. I strolled up and offered to hold her bouquet. When she declined, I offered to hold her microphone. She excused herself and left.

The reception at Brussels was more formal. King Baudouin and Queen Fabiola, our second monarchs of the day, were gracious but, it seemed, careful. Almost cool.

Before our arrival we were informed that there were relatively few rules of protocol concerning us save one: It was a custom that at no time should we turn our back to either the king or the queen.

Poor Mike Collins. We were about to march up the stairs into the palace dining room when the king decided to take Mike by the arm and personally escort him up the long flight of marble stairs. The queen fell in line directly behind Mike, escorting Neil. We all looked up with barely suppressed smiles as it occurred to Mike he had turned his back on the queen. Somehow, he managed to remain arm-in-arm with the king and still turn sideways. He walked up the entire stairway that way, looking like the kid who forgot his lines for the school play.

"I think I broke my goddam ankle," he said as we drove back to the hotel.

Infrequently throughout the trip the NASA press people or the crew of the plane issued short little news bulletins. When we got on the plane the next morning the bulletin announced that Mike had been awarded the Absorbine Junior Medal. The citation read, "For athletic prowess and skill in covering a fifty-foot expanse in Brussels sideways while not turning back on the queen."

I was given the Jim Webb Medal. Jim Webb, our boss, was famous for his effluent propensity for public-speaking. My citation read, "For the torrent of words that flowed from his tongue." I thought it an ironic and clever award. A Jim Webb I definitely was not.

Stretch Flanagan, one of our harassed security men, was given the Mayor Daley Memorial Award, "For displaying those remarkable qualities of the Chicago Police Department in crowd control situations."

Neil was presented the Georgie Jessel Medal: "He didn't sell bonds for Israel, but he topped Georgie in toastmaster roles."

The Patricia Nixon Medal was given to Joan, "For displaying the qualities of quiet and determined restraint most evident in our First Lady in not upstaging her husband when the public obviously wanted to see her, not Buzz." It turned out Joan had had a grand time accepting my decorations in South America.

While we read the awards list we flew the short distance to Oslo, where King Olaf would be our host and our third monarch in two days. None of the six of us had ever been to Norway and we looked forward to it if only because it included a one-day rest stop.

I looked forward to it especially because it would be a country near Sweden where my family originated. Sweden had been considered as a stop, but was ruled out because of the delicate situation involving Sweden's acceptance of men deserting the armed forces. Well, Norway was close.

And a surprise. The people who lined the streets were exceedingly polite but not at all enthusiastic. They waved, as if on cue, but there was little shouting or excitement. It was kind of depressing and the three of us fell into a conversation about how clean Oslo was compared to the other cities we had visited as we dutifully waved.

King Olaf put on a lavish lunch and laughed boisterously at every remark anyone made. It was Joan's turn to pull a booboo. Before arriving we were informed that Crown Princess Sonia was married to the Prince Harold, a commoner, but nevertheless both were addressed as "Your Highness." Also at the lunch were Mr. and Mrs. Eric Tandberg. Tandberg was the Walter Cronkite of Norway, right down to his sincere eyebrows. Joan got her ladies mixed up. All through the lunch she said she neglected to call Princess Sonia by any title—"Would you pass the salt, please"—or addressed her as "Mrs. Tandberg." Mrs. Tandberg, meanwhile, moved up in position to "Your Highness."

We flew by helicopter into the mountains to a beautiful old farm where we were the house guests of the minister of defense, Otto Tideman, and his wife for our rest day. Our quarters were separate from the main house, but our host and hostess, real fresh-air fiends, were ever-present and enthusiastic.

The night we arrived they announced an informal dinner for the six of us. Before the dinner we had time to nap.

Joan and I fell to discussing the lack of enthusiasm of the crowds. I remembered a thesis a general I had known wrote on the people of the northern climates. He speculated that the cool air over several generations caused a certain reserve and coldness of personality. They also spoke languages not taken from the more passionate Latin or Romance languages.

Whatever it was, it really bothered me and I asked Joan to convey my regrets at dinner. She was annoyed with me, but she went on. I stayed in bed the entire evening and for some reason remembered how I had loved to read the comic strip of Terry and the Pirates when I was a kid. Terry had a broad, open Scandinavian face. Here I was on the continent of my ancestors and the response seemed blah.

Joan, still annoyed, returned from dinner and found me sulking in a chair. She poured a nightcap for us from the bottle of Scotch we found in nearly every room we stayed in on the trip and sat down to offer a bit of philosophy. She believed, she said, that life would eventually return to normal. I countered by saying I didn't think it ever would, such a hope was now an impossibility. She insisted and I became angry.

"Joan, I've been to the moon and I'm never going to be allowed to live the way I once lived. Neither are you and neither are our kids. Your belief isn't right, it's only a hope and it won't work. Let's just try to make it as worthwhile as we can."

We fell into an uneasy silence which I ended by saying I felt all six of us were fakes and fools for allowing ourselves to be convinced by some strange concept of duty to be sent through all of these countries for the sake of propaganda, nothing more, nothing less. Joan tried to reason until she finally gave up and began to cry. We proceeded to get drunk and we both cried. That night we slept like two frightened children, hanging onto each other.

October 12, Bonn: The Germans may not be emotional like the Latins, but they love technical achievement. The crowds were so thick and enthusiastic, our security men nearly gave up in despair. Instead, the wives were sent directly to the hotel while we went on to City Hall. Pat and Mike missed this enthusiastic reception, since they had skipped Bonn and went instead to Genoa, Mike's birthplace.

Joan and I had not been in Bonn since 1958, when I was stationed as a fighter pilot in Germany and she was pregnant. At that time we got lost driving around the city, then later took a boat down the Rhine River to Cologne. Joan remembered that she took her shoes off to relax and her feet swelled so she couldn't get them back on. She got off the boat barefoot, which just wasn't done in 1958. Bonn has memories for us; it is a fixed point in our lives and we like it.

Leaving the hotel to go to tea with President Gustav Heinemann, we encountered a massive crowd. I looked back at Joan and there she was, tears streaming down her face, struggling to get past the police into the crowd. I started after her, then looked up to see who she was reaching for. There, also in tears, was Waltraut Sell. By the time I got there, they were embracing and crying.

Wal was our part-time babysitter when we lived in Bitburg, and all of us liked her a lot. She was Joan's age and devoted to our children. Wal and her husband had driven up all the way from Bitburg and must have stood in the crowd for hours on end hoping to see us.

We all spoke briefly, but conversation was impossible and we were holding everybody up. Joan asked one of the German security people to see that Wal was taken to our room and given lunch while she waited for us. We rode off to the tea, anxious to get back to the hotel and Wal. When we returned she wasn't there. The security guard couldn't be found either because we didn't know his name. We decided Wal got lost in the crowd. Joan sat down and wrote her a letter, starting a correspondence that goes on still.

October 13, Berlin: We left the president's plane in Bonn and flew through the Berlin air corridor in a government DC-6 which was safer and slower for crossing East Germany and could land at Tempelhof airfield. Pat and Mike were waiting when we landed.

The motorcade hardly missed a street in all of Berlin and Mayor Klaus Schuetz was with us the whole time. No wonder, because he was up for reelection and was favored by Willy Brandt. We stopped at City Hall for lunch, then drove to the Berlin Wall. Joan simply refused to believe it was against the law for East Berliners to open their windows and look across the wall. It was the only time we ever stood on a platform and faced buildings without people. Even the guards turned their backs.

The motorcade and mother nature finally got the best of Mike. We stopped while Mike dashed into a factory to test the plumbing, while the several carloads of photographers rushed about trying to find him. The official explanation was that Mike stopped to shake hands with the factory workers. From then on, whenever any of us had to go to the bathroom during an official function, our handy euphemism was "going to shake hands with the factory workers."

October 14, London: Roughly the halfway mark. On the plane crossing the English Channel we received a communication stating the British press expected us to give two additional press conferences. We were already scheduled for our prearranged quota of four major events per day. The idea of two more sandwiched in annoyed Mike and me, but Neil was really pissed off. He said no, definitely not, and we supported him completely. If we started changing the rules barely halfway through the trip we'd really be in a mess. In addition, it was physically a near impossibility to hold so many press conferences and attend the other scheduled functions.

How best to say no and cause the minimum of offense to the people who were to communicate the news of our visit? Bill Carpentier came up with the best idea. He advised the American embassy, which in turn communicated with the British officials, that we wouldn't be doing the two extra press conferences because the rigors of the trip had practically worn us out.

Bad move. The press wasn't unfriendly, it was hostile.

The reception at Buckingham Palace was impressive. Queen Elizabeth, surprisingly small and buxom, was very friendly. Prince Philip, an aviation buff, was full of questions.

While we were at Buckingham Palace, Bill Carpentier

was conned into going on television to state that we were exhausted. It was, he said, the only way out of big trouble with the television networks. He then had to sit still for a question and answer session which no one had warned him about.

News travels fast. Chuck Berry, the head NASA physician, called to chew Bill out for going on television. We tried to calm Bill down by saying that Berry was jealous because he wasn't the guy on television. Chuck Berry, the astronauts' doctor, travels a lot, gives speeches and lots of interviews stressing his part in the space program.

Dinner at 10 Downing Street. There were lots of toasts and plenty of the "hear-hear" business. The recently deposed Labour leader landed in his cups and gave a speech ripping his country's present administration, concluding with a toast to us. If it hadn't been so uncomfortable, it would have been funny. Neil was not at all amused.

Following the dinner we were all escorted to another, larger room and several hundred people were waiting as we formed a reception line. It was nearly impossible to move in such a large crowd and I noticed Joan wasn't moving at all. No wonder. She was wedged in next to Sean Connery.

We were on the plane for Rome the next morning before we realized something peculiar had happened. In every city we had visited, the three of us had been given some sort of award or decoration. The plane by now was loaded with awards and gifts of various sorts. In London, no official award or decoration had been made. Odd. We never figured out why.

October 15, Rome: We stayed three days, a day and a half on official visits, a day and a half to rest. Rest? After a long motorcade with several stops, we changed into formal clothes for the official state dinner.

Terrific dinner, a first of sorts. Hadrian's Tomb, now called Castel Sant'Angelo, is a musty ancient building crumbling

in places. An elegant state dinner was served in these surroundings. The contrast was unforgettable.

We never knew who our dinner partners were to be, and
as often as not, we still didn't know who they were after
we'd eaten with them. My dinner partner at Castel Sant'-
Angelo was an elegant older woman, a Mrs. Marconi.
Marconi? Could it be? I thought it impolite to ask and I
don't know still. Neil acted as our spokesman and gave a
marvelously eloquent speech, the best he gave on the entire
trip. It began with Galileo and worked on through the Italian scientists whose brilliance so many years ago made so
much possible for our voyage. I liked it even more because
I knew no one was going to put the finger on me for a
speech. Usually we didn't know until the dinner started so
we always had to be prepared. This time we were informed
well in advance.

October 16, the Vatican: Pat Collins, who is Catholic,
was terribly excited about this particular visit and her enthusiasm caught us all. It turned out to be one of the most
striking and stirring moments of the trip when His Holi-
ness, Pope Paul VI, a frail, warm man, presented us with our
gifts.

He unveiled three magnificent porcelain statues of the
Three Wise Men. He said that these three men were directed to the infant Christ by looking at the stars and that
we three also reached our great destination by looking at
the stars.

Joan became the first victim of *turista*. She went to bed,
and the rest of us went to Gina Lollobrigida's party. I went
with Nick Ruwe, a lively bachelor who was on the trip as
a representative of the president. We had all met Nick at a
dinner in Houston shortly before we left, and he had
quickly settled into the spirit of the trip.

That night, at an elegant party right out of *La Dolce Vita*,
the spirit—and spirits—flowed until dawn. I flowed in shortly
after dawn, where I began a day-long stay in the doghouse.

I slept most of the next day and while Joan wasn't in the bathroom she toured the catacombs beneath the embassy. I showed up for a late lunch and by 6:00 p.m. we were back in our hotel room getting ready for bed.

October 18, Belgrade: The official word for Yugoslavia was that we not mention politics and such at all, not even in our hotel rooms. They just might be bugged.

We stopped our motorcade and laid a wreath on the tomb of the unknown soldier, something we had not yet done on any of our stops but repeated with increasing frequency for the rest of the trip. This first ceremony in Belgrade the Yugoslavians took with great seriousness. The tomb was at the top of a long flight of stairs and we had little help lugging the heavy wreath to the top. Joan, who was now really in the grip of the *turista*, looked faint. Pat Collins noticed this and moved to stand behind her. Joan's stomach became one of the great medical mysteries of the trip. In Belgrade we called it the Belgrade Belly, while in Rome it was determined to be the Roman Rumbles. Two days later it would become the Turkey Trots.

Our welcome in Belgrade was tumultuous. President Tito, a down-home country boy, was so carried away with enthusiasm that he interrupted our six-course luncheon to order a seventh: a dish from his home town. It turned out to be pig hocks smothered in sauerkraut. Good old Joan, she got it down, but it came back up a few hours later. Our constant companions in Belgrade were a Mr. and Mrs. Job, whose exact title in the government was never explained to us, but they proved quite interesting. Mr. Job, naturally, was a hard-line party member and rather aloof. Mrs. Job, on the other hand, was decidedly pro-American, curious about our visit with the pope, and interested in football. There was much conjecture among the six of us about the Jobs.

October 20, Ankara: Turkey is arid with low, rolling hills and many Turks turned out to wave politely. It took several minutes before we realized there were virtually no women watching the motorcade. They might have been freed from their veils, but they hadn't been freed from their kitchens.

That afternoon there was a tea at the presidential residence and the big surprise was that tea was exactly what they served. It was thick and full of sugar.

It is curious what one remembers and observes during a trip such as this. All of us later mentioned the tea, simply because it was the first tea we had attended at which Scotch or champagne were not the only liquid served. The evening receptions and dinner also included liquor, but that was a natural occurrence. My prevailing memory of the whole trip is that there was liquor everywhere. There were almost always bottles of Scotch or gin in our hotel rooms. With the exception of that night in Oslo, neither Joan nor I got drunk. Even when I stayed up all night partying in Rome, I didn't really get drunk. Still, what we remember most is drinking. Our emotions were at such a pitch that perhaps fast-flowing adrenaline kept us sober. I simply don't know, but I marvel at how we all got through so much liquor with so few consequences.

That night, after a reception given by the prime minister, we returned to the hotel and found a telegram waiting for us.

It was from Tom Stafford, who by now must have been regretting his offer to keep an eye on our house and children. He had tried to call but couldn't get through.

We rushed to the telephone and the call somehow went through; slowly the story unfolded. Mrs. Gilder, when she came to stay, had asked that the animals, Slodey the goosing Russian wolfhound in particular, remain outside during her stay. We agreed, although Mike had objected strenuously to this arrangement.

It seemed Mrs. Gilder had a heart attack while doing some straightening up in the kitchen. She was alone except for Slodey, who had been sneaked into the house by Mike to stay in his room while he did his homework. Mike left the door open and Slodey got out. Both Joan and I were convinced Slodey had caused the poor woman to have a heart attack by pressing his nose against her backside. It was at once funny and horrible. We have never learned if this is what happened. We were afraid to ask and Mrs. Gilder never volunteered the information. She was in the hospital and the kids had been sent to stay with friends.

The news from home was almost too much for Joan. She began making plans to go home while I got busy on the telephone trying to find another sitter so that she would stay. Slodey was sent to a neighbor's backyard for the remainder of the trip, and four days later another woman moved in and the children moved back. Joan stayed with me. From then on, our neighbors checked the house frequently and we were in almost daily contact by telephone. Mrs. Gilder was soon on the mend.

October 22, Kinshasa: The flight to Africa took almost all day, and we all used the trip to sleep. Joan officially stopped eating, explaining it was simply no use. She was adjusted to the condition but could endure it more easily by not eating.

We arrived at 4:00 P.M. and stepped off the plane into the incredible heat. We stood dripping with sweat while the band played "The Star-Spangled Banner" and the Congolese anthem. I delivered my airport speech in French. It was a big success with the natives. The motorcade lasted for two unair-conditioned hours.

We stayed at a compound built for the 1967 meeting of the Organization on African Unity. Each couple had a private villa equipped with kitchen, living room, bedroom, houseboy, cockroaches, and insecticide. The outdoor shower, a three-nozzle affair, was open and designed to be used in groups. When in Rome.

The villas were located along the Stanley River, named for the newspaperman who found Dr. Livingstone. We had expected to find ourselves in a lush jungle and were surprised by the pastoral countryside and rolling hills.

Joseph Mobutu, our host, occupied the villa in the center of the compound. He both worked and lived in it and for company he kept two tame lions who could be found dozing in the sun near his door.

Mobutu presided over ceremonies the next day in the searing heat. The three of us received canes engraved with the symbols for bettering and thriving of men and we were decorated with the Order of the Leopard and, appropriately warm enough for winter in Moscow, leopard hats to go along with it. Then, in a gracious and unexpected ceremony which had not been announced, he decorated each of our wives with the Order of the Zaire, an award reserved for those with grace. The wives were delighted and happily stepped forward where Mobutu kissed them on the cheek three times each and decorated them. They deserved an award for grace, they really did, and they deserved another for standing at attention in the heat as the band played the Congolese and American anthems through a total of seven times that morning.

Bill Carpentier had finally run out of medicine for Joan and, in desperation, brought in a local doctor to see what could be done. The African doctor prescribed a medicine not approved for use in the United States but readily available throughout most of the world. Joan by now was ready to try anything, and the medicine began to work. Within a week, by the time we got to Australia, she was cured.

That night we ate informally at the compound restaurant and then went to a native celebration and dance dedicated to *Apollo 11*. It was a high-spirited, terribly hot but fascinating evening.

When Western-style dancing began, and before we had been invited to join in, I jumped from the dais and cut in on Miss Congo and her escort. The band leader noticed and picked up a faster beat. The dancers all moved back to watch.

Neil, it turned out, disapproved of my obviously spontaneous participation. Nick Ruwe and Bill Der Bing settled in the opposite camp: they thought it was a genuine and honest move. The newspapers loved it. Neil subsequently came around.

October 24, Tehran: A long flight to Tehran, which we passed by dozing or watching the movie *Tony Rome*, with Frank Sinatra and Jill St. John. Joan used the telephone on the plane to call the children one by one and missed them all.

Because of our relatively late arrival, we made it easily and quietly to our hotel. In the middle of unpacking Joan turned to me and said, "Buzz, I know what city this is, but what country is it?" I was beginning to feel the same way. I was also certain I had a fever and Joan felt my forehead and said I was manufacturing a fever to get out of some official functions. When it seemed to be worsening, I called Bill Carpentier, who took my temperature, 98.3. I was manufacturing a fever.

The next day we were received by the Shah of Iran and his wife, Farah Diba. The Shah was a stately but friendly man with a great patrician nose and beautiful gray hair. Farah Diba was, quite simply, one of the most beautiful women in the world, a condition enhanced by the fact that she was five months pregnant. Their young son also attended and took great pride in showing us his model of the Apollo Saturn rocket. Like nearly all the young people we encountered, he was enthralled.

Farah made a presentation we would remember as one of the most thoughtful of the trip. She had inquired through the embassy about our children, their interests and ages. For each she had prepared a gift—eight in all.

The reception must have pleased the Shah because as we left, he insisted we all come to his birthday party that night. It would not be an official function, and we all accepted.

The Shah's birthday party was memorable because it was a lavish party throughout which Joan was miserable and I was smiling, but only for effect. I quickly became a social wizard, something I definitely am not, and determined to meet everyone there. Joan was stranded.

We were caught in the ebb and flow of a changing world within a world. That night we had one of the more memorable fights of our marriage. I know now that we were both resisting the vastness of the changes together, but we were fighting in different directions. I was informed that I either begin to stay at home or plan to move out. A divorce would ruin my career so she wouldn't ask for one. If I stayed at home I wouldn't be required to pay attention to her, but I would have to spend time with my children.

At this point I screamed that I loved my children and was answered in equal volume: "Then show it!"

October 26, Bombay: We observed a sullen and reproachful silence on the plane from Tehran to Bombay. The reception here was the largest of our trip. Three-hundred thousand people flooded the center of the city, though it was some time before we had a count. We were told there were three *leks* present. The condition of humanity in India is so low that people are counted by how many fit into one area called a *lek*. They have no identity other than that. As I remember, 100,000 people can be squeezed into a *lek*. It was a terribly depressing country and it was also an awkward stop from a diplomatic standpoint.

Indira Gandhi had suggested we come to the capital, New Delhi, but the State Department felt we could be seen by more people in Bombay. Mrs. Gandhi, miffed, did not attend.

October 27, Dacca, East Pakistan: We were advised to avoid eating any food and I very nearly didn't get off the plane. En route, we received a cable saying that a group of dissidents were threatening to cause trouble because one of the American astronauts, a Colonel Aldrin, had Zionist leanings. They would not be responsible for my fate if I dared step off the plane.

Julian Scheer nearly dissolved when he saw it. What in hell do they mean? he kept asking. I had no idea at all. I sat staring out the window, wondering how I could endure the nightmare this trip was becoming. I racked my brain trying to figure out what was going on. The best I could do was recall that a Masonic Lodge in Tel Aviv had sent me a very elaborate plaque and I had responded to them.

Julian, ever insecure, refused to make any decision or even to suggest one. Mike and Neil urged me to get off the plane and pretend nothing had happened. I did just that and there were no incidents of any kind. I jumped at the slightest noise.

If Bombay was depressing, Dacca was even more so. The country is now known as Bangladesh and I can see why a revolution was inevitable. The poverty was extreme and thousands of people were starving and homeless.

October 28, Bangkok: A welcome relief. The streets were lined with beautiful smiling children in blue and white school uniforms who not only weren't starving, they were on the chubby side. Joan began to cheer up—the children were a perfect tonic. On the plane to Bangkok, as all the wives customarily did, Joan had telephoned home. Our son Mike, who does not put up with much interference from anyone, got on the telephone to complain about neighbors dropping in and checking up on him. Andy got on to announce he had sprained his ankle. Jan got on to announce she was sick and tired of her brothers. When Joan finished the conversation she sat down next to me and spoke to me for the first time in nearly three days: "I'm never going to call home again."

We stopped the motorcade a number of times while the children ran forward to present us with flowers and balloons. Following our official reception, we went off to our press conference. Joan went off for a nap and a visit to Johnny's Gems.

Johnny's Gems is a discount jeweler who is famous in the military for the care he gives his customers and the honesty of his dealings. Joan had been given a moonstone in Dacca. Johnny designed and made a setting for it. Later that afternoon we attended a reception given by the prime minister.

The next day we were received by King Phumiphol Aduldet and Queen Sirikhit in a stiff, formal, and uncomfortable ceremony. I had the feeling he didn't really want to do it and then didn't know what to say to us once he met us.

The Thais have a reputation for being a happy people who are exceptionally good with children. We toured a school and could see why: the classrooms and teaching methods were extraordinarily advanced and the whole school was obviously built for children—even the shrubbery was trimmed into the shapes of animals.

Joan was soon back at Johnny's and reappeared at the hotel loaded down with bronze flatware, salad bowls, a large candlestick, and $70 worth of Thai silk, shirts, and robes. With a happy grunt she thumped it down on the bed and announced that her Christmas shopping was done.

I still find it incredible to believe, but Joan, Jan, and Pat all did their Christmas shopping on the world trip and all of them completed it. They had more free time than we did, but not that much more. I hauled her back to Johnny's and bought her a blue star sapphire ring set into white sapphires.

October 31: Up at 5:00 A.M. and off for Perth and Sydney. It was Mike Collins' birthday and we held a celebration on the plane. By late afternoon we arrived in Perth, which was not on the original schedule, but the three of us had asked to stop there. This small city on the western tip of the Australian continent is a vital link in the space program. It is the home of one of the major tracking stations and, some-how, all of us were adopted by these friendly people. When John Glenn made his flight, the entire city turned its lights on and he saw it and thanked them. The citizens were de-lighted to have guests, listened attentively as we spoke in a small park in the center of town, and sang "Auld Lang Syne" to us as we left.

There is a great rivalry between the west and east in Australia, and the people of Perth were pleased we stopped there first. So were we.

It took nearly the rest of the night to fly across the con-tinent and at 2:00 A.M. we arrived in Sydney and went to bed.

November 1, Sydney: A beautiful clear harbor and the girls favor very short skirts. Luncheon was presided over by the newly elected prime minister. The ex-prime minister was seated by Joan and he told her the luncheon would have been much better if he had given it. When it came his turn to speak, he told us all how much better it could have been. We were all very uncomfortable.

November 2, Guam: Another of the infamous rest days. We were offered the home of Captain and Mrs. Beadles who were under the impression there were just six of us. They were absolutely mortified when twenty-two people showed up for dinner. By the time everyone had located a place to sleep, we settled down to a crowded dinner.

November 3, Seoul: Another city fitting into my past and one I now could share with Joan. It was freezing cold when we arrived and I said at the airport I was glad to be back and to see that Korea was now at peace.

We were given a reception and a luncheon by the prime minister and received our first decorations in the Orient. I was struck by the colors of the ribbons and decorations. All the others had been bright and covered with primary colors. Here, they were pale and delicate, almost subtle.

November 4, Tokyo: Last stop. We were decorated by

Prime Minister Eisaku Sato, and it was rather amusing. He couldn't get the ribbons over our heads, so we all stood around while they were unpinned, draped around our necks, and pinned again. We were presented with the Japanese Order of Culture, the first time this honor had been given to foreigners.

Our motorcade through Tokyo was tumultuous. The Ginza is even more Americanized than when I was there last. Joan is willing to bet it looks more like Broadway than Broadway does.

Our next stop in Tokyo was at the moated Imperial Palace for an audience with His Excellency, Emperor Hirohito. Here we were, in the public chambers of the one surviving Axis ruler of World War II. So much had happened since December 7, 1941—Japan had risen from the atomic dust of defeat to become one of the most industrialized nations on earth. It is still impossible to judge the influence of Hirohito on Japan's military might then, and its phoenixlike rise in industry now, and I wonder if it will ever be known. Hirohito himself appeared to me as a bookish, shy man more at home in his gardens and his beloved seashore than in the imperial counsels of war.

Prime Minister Sato gave his official dinner for us in the best Japanese tradition. No state banquet, no Western ceremonies. We were taken, one and all, to Shiu Kikura, the best geisha house in town. We took off our shoes and feasted on egg-drop noodle soup, chicken livers prepared Japanese style, and the culinary works of the Shiu Kikura kitchen. Joan was surprised to see that some of the geishas were quite old. Mr. Sato told her they could work well beyond their youth if they had a particular talent, especially if they were good musicians or dancers. Some of them appeared to be grandmothers and were very gracious indeed.

Following the dinner, the crew, principals, wives, and support team held an all-night celebration in honor of the completion of Giant Step. Joan and I stayed for one drink, then collapsed in a heap. The party lasted all night.

November 5: We left Tokyo at 2:00 P.M. to begin the long flight to Washington with a 2:00 A.M. stop to refuel in Anchorage. I slept fitfully, watched a movie, and ate. Neil, Mike, and I were sleeping when we arrived in Anchorage, but Joan, Jan, and Pat got off the plane and threw snowballs. The three of them were friendly before *Apollo 11*, but by now they were fast friends—all that had happened since the day we splashed down in the Pacific had strengthened their bond. Their husbands were slowly drifting apart, while they grew closer. It is a peculiar irony, but our wives remain close while I see Mike infrequently and Neil hardly ever.

It didn't take much time to refuel, but it took most of the allotted two hours to check us through customs. The plane was loaded down with awards and gifts, plus our personal purchases.

We had been told this complicated procedure would be expedited, if possible. Many of the gifts were put in storage until the various government committees involved could decide if we should have them, and some of the others would go directly on to Houston with us.

The children, naturally, were anxious to see what the Farah of Iran had sent. So were we. It proved impossible to find the gifts in the vast assortment of treasure; so we simply hoped they would come directly to Houston with us. Instead, they were placed in special storage with most of the gifts we had received. A year later, when we had all but forgotten about them, a crate of packages was delivered to our house. The gifts for the children had vanished.

Shortly before landing in Washington we were presented with a memo from our support crew.

PERSONALITY OF THE DAY

Your next stop is Washington, D.C., U.S.A. Here are a few helpful reminders:

The water is drinkable, although that is not the most popular native drink.

You can always expect student demonstrations.

Never turn your back on the president.

Never be seen with the vice-president.

If you leave your shoes outside your door, they will be stolen.

It is unsafe to walk on the street after dark.

Do not discuss the following sensitive issues with the natives:

Vietnam War
Budget
Foreign Aid
Import-Exports

Rate of exchange is .05 cents per one dollar (American).

We were welcomed home on the lawn of the White House by the Marine Band and a number of dignitaries, including President and Mrs. Nixon. It felt truly good to be home, and one and all, we said so. The president invited us to dinner and to spend the night at the White House.

We had three hours before joining the Nixons for dinner and I spent most of it in the basement of the White House where the president's dentist replaced a filling I had lost shortly before we landed.

So much had gone before this last dinner that it was almost incomprehensible. Yet within hours it had drifted into the background. The six of us and the Nixons were the only people at dinner and it was a friendly, warm evening. We all had cocktails and Mrs. Nixon, as affable and friendly as she had seemed reserved in Los Angeles, smoked a cigarette.

He thanked us for our trip and for being ambassadors of goodwill. He turned to Mike and said that he understood from the State Department that Mike would like to continue this work. Mike said he would. The president stepped to the telephone and was instantly connected with Secretary of State Rogers who said he would do his best in Mike's behalf.

He then turned to Neil. Neil too would be honored to serve as a goodwill ambassador, but he wasn't exactly sure where he could serve the best. The president advised him to think it over, then let him know personally.

He turned to me and asked the same question. I thanked him and said that I really wouldn't care to do that sort of thing and that while I was gratified by the success of the trip, I honestly felt I could contribute more by technical studies and work than public speaking before large numbers of people. I think I said "sir" after every other word.

The president excused himself after dinner to work on a speech, and Mrs. Nixon took us on a tour of the private quarters. We saw her porcelain collection and the president's collection of gavels.

The tour ended with our quarters, where a bucket of ice and a bottle of Scotch waited. The six of us sat down and, for the next two hours, talked over our experiences.

We continued our talk at breakfast the next morning and on the plane back to Houston. We arrived home in the happy glow of a major undertaking completed and began what Joan referred to as "the process of bouncing from princesses, emperors, and kings back to the kitchen."

Most of the country reacted as though we'd never been gone. Little press coverage of the trip appeared in the United States—a situation which, in retrospect, is sad because it would have been nice for the general public to share in this particularly American triumph. Yet at the time we were asked to carry members of the press on the plane, one and all we refused. On board the plane was the only place we had privacy and could relax. The press had been along during our one-day cross-country tour and had proved a bit bothersome.

A few weeks later, Operation Giant Step would resume for a two-day trip to Canada. As for me, I had two days of rest before I would be off on the banquet circuit. I spent the days in my office making hopeless little dents in the gigantic pile of mail.

4

A few short months before the Great Depression began in 1929, my father withdrew from the stock market and bought a rambling, gabled, three-story white and green house on Princeton Place in Montclair, New Jersey. Previously a rather rootless man, he had been persuaded to settle in Montclair by the high school principal, Harold Ferguson, an old friend. At the time my father had a three-year-old daughter, another who was one year old, and a pregnant wife.

On January 30, 1930, I was born in a somewhat gerry-mandered hospital. When my mother entered the hospital, she entered via Montclair, but when she arrived in the maternity ward she was in Glen Ridge, a city listed appropriately on my birth certificate. They named me Edwin Eugene Aldrin, Jr. At home I became known as "Brother." My sister, Fay Ann, a year and a half older, could not quite manage that: Her version came out "Buzzer" and it stuck until it evolved into Buzz.

My mother had blonde hair, blue eyes, and an independent will which often conflicted with my father's own strong determination. She was the daughter of a strict Methodist minister who served as a chaplain in the army. Her name was Marion Gaddys Moon until the day in the Philippines when she married my father, who at the time was a dashing aide to General Billy Mitchell.

Mom, perfectly groomed, presided over a busy household but did little of the actual work. The kitchen was supervised by Anna, a robust black lady who could not be intimidated by anybody. The remainder of our large house, me included, was under the direct supervision of Alice, our black housekeeper and my best friend. Together we shared the third floor of our house. Her enthusiasm for my world made it grow, and more by demonstration than by words she taught me tolerance.

My father was an executive with Standard Oil of New Jersey and famous as one of the country's first flying executives. As such, he was away from home a good deal of the time and when World War II began he was gone even longer. From time to time, on his way from being inspector general of the Thirteenth Air Force in the South Pacific to Europe to study anti-submarine missions, he would come home in his colonel's uniform. The visits were always short and, it seemed to me, rather remote.

Our family life included my mother's sister, Madeline Sternberg; her brother, Bob Moon; and my grandmother. The Moons were as close as the Aldrin family was mysterious. My father seldom mentioned his family. All I knew was that his brother and two sisters had been born in Sweden but that he, the youngest, was born in America. I visited with his family once, when he took me—still very young—to Worcester, Massachusetts, where they lived.

My father never gave direct instructions nor stated goals, but what was expected was somehow made clear. I also knew he was more important than most of my friends' fathers. My parents, somehow, were inhabitants of a world larger than the one provided by Montclair, New Jersey. When the *Hindenburg* burst into flames while trying to land in New Jersey, I could tell my friends with certainty that my father had crossed the Atlantic on the gigantic dirigible and had, in fact, predicted that it was neither safe nor practical.

When I was two, I took my first ride in an airplane. My father was the pilot, Alice and I passengers. He flew us to Florida in Standard Oil's Lockheed Vega, a sturdy plane painted to look like an eagle. My father must have been distressed to see his only son throwing up for most of his first plane ride. He tells the story now with a look of wry amusement.

My interest in mechanics and design started early—with a mouse cage. I designed a three-story cage of wire and plywood, complete with an exercise wheel, teeter-totter, and tunnels. When my design was complete, my mother drove me to the hardware store and helped me buy the necessary materials. Once the cage was complete and I had shown off my miracle of construction to my family, a white male and a black female mouse were acquired and immediately obliged with a litter of the tiniest, cutest little creatures I had ever seen. I sat and watched them for hours, and even built a special compartment in the cage for them.

One morning I went to the cage and found I had left the door between the big cage and the baby cage open. The mother was feasting on the last of her young and I was weeping. Whatever I understood about the reproductive process by now was influenced by this horrible sight. I felt personally responsible and would not be consoled. Not even my mother's insistence that accidents will happen helped.

I was small for my age and naturally anxious to appear as tough as the bigger boys. I decided a good black eye earned in a fight would suit my image perfectly. I picked a number of fights and came home with various wounds and bruises, but never a black eye. When I finally got my much-wanted shiner, I nearly went into hiding. I got it in a nasty collision with the kitchen door and was horrified the bigger boys would discover how I got it.

Some of the older boys who occasionally included me in their games often played football after school at Anderson Park. It was my extreme good fortune that Anderson Park was located directly across the street from my house. I did my homework in my room at a desk that faced two windows looking directly across the park. As soon as one or two of the older boys appeared, I was down the stairs two at a time and out into the park. They called me Little Whitey because I was short and towheaded. I was also full of wiry energy and enthusiasm. They let me join in.

We were continually organizing one game or another. In those days there were no structured athletic teams for youngsters. I think we learned a good deal more by doing it for ourselves than we would have if there had been a Little League or any other kind of structured organization. Doing it for ourselves helped develop leadership abilities and the kind of competitive spirit that I would eventually discover characterizes so much of later life.

Baseball didn't particularly interest me, but tumbling did. So did pole vaulting. The tumbling wasn't especially sophisticated, but we did learn to do handsprings, hand stands, and to dive over people. We acquired a small reputation for our expertise and the crowning moment of glory came when we were invited to put on an exhibition for the students at Lady of the Lake, a parochial school located in the adjoining town of Caldwell. I returned from the exhibition exhilarated and full of curiosity about Catholicism.

Pole-vaulting I particularly liked, although I wasn't at the time aware of why. I have since decided that I preferred it because it is a solitary experience. You are not truly a member of a team and your achievement is strictly your own. It is also a sport that requires much practice, and I practiced religiously. With great effort I installed an exercise bar next to a sturdy oak in our backyard and whenever I wasn't in school or at Anderson Park, I was working away in the Aldrin backyard.

Another favorite activity was sneaking into the movies. The most effective method at the Bellevue Theatre was to climb up the fire escape and quickly pull open the door and duck in, hoping you hadn't let in too much light. Usually we were caught, and the requirement then was, as you were being escorted out past the box office, to say to the manager, "I'll never do it again," with your fingers crossed behind your back. Then, as he released you, you said under your breath, "Today," thereby appeasing any gods that might not accept crossed fingers.

Saturday afternoons they showed serials at the Bellevue and whenever possible I was there. The first I remember seeing was one in which Jackie Cooper was forever in one great peril or another. One particularly exciting segment ended with Jackie falling off the roof of the barn, obviously to certain death. We discussed his fate endlessly the next week and eagerly returned the following Saturday. The gasp of relief was loud and sincere when Jackie, instead of dying, landed in a rain barrel.

My favorite serial was *The Lone Ranger*. The first series ran for ten weeks and began with ten rangers, one of whom would be bumped off each succeeding week. They didn't wear masks, and I speculated continually on which one would become the Lone Ranger. At the end of the series, only one Ranger was left and we never knew which he was. Tonto appeared soon; from then on I was enthralled with their independence and great sense of justice, and worshiped the Lone Ranger.

I pretended to be a latter-day Lone Ranger and felt very much like him when I set off one day to ride my bicycle to the George Washington Bridge. I wasn't off to dispense justice, but I did go alone and it was a half-day bicycle ride fraught with hazards.

Scholastically, I wasn't exactly the star of my class by any means. My two sisters, however, had a bent for academic excellence of which I was constantly reminded. I was not a poor student, but I was average. "Average" was the kind of word one didn't use at our dinner table unless referring to others, and it wasn't long before I was being pressured about my grades. At the time I had skidded through a Latin course on my sisters' reputations by getting a B and C the first half-year. My own disinterest showed clearly by the third semester and I sulked home with a D, my first. It wasn't until the ninth grade that I made my scholastic turnaround and, from that time on, I was crushed whenever I received a grade as low as a B. In my junior year of high school, scholastics ascended over athletics in importance and I spent my first football season in the stands.

Summers we usually spent in the mountains at Culver Lake, which was about a two-hour drive from Montclair. We rented a cottage from Dr. Jimmy Wolfe, a family friend and the physician who brought me into the world.

One early summer, my tenacious nature nearly caused me to drown. I hadn't yet learned to swim, but I had become an avid rock collector. The best of my collection I placed in my bucket one day and took it down to the dock to show to my friend Stevie. Stevie was my age but bigger and on this particular day, meaner as well. When I refused his offer of an important but obviously one-sided trade of rocks he pushed me, pail and all, off the dock. I wasn't about to give up my pail for love or money and the last thing I remembered was looking up and seeing the daylight above the surface slowly drifting away. Stevie's father, meanwhile, realized the danger and dove in after me. He finally pulled me ashore, my bucket still clutched to my chest.

During a subsequent summer when I had learned to swim, Dr. Wolfe built a box with two pieces of glass in it, which we could put over our heads and then look around beneath the surface of the water. I was fascinated and used the box continually. I liked swimming, but I loved diving below the surface. This fascination grew into my hobby of scuba diving and would eventually have a noticeable and surprising effectiveness when I wanted to simulate space walking here on earth.

My sister Madeline, four years my senior, and I got along quite well while my relations with my immediate sibling, Fay Ann, fluctuated considerably. My opinion of her as we grew up was: "She did it, she did it. And she'll do it again."

During the winters the porch on the side of our house could be enclosed and made into a separate room, accessible to the main living area by French doors. One day Fay Ann, after a merciless teasing by me, marched into the house and locked me on the porch. When my demands that the door be unlocked went unanswered, I kicked in one of the windows. The discipline, as I remember it, involved both a spanking and banishment to my room. Whatever it was, the message didn't get through, because within a week the entire sequence was repeated.

Fay Ann and I must have been tiresome and troublesome at times, but the past has grown into a bond between us and we are close still. Madeline, older and more independent, remained aloof from all of this until one night when, in her appointed job as babysitter, she simply had had enough and took after me with a hairbrush. Hours later, that same hairbrush was used on Madeline.

In the sixth grade I fell in love with Ann Lang. It involved, I regret to say, much anguish on my part since little happened but my first broken heart. It was devastating at the time because Ann Lang's favorite was Malcolm Minor. Malcolm was a social get-around, which in the social hierarchy of our particular school, was tops. I was a lowly gymguy. Today we call gymguys "jocks," but at that time I not only didn't know what a jockstrap was, I was unaware there was anything down there worth protecting. I did have an ego and I wanted to be "in." I longed for the day somebody would refer to me as a social get-around. Nobody ever did.

My knowledge of sex was, at best, hazy and vague. In time I acquired the vocabulary but I had no idea what deeds accompanied the words. The summer I was nine years old and literally out the front door to catch the train for my first trip to camp, my father hastily retrieved me and, for reasons of his own that remain unclear to me to this day, took me into one of my sisters' bedrooms, sat me down, and we had a chat. I paid polite attention as he explained to me the engineering wonders of pipes. They had one part which was called "the male" and it fit . . . er, ah, assembled . . . well, was screwed . . . into another part called "the female." I thanked him and went off to camp wondering vaguely what he was talking about. The subject of the birds and bees was woefully imprecise to my father compared with the exactness of fitting pipes together.

I returned from camp somewhat more enlightened. Meanwhile, a new family had moved into the neighborhood. They had a son a year older than I. On a musty fall day in the coal bin of Osborn and Marcelles Coal and Lumber Yard he demonstrated his prowess at masturbation before a fascinated onlooker.

Subsequent adventures in the coal bin involved as much cloak-and-dagger activity before the event as there was guilt afterward. There was, from that day on, great speculation about "doing it."

Things naturally progressed and before a few more years passed we were all having serious dates at the movies. What was serious was our intention. We aimed to get a feel, and there were two major methods for accomplishing this according to various, no doubt self-appointed, experts. One was called "the armie," and it involved placing your arm around the shoulder of your date then allowing your hand to slip surreptitiously down her arm and over. The other was much more direct. It was called "straight on in," which was exactly as it sounds. The first time I ever tried the much more subtle armie—after what seemed like hours of nervous anticipation—the young lady turned to me and nearly sent me running in fright and embarrassment: "Buzz Aldrin, you're going to get in Dutch!"

I eventually succeeded for one brief moment and wondered, for hours afterward, what all the excitement was about. I soon found out, but "doing it" was still a long way away.

The big song when I was in junior high school was called "Popularity," and it proved rather enduring because I still hear it occasionally. The concept of popularity remained fuzzy and had, I think, more to do with the size of a girl's breasts than any other attributes, physical or otherwise.

The first time I fell in love when it was reciprocated was in the eighth grade. Carolyn was older than I, and a friend of Fay Ann's. She lived in Cedar Grove which was sufficiently far away so that my mother insisted on driving me to my dates, much to my displeasure. It was a very brief love because fate soon stopped it. Fate was high school, where Carolyn soon went, promptly forgetting anyone she had ever known in a lesser school. Fay Ann helped by teasing me about running around with her gang instead of my own and I countered with detailed reviews of Fay Ann's complexion.

Overshadowing all activities—scholastic and social—was sports. Sports, in turn, developed my natural competitiveness which grew considerably during the seven summers, from my ninth to fifteenth years, when I went off to Trout Lake Camp in Maine for eight weeks.

Camp was supervised by Charlie Hamilton, one of Elizabeth, New Jersey's more upstanding citizens, and was divided into two four-week sessions. The division was so any parents worried that Maine was too far from home could retrieve their sons after four weeks. Several weeks before departure, my mother finished sewing my name into just about everything, checked her list of supplies against the list provided by the camp, and packed everything into the duffel bag and reinforced trunk. They were shipped ahead while I waited restlessly for my departure. We were driven to New York, where we boarded a boat for the all-night ride up to Boston, finally ascending through the cranberry bogs along Cape Cod where some of the guys invariably got sick. Disembarked in Boston, we headed for the train station for the train to Portland. In Portland we were met by chartered buses or, if it was a lucky day, a Packard or Chevrolet sedan, vintage 1936, with black shiny paint and running boards. Six boys were packed in per car and the rest went by bus. Those who didn't get seasick now had their chance. The roads were winding and caused frequent nausea among young boys going away from home for the first time.

The first few days we bunked wherever we chose while the camp instructors tried us out at various forms of recreation and sports. Once they could divide the camp into two roughly equal teams, we were set—one team to be called T for Trout and the other L for Lake. Once assigned to one or the other team you were on that team on all subsequent visits to the camp. I became once and for always an L.

Each cabin held six boys, roughly the same age, three from T and three from L. We were supervised by a counselor and a junior counselor. It was regimented, yet there were many opportunities for individual freedom and activity. Reveille was not long after sunrise, followed by flag raising and breakfast, which was served in what we called the Lodge. While the counselors were making men of us, they were also teaching us manners. Breakfast frequently included a whole orange, served sliced in half. It was strictly against the rules to pick up the orange and eat it in the usual way. Instead, we were taught to scoop out the pulp with our spoons.

The first summer at camp I remained constantly on guard against "quickies," or "funsies," anxiously waiting for the next year when I could cause them to happen to others. A quickie, or funsie, was, in effect, pulling a fast one. One of the more popular was to say to a new camper, "Would you do me a favor? There is a light switch on the fireplace mantle. Could you climb up and turn it on?" The fireplace mantle could barely be reached by full-grown men and it was a major undertaking involving piling chairs and furniture together for a nine-year-old. The word would spread quickly and by the time the quickie victim was up on the mantle and realizing there was no light switch, there would be a gathering of smiling faces forming to watch his humiliation.

By dinner time, the call to gentlemanly behavior was, whenever possible, sabotaged. One sure way was to get your table mates giggling and there was no surer way to do that than by flatulence. We all envied the best at this dubious talent and soon fell to imitating them by cupping our hands under our armpits and pulling our elbow directly down and to the side.

The competition to see which was the best team was constantly emphasized to us all. Whenever your team was ahead, it wasn't ahead by enough. When you were behind you really worried. Winning was important, yet I cannot now remember which summers my team won and which the T's won. There were also individual awards given, and I received many. The National Rifle Association, as full of advocacy then as now, issued the marksman awards. The great trophy, the one for best all-around camper, became mine the third year I was there and I have it still.

One highlight of the summer was an overnight trip up the mountains along the opposite shore of the lake. The lake was only three-quarters of a mile long, but it loomed before us as great an unknown as the Pacific Ocean. We hiked to Flag Tree Mountain, which may not have been the actual name of the mountain, but that was how it was known among the campers. It had a uniform skyline but for one tree that loomed larger than all the others. We climbed the mountain each year in search of that tree and continually failed. We'd sit around and plan our approach to it and invariably it would not turn out to be where we had thought.

If we found what we suspected to be the flag tree, a climbing party with a flag was organized. There must have been flags flying from half the trees on the mountain each summer, but never from the Flag Tree. My last year at camp, we figured out that while it was the tallest tree on the mountain, it didn't necessarily have to be growing at the top. We picked a point slightly short of the top where it seemed likely the tree would be and sure enough, it was there where we figured. It was never destined to wear a flag, though, because the first branch was over seventy-five feet above the ground.

Years later, in Acapulco with my own son, the Flag Tree came alive again. Andy, during a boat ride across the bay, pointed out one tree that was larger than all the others and announced that since it was the biggest, it must be on the top of the mountain. I challenged his reasoning and he contested me. We spent two hours, first his way and then mine, before we found the tree where I figured it would be. I had bought a flag. This time Andy and I got the flag atop the flag tree in Acapulco. It wasn't easy.

As I grew older and more experienced in the ways of summer camp, I became eligible for the three-day canoe trip up and down the Songo River. The trip ended with our first sighting of civilization since we had arrived at camp. Civilization? It was a Howard Johnson's located on the outskirts of Naples, Maine. The return to the world of sophistication was celebrated at the candy counter by buying a round hard candy which one year cost me a tooth.

The eight weeks raced by each summer and I was never once homesick. The first summer in camp my parents and sisters came to visit, but mostly they spent their summers at the New Jersey shore.

One of the last nights at camp was celebrated with the Turkey or Beans Banquet. The team winning the summer competition was served turkey, while the losers were served beans. Following this dinner came the awards night accompanied by testimonials of our undying loyalty to Trout Lake Camp which, the next morning, we would all reluctantly leave for another year of—"no funsie" was what I called it to myself—school.

Clary Anderson was my high school football coach and friend. Although scholarship was by now terribly important to me, I nevertheless became a willing quarterback on the sophomore team at Montclair High. In those days the quarterback wasn't quite the glamorous position it is now. Too bad, because I was too small for any other important positions. The box formation was the big news in 1944, and we performed the shift away from the T formation with precision, almost as though it was ballet.

Teenagers, I have since discovered from my three, wear their parents into cooperation more by attrition than by logic. I was rather good at it, especially with my mother. My father also acquiesced, but only if it fit somehow into his particular scheme for my future. We didn't discuss the future much, yet it wasn't difficult to know what was expected of me. Whatever I did had to be done well and after high school I was going to a military academy. Without my knowledge, he was laying the groundwork for my eligibility to go to Annapolis, while I independently set my sights on West Point.

By the eleventh grade my dreams about West Point took further flights of fantasy when Madeline came home from Hood College with her boyfriend, Max Ullrich. Max was a West Point cadet, and I was in awe. He couldn't have been in our house for more than fifteen minutes when I realized I was staring at him. A couple of months before, Max, the color guard parading behind him, had been on the cover of *Life* magazine. And now here he was in my house on Princeton Place. He was even going to spend the night. He had forgotten to bring a sport shirt for casual wear and asked to borrow one of mine. My interest at the time in matters sartorial was virtually nonexistent, but I spent what seemed like hours selecting my very best shirt for our guest. He returned it with thanks the next day. I took it immediately to my room and put it on, no doubt thinking it would bring about a metamorphosis in me, a dramatic prescience of a future West Point cadet. The balloon was punctured moments later when I got a whiff of the shirt: heroes had body odor just like sweaty high school kids. I was surprised, I really was.

My last summer vacation of high school I didn't go to Trout Lake Camp. It was time to start preparing for a military academy. Young men of respectable families who want to go to important colleges go to prep school. Young men of respectable families who want to go to important military academies go to poop school. The poop school selected for me was in Maryland and it was called the Severn School. It was suspiciously close to Annapolis, but it didn't occur to me to ask why it had been chosen.

The purpose of a poop school was to provide a four- to six-week cram course to prepare students for their congressional exams which, if all turned out well, made you eligible for an appointment to sit for the entrance exams. The congressional exams take place in the middle of August, just after the end of the poop school course.

At Severn, students took courses in math, physics, vocabulary, and English. Math and physics presented no problem at all—I enjoyed them. English and vocabulary, however, required a concentrated effort from me. We also went over exams from previous years. To my chagrin, they emphasized vocabulary. We started through the dictionary and by the end of the cram course I was marooned in the M's, knowing I'd never complete the task in time for the examination. We also worked endlessly with synonyms, which seemed to be a large part of every old examination.

One afternoon, one of my poop school mates and I pooled our resources and bribed the school janitor to go into town and buy us a bottle of, as we called it, hootch. We had in mind bourbon, but he came back with gin.

The ensuing experience has taken on the aura of an exciting adventure over the years, a kind of poetic memory in which, "We drank that bottle of gin, the two of us, and down it went. Laughed a lot, stumbled, and got sick. And that was the name of the game. Bottle of gin and two big guys. We killed that bottle of gin."

Realistically, the bottle of gin almost killed us and though we looked upon ourselves as two big guys, we were actually a couple of stringy sixteen-year-olds. We took our illegal bounty down to the Severn River and proceeded to drink—straight—the entire fifth of gin. I can recall walking out on the diving board and suddenly being afraid I'd fall in. Then I became thoroughly sick, all over the place.

The next morning I somehow managed to get out of bed. I fully expected to go to my classes, but first I wanted to wash my face. I took out my Yardley soap and scrubbed. I was immediately sick all over again and I have never used Yardley soap since that day. I went back to bed and the official explanation given the counselor was that I had had a bad hamburger the day before.

That August, in the United States Naval Academy, Navigation Hall, Annapolis, Maryland, I sat for my congressional exams. The Naval Academy tradition was that, on the way to take an exam, you threw a penny at the statue of Tecumseh. We all tossed pennies over our shoulders and walked grimly to the hall where the test was being given.

My first reaction when I saw the exam was one of unqualified terror. The synonyms I had worked hours to memorize were nowhere to be found. They had all been changed to antonyms. The test took two hours. I think I spent fifteen minutes on the physics and math, and the remainder sweating over the English antonyms.

I did well enough. The purpose of the exams is to provide a guide for the necessary congressional appointment. I scored well and Senator Hawkes, at the behest of my father, and the results of my exam, gave me a principal appointment to Annapolis. If I passed the entrance exam, I would go to Annapolis.

My father by now knew I preferred—wanted desperately, is more accurate—to go to West Point. He nevertheless suggested Annapolis to the senator. When news of the principal to Annapolis came through, my father and I held a brief confrontation during which I stubbornly insisted he go to Senator Hawkes and say that my choice was West Point.

I sat for my West Point entrance exam at Governor's Island, a forbidding fortress off the tip of Manhattan. The tests seemed endless and I was worried I wouldn't sleep that night and be tired the second day. It was an unnecessary concern—I was so exhausted from the first day's testing that I fell asleep that night while lying on my bunk and cramming.

A month after the exam, shortly after I began anxiously waiting at the mailbox each day for the postman, the letter came. I was appointed to West Point. I could hardly contain myself. I immediately became The Cadet of the Future except for one immediate unmilitary action. Tears were streaming down my cheeks.

On July 1, 1947, I reported at West Point. I had been advised that it was wise to bring as little luggage as possible, so I arrived carrying a small, rolled canvas bag. I stepped off the train at the Point station and walked—my last walk anywhere for a year, hereafter I would be required to run—to the reception area at the east end of the main campus. As far as memorable days in the lifetime go, this would be recorded as one in which the changes were abrupt and dramatic. I entered the campus at 10:00 A.M. and promptly ceased to be an individual. There we were, guys who had lived in the city, guys from farms, guys from military families, guys from rich and poor homes: the whole spectrum of America. That was at 10:00 A.M.

We were immediately ordered to roll the pants of our civilian trousers up five inches, no more no less. They were rolled up so that we could see that our feet were pointed properly. It was mostly a psychological ploy—plebes aren't bright enough to know where their feet are pointed.

By 4:30 P.M. we were all exactly the same: frightened new plebes, hair shorn, and in regulation clothing. All day long, at any possible moment, we were browbeaten by the upperclassmen. We drew clothing, blankets, and sheets. We were measured by the tailors for the blue-gray dress coats, and I looked on in awe when I saw the black academy stripes on the front and back. What little time we had to ourselves, never more than five or ten minutes usually preceding meals, we frantically polished our shoes. The effort was fruitless because we'd no sooner start shining than an upperclassman would enter our room and give us another lesson in bracing. Plebes at West Point are required to be at brace whenever an upperclassman enters the plebe's room and whenever the plebe leaves it. Bracing is a form of standing at attention, chest pulled up, shoulders pulled back, and chin stuffed in hard against your neck.

Companies were formed on the basis of height. We were regimented into eight companies with First Company being the tallest and Eighth Company the shortest. When I pushed it, I could get by at 5 feet 10 inches. Being slightly on the short side of average, I landed in Fifth Company. At 4:30 P.M. that afternoon we marched in formation to Battle Monument on the Point by the Hudson River, where we were sworn in.

The next eight weeks, before officially starting the plebe year, we would be in what is euphemistically called "Beast Barracks." What we were being taught, in addition to regimentation, is that you cannot be a leader until you have learned to be a follower. Some of what we had to do was ridiculous, and it was soon obvious that in order not to go mad it helped a good deal to have a sense of humor. Fortunately, I could laugh and I frequently did. The particular image of me trying to get a spoonful of jello to my mouth, while taking my meal at braced attention struck me as funny. When jello was served I was at considerable pains not to look at any of my table mates nor to contemplate the ridiculous sight of myself. My particular duty at the table, as water corporal, and the only time I was permitted to speak, was when the water pitcher was empty. Then and only then could I ask the waiter for another pitcher of water. At that time I was a fairly garrulous person and whenever the urge to speak came upon me, I swilled down the water so that I could ask for more. I now credit the fact that I have a weak bladder to that year of water-pitcher duty at West Point.

The regimentation was so thorough it even included our shaving kits. We were presented with photographs on how our beds should look, how pajamas should be rolled, and what items—bathrobe, towel, and so on—must hang on which hooks of our alcove. Each item, socks and underwear included, were to be folded in a prescribed way and stored in a proper place. We began to learn the system and at the same time how to maneuver within it, if not beat it on occasion.

Minutes could be saved every morning if a way could be found to avoid the complicated procedure of making the bed. Regulations required that the mattress be folded in half, and on top of it the bedding had to be stacked in a precise way. Folded perfectly, from the bottom up, the order was two sheets, pillow, two blankets, and comforter. We hit upon a method, no doubt the same method as plebes had used for years. The complicated stack was placed beside the bed each night, and a separate set of sheets was pulled out of the laundry bag. The comforter, on the top of the pile, was the easiest to refold. It doubled as a blanket. The risk was that after a week or so the prefolded sheets got dusty and, as such, could cause trouble when the inspecting officer came around. Once a week, the sheets were refolded.

Pajamas were a particularly difficult folding job. They had to be folded and rolled in the shape of a croissant, an involved process. An extra pair helped, but they were hard to come by. You could sleep in whatever you wanted, but the regulations said pajamas and if caught without them you were subject to a delinquency report. I preferred risking punishment to laborious folding.

I am amazed at all that we learned on that first day. By the time we were sworn in, we had learned to march, turn corners, move to the left or right flank and to the rear. We had even acquired a bit of knowledge about handling rifles and going through the manual of arms. Somehow we found time to shine the brass belt buckles we had just been issued.

It helped, of course, to be a bit naïve—the harassment was somewhat less painful. I had completed high school, which was the minimum requirement for entrance to the military academy, and I was hopelessly naïve. Others were older. There were numerous people in our class who'd been in the service as enlisted men and a few had been officers. These guys formed a clique because many knew each other and had had previous military experience. Some had one or two years of college. They had a distinct advantage over most of us. This caused a somewhat unfair situation, but there was no way to get around it. One and all we were to compete.

Beast Barracks' summer progressed with a wide variety of training courses and lectures. We learned infantry tactics and our mettle at cooperating with the military way of doing things was constantly being tested. If there was any one thing I found intolerable at this time, it was the aching fatigue brought on by the drum and bugle corps at exactly 5:50 A.M. each day. I never did get used to it.

We were indoctrinated in the labyrinthine West Point Honor Code. At its core, the code essentially says that your word, given either verbally or in writing, is the truth. In each of our rooms we had a card with our name on it and next to the name were listed several categories or places you might be at any given moment. Our time and whereabouts had to be always accountable. If somebody in authority came by your room and found your card was unmarked and you not there, you could be written up for being absent at that particular time, a violation of regulations. If you later said you were on an authorized visit or at some place where you were permitted, your word was accepted. If you weren't telling the truth, your fellow classmates were honor-bound to say so. And you, in turn, were honor-bound to report yourself to the honor committee. The committee, on which each class had representatives, is completley separate from supervision by the academy's officers. Enforcement of the code is by the cadets only through their own chain of command. It was—and I understand still is—rigidly enforced. It can, of course, be argued that the code is too strict to have any application to living in the world at large. Nevertheless I became committed to it and believed in it. By my junior year I would have grave doubts about it, but for now it would be my way of life, a way of life I would faithfully observe all my years at West Point, in spite of my later misgivings.

One common thought during those eight weeks is, "Will I make it?" It is a valid worry because the plebe class is trimmed by between 15 and 20 percent of its members by the time the school year starts.

After four weeks, we were permitted visitors. My folks drove up from Montclair. Fred Henney, one of my roommates and by then a good friend, didn't have any visitors—his family lived too far away to come for a weekend. I invited him to share my family from then on. Both Fred and I had a taste for candy bars—we firmly believed they provided us with nourishment and, most important, added energy—but candy bars were strictly rationed for West Point plebes. Thus, my parents arrived with bags of candy bars for each of us and our first session off the grounds with visitors was spent conspiring how to smuggle the candy back in. We had to carry it on our person, since we were prohibited from carrying paper bags or the like. They had to be anchored to us somehow, because we had to double-time to our quarters. We ended up with candy bars stuffed in our garters (required apparel) and on top of our heads, under our hats.

Fred, whose father was a colonel who had assiduously taught his son the military ropes, could be counted on for one thing above all: whatever was the wrong way to do something, Fred would find it first. I can only ascribe this to his innocence, and the results were often hilarious. Sure enough, Fred dropped a candy bar on the way back. He stopped briefly trying to decide what was the best thing to do while I sped on. Fred didn't get caught smuggling candy into his quarters, he got caught standing still—a more serious offense. For his excuse he compounded his disaster: "I was looking for my candy bar, sir."

Toward the end of Beast Barracks, I took a brief break from a touch football game and sat down to rest on the green area surrounding the field. I didn't think much of it at the time, but within two days my arms, legs, knees, and face bloomed with poison ivy. It got so bad that when I was dispatched to the hospital I couldn't bend my knees to get there. I spent the next ten days in the hospital and it turned out to be a mixed blessing. I was fairly well out of the running for the plebe hike, a five-day trip through the countryside of grit and grime, roughing it. When my bedraggled, exhausted, and filthy roommates returned, I was in bed resting.

The day after Labor Day the school year started. The harassment increased because all of the other cadets had returned from summer vacation, but academics were now introduced and the change was welcome. A class would usually begin with a quick quiz to see if we had done our homework the night before. This would be followed by a lecture on the next day's assignment. When there were fifteen minutes left in the hour, we'd be ordered to the blackboards. Three walls of the classroom were covered with blackboards which were alternately numbered odd or even. The odds and evens were each given different problems to solve. At the beginning of the plebe year we were all arranged alphabetically. My last name put me in the first section. After the first three weeks, our order began to shift slightly as our academic abilities emerged. My firm resolve was that I wasn't moving anywhere. My name put me in the first section at the beginning and my work would keep me there.

Fully one-third of the plebe year is mathematics and that part was easy for me. I had spent all of my last year in high school reviewing math and, whenever possible, moving ahead of the class with my work. It proved to be time well spent.

I had also taken French in high school and though I found it difficult, I retained what I had learned. I chose French at West Point and the first year was pretty much a review of what I had already learned.

English, history, and social studies were my stumbling blocks; so they were given extra emphasis when it came time for homework. History, in particular, seemed so intensely taught that if I had blinked, I might have missed the French Revolution.

Athletics were considered of nearly equal importance to scholastics. If you weren't involved in intercollegiate athletics, you were required to participate in intramural sports and I, as always, was a willing participant. I had missed trying out for the plebe football team because of the poison ivy, which really hadn't upset me much. I had already resolved to abandon football for studies as I had in high school. I went out for swimming; specifically, the fifty-yard sprint. Before long it became obvious that though I was a good swimmer, I had no great future in the sport. After a similarly unrewarding attempt at hurdling, I returned to pole-vaulting and there I pretty much stayed. I eventually vaulted 13 feet 9 inches, which in the days before the fiberglass pole was quite good.

That spring, when the track season was seriously underway, I was reassigned from an at-brace dining table to a training table. It was a great relief—I could relax and talk.

On Saturday nights dances were held. They were called "hops" and you attended in your formal uniforms. From the time the dance ended at 11:00 P.M., we had one hour to return to our barracks before being in violation of the honor code. Attendance at the dances was not mandatory, and I attended a good many of them with a number of dates. Mostly, though, I remember spending Saturday nights studying. As soon as the first academic listings had been published I started a graph of my progress. At the end of the year I was the first in my class.

The first taste of freedom came after the West Point–Columbia football game, which that year was played at Columbia. From the time the game was over until 11:00 P.M. that night, when we would report for the bus ride back to the Point, we were out on the town. Since we were more than fifty miles away from West Point, we could drink. If any of us turned up drunk, though, it meant big trouble. This first shot of independence proved too much of a temptation for several of my classmates. When they arrived for the bus, they were slugged ("slug" was the term for punishment in cases of serious offenses). The lowest slug you could get was eight and four, representing eight demerits and four punishment tours. The demerits remained in your records while the punishment tours were served either by walking a specified area for two hours every Saturday and Sunday afternoon or working on a rock pile, which at that time meant helping to build a golf course for the officers. A large accumulation of demerits could bring an official hearing and the possibility of dismissal.

There was one disappointment that year, one we all endured together. Although Annapolis had already declared the tradition archaic and had discontinued it, West Point plebes were still required to remain in their barracks for the Christmas holidays. A few years later the rule was invalidated, but we were a lonely group of people that Christmas. I telephoned my parents on Christmas Eve, and after the conversation I went to bed feeling empty and desolate.

Toward the end of the plebe year, one by one we began to be recognized. An upperclassman would acknowledge that we were, after all, human beings. Until this time we were ordered here and there—and harassed during the process. One day during track practice, one of my upperclass teammates gave me a particularly rough tongue-lashing. When he was finished he smiled broadly and stuck out his hand. We shook. Thereafter, he addressed me in a normal tone of voice and no longer harassed me. Other upperclassmen could still harass, but the knowledge I had received my first recognition was comforting in the extreme. Acceptance is something I sought no matter what I was doing.

At the end of what we called June week, we were given a thirty-day leave, following which we were to report for the rest of the summer at Camp Buckner, on the military reservation some ten miles away from the Point. I spent my leave with my family and visiting fraternity brothers from high school on the Jersey shore, but mostly I was filled with anticipation for what would come next.

At Camp Buckner we were officially deemed yearlings, the equivalent of sophomores. For the rest of the summer we were indoctrinated primarily in military command, environment, and tactics. Our instructors were mostly first classmen and we were given our first opportunities to exercise certain leadership positions. For one period of the stay I was company commander and the lesson to be learned became clear: if you wish to lead, then you begin by taking on one of the most difficult leadership roles of all. You lead your contemporaries. Leading people who are some-how subordinate to you is, by comparison, relatively easy. We were put in an order of merit to compete with equals for the command positions.

Afternoons we scrambled through infiltration courses, learned from the engineering corps how to build pontoon bridges, and studied artillery. Then came the swim period, a euphemism for horseplay water-polo style.

As always, there was the honor code. One of my class-mates was caught in an honor violation and was brought before the honor committee. The committee recommended he be court-martialed but was informed by the school au-thorities that the grounds for court-martial were insufficient. The honor committee reconvened and the cadet was silenced, which meant that no cadet could speak to him and he, in turn, could speak to no one but his professors until graduation. It was a pretty drastic life to live. It only hap-pened once while I was at West Point and once was enough. It was even a painful thing to see going on.

For me, the West Point system of education was good. I wouldn't venture so far as to say it's the best way of educat-ing people, because its intention was to place all students under the same set of rules with the purpose of arriving at some order of merit. The system does not take into account the variety of backgrounds and degrees of individuality peo-ple inherently have. I'm pleased to see that the military academies are now moving away from this complete stand-ardization of education.

Nevertheless, I fit in well. To me, the beauty of that system was that you knew exactly where you were at all times. You could measure your progress. You also knew what was expected of you from day to day. You did your lessons, went to class, and performed. Part of what you learned you stored away for further use, some you dis-carded.

Would I do it again? The question is impossible to answer, because I suspect that the educational system at West Point has perhaps changed almost as much as I have in the intervening years. I experienced a certain sense of bitterness when the honor system proved fallible, but I was young and I continued to believe in it. Yes, it was unrealistic, but then so was so much that we believed in those days. At the time, the tradition of West Point and the malleability of a boy from Montclair, New Jersey, fit together well. I was unformed, and West Point, for better or for worse, fit me into a form.

Because I had done so well in my first-year academics, I was asked by the football coach, Red Blaik, to be one of the tutors for the football players. I declined this flattering offer for two reasons: I was already tutoring several of my classmates who were personal friends and I preferred to use my remaining free time for my own studies. A cadet who ranked below me in class academics was asked and he accepted. Let's say his name was Herman Thomas. It didn't seem of any importance at the time, but it would evolve into one of the most discouraging and disappointing events in my years at West Point. It would eventually affect my faith in the system.

One day in physics class we were at the boards taking exams when I had the distinct impression through my peripheral vision that one student was studying my work and methodology of solving problems. I was rankled by this experience. The cadet was Herman Thomas. I kept my silence until sometime later when the incident was repeated, again in a physics class, again by Thomas. By this time I figured I was in violation of the honor code for not reporting the incident to the professor.

The custom in matters such as this was to inform the professor, who, in turn, would be especially watchful and attempt to catch the cadet in action. I remained after class awkwardly waiting my turn to speak to the professor. I was hampered by the presence of another cadet waiting to speak to him. It turned out the other cadet who was on the other side of Thomas was waiting to report a similar infraction. The two of us went on record and the matter was referred to the honor code representative who adopted a wait-and-see attitude.

The incident was fairly well forgotten by the next year, my third year at the academy. But not for long. Second period one morning, we sat down to take a chemistry exam. The professor passed out a list of ten questions and we set to work solving them. As was customary in such a situation, the cadets all shifted their desks and chairs slightly so as to avoid any temptation. As we shifted about, I noticed Thomas briefly referring to a piece of paper in his notebook, but I wasn't at all sure he was doing something dishonest. Moments later I looked up again and saw him looking at answers to what I could now see was an exam completed by a cadet and graded during the first period that morning.

I was stunned. My immediate reaction was to stand up and call for the professor, but I hesitated. It seemed a terribly drastic action. I would eventually wish I had acted immediately. I waited until after the class was dismissed, reported this serious infraction to the professor, then went back to my company and found our honor code representative.

What puzzled me most was how the exam could have got out in the first place. The implications were large and well beyond me. It wasn't unusual for an identical test to be given the previous period, but how did Thomas get one of the graded exams?

I told my company rep what I'd seen. He listened uncomfortably and said he'd look into the matter. I saw him less than fifteen minutes later at lunch where he took me aside and said he had gone to Thomas's room and there, in a notebook on his desk, was the test with the answers. He'd found it in the first place he looked.

But he hadn't taken the evidence. Why, I asked? Because

two now knew about the infraction, not counting the professor. Thomas was, therefore, honor-bound to report the truth when confronted with our accusation. My belief in the merits of the honor code were such that I readily accepted this.

My company honor rep, however, must have been somewhat less the innocent than I was because a few hours later he found me to tell me he had gone back to collect the evidence. It was gone. I was undisturbed—I had actually been surprised the exam was there the first time he looked.

Rumors began to fly through the class that some sort of complicated confrontation was going on between me and Thomas. I kept my silence, secure in my belief that it would all be resolved satisfactorily.

When cadets are faced with severe infractions of the honor code leading to the possibility of dismissal or a court-martial, they usually call a lawyer, generally a lawyer in New York City. That night Bob Pursley, a good friend of mine, overheard Thomas talking with his lawyers.

For several nights in a row, I was summoned to honor committee meetings to tell my story, as were the others who were by now involved. The meetings were necessarily kept secret, but the rumors nevertheless continued to circulate.

One of my classmates, in a burst of candor, told me one of the more significant rumors circulating among various of the cadets. It was that Thomas and I were involved in a somewhat dubious competition. The rumor strongly implied that I was out to get my competitor. This quite literally stunned me, and I replied that I could compete with anybody, but that there were rules for all competitions and they did not include cheating. I was not going to be defeated by unethical moves by anyone. I was competitive, but more than that, I was honest. In fact, I was a square about such matters.

Within a few days, the honor committee, consisting of

the first classmen from all twenty-four companies, voted unanimously that this was a severe honor violation and presented the case to the commandant of cadets. I felt vindicated from the disturbing rumor.

The commandant, Colonel Paul D. Harkins, called me to his office and said he had looked at the evidence but felt that we didn't have a case for a court-martial because we lacked the most tangible evidence of all: the exam. The normal procedure would then have been silence treatment, but the commandant—for reasons never explained to me—elected not to have it enforced pending more evidence or additional infractions. He did have a number of meetings with Thomas but their nature was not disclosed to me. Thomas is now a very high ranking career officer in the armed services.

My confidence in the system was severely shaken, but I nevertheless accepted the decision of Colonel Harkins, who went on to become a lieutenant general. I felt bitter that Thomas had not summoned his courage and faced the consequences by admitting what had seemed to me to be an obvious case of cheating. I never forgave him, but I kept my silence. Later that year I determined that our working relationship would be cordial, and that is how it was. We would never be friends.

I had learned an important lesson: no matter where you go or what you do, you'll find people who won't abide by the system, the rules. I realized this quirk of human nature existed in spite of my own rather naïve idealism and that I had to live with it. I also realized that the honor code was fallible.

I remember vague thoughts about the possibility of some sort of organized cheating ring. Could it be? No, not at West Point. But then how did the exam get into the hands of a cadet who was also a tutor?

My solace was that at graduation, Thomas placed behind me in class standing. The solace was short-lived, because the year after our graduation the West Point cheating scandal exploded all over the newspapers. There was indeed an organized cheating ring and my only regret was that it had not been resolved within the academy itself by the cadets and officers. Instead, it became public knowledge and did considerable harm to a tradition built over many years. Whether or not the incident in which I was involved was in any way connected with the subsequent scandal, I have no idea.

One of the larger mysteries of life was solved during the summer of my sophomore year, my "Summer of '49." A number of cadets, mostly those contemplating joining the Air Force after graduation, were invited on a tour of air bases around the country. While at Fort Bliss in El Paso, a group of us slipped across the border to Juarez, Mexico, where for a reasonable fee we were relieved of our virginity. Afterward, we stood in embarrassed silence as a woman purporting to be the health official in residence inspected us and washed us off. For weeks afterward my guilt was so strong that every time I urinated I waited for it to hurt. I remained on constant guard for the telltale sore. Nothing happened. At nineteen, I finally learned about "doing it."

The next summer, twelve of us were invited on a trip to the Far East. We would go to Japan and the Philippines to study the occupation governments created by General MacArthur as examples of the military cooperating with the establishment of government, the creating of new laws and constitutions. We flew in an old air force, propeller-driven plane to Hawaii, spent the night, and continued on to Tokyo. The day after we arrived in Tokyo was June 25, 1950. That morning the newspapers contained the news that the North Koreans had invaded South Korea. The study tour of governments was canceled because our aircraft was needed to begin ferrying in troops from the United States. We did remain long enough to attend serveral briefings on the nature of the fighting in Korea. High altitude F-80 jets were already flying out of Japan until bases could be established in Korea.

That same summer, obediently following a recommendation by my father, I applied to be a Rhodes scholar. As was the custom for West Point cadets applying for the scholarship, I asked for the field of philosophy, politics, and economics. These weren't my strongest subjects, but I felt that they would help my education to become more well rounded even though I suspected they would be of little help to my military career.

The interviews took place at Princeton and among those on hand to tutor us was a social science professor from West Point, George A. Lincoln, who had at one time been a Rhodes scholar. Lincoln would eventually come to occupy a somewhat dubious place in history: he drew the line across Korea, the 38th parallel, at the end of World War II, the same line which would be credited by many as one of the more significant contributions to the beginning of hostilities in Korea, and one of the most easily infiltrated by the enemy.

I was not accepted and, tail between my legs, I sulked home to Montclair to announce I had met my first academic Waterloo. I fully expected my father to be disappointed and was not at all prepared for his immediate rationalization. I didn't really want it anyway, he said, because it would do virtually nothing for my military career. His words were small comfort, for in my imagination I was already in a tweed jacket strolling the grounds of Oxford with a pipe in one hand and a book in the other. There were leather patches on the elbows of the jacket.

Dad and I agreed that following West Point I would enter the Air Force, but there the agreement ended. He wanted me to go to a multiengine flight school and I wanted to be a fighter pilot. Whatever my choice, there was little likelihood it would be refused. The Air Force had openings for nearly a hundred students interested in flight training and my standing in my class virtually assured me any assignment I wanted. I chose the Air Force, was immediately accepted.

The last year at West Point passed without any particularly memorable events and had about it a sense of anticipation about the future.

5

I graduated from West Point feeling on top of the world. I was twenty-one years old and thought of myself as worldly, sophisticated, and somewhat accomplished. I had a forty-day leave before reporting for basic flight training, and I decided to go to Europe. I hitched across the Atlantic on Air Force planes and was no sooner in Paris than I discovered how unworldly, unsophisticated, and unaccomplished I really was. I was just a typical American kid who had graduated from West Point, and as far as the rest of the world was concerned, still wet behind the ears.

For someone who had always lived in groups and who had marched to definite orders, the sensation of casually wandering around Europe was strange indeed. I had a vague schedule that permitted me to stay with various business friends of my dad's, thereby saving hotel money, but mostly I wandered. The wraps of a sheltered life fell away as I wandered through Wiesbaden, Frankfurt, Munich, Stuttgart, Vienna, Salzburg, Rome, and Switzerland. It was, as I remember it, the first time I ever had a sense of the continuum of civilization. I wandered museums, castles, and government buildings, my eyes wide with curiosity. I had never spent much time alone—now I did, and I liked it.

My basic flight training took place in Bartow, Florida, an ideal location that permitted us to work through the week on training, then spend our weekends watching the ski maidens in Cypress Gardens. I drove there in a 1951 Chevy coupe, my first car, which I customized by painting the roof white and installing a sun visor on it.

I spent six months at Bartow, most of it in the cockpit of a T-6 trainer, a sluggish but maneuverable propeller-driven aircraft. Student officers from West Point, Annapolis, and ROTC formed one group and aviation cadet student pilots another. A further division was made between the married men and the bachelors. Since the pecking order was fairly well established, I started out spending most of my time with West Point bachelors. Then I met Sam Johnson, a fellow student pilot who was both ROTC and married. Our friendship began in Bartow and continued on through subsequent assignment to Texas, Las Vegas, and Korea. Sam, Shirley, I, and my date of the moment were frequently together. From 1966 until the Vietnam war ended, Sam was a prisoner of war. We saw Shirley and their children frequently during those years when we were in Houston and she was living near Dallas. When he heard we had landed on the moon he went up to his guard, pointed at the moon, and said, "That's ours now."

I had an instructor in Florida who had done extensive B-25 flying during the war and didn't particularly like acrobatics. In our T-6's—known as Terrible Texans—acrobatics were about the only source of excitement. My instructor rode along with me several times and one day, during a couple of steep loops, I think he blacked out. When we started up the next day he told me that as far as he was concerned, I knew how to do the acrobatics and from now on he'd sit on the ground and watch.

If you scored well, you were on your way to becoming a fighter jock. If not, or if you didn't want to fly a fighter, you went on to multiengine school which, though more secure, tended to be less popular. Multiengine training, which my father advocated, led to positions of leadership—you eventually commanded a crew. But for individual accomplishment, exhilaration, and just plain drama, the fighters had a clear edge. I scored near the top of my class and was assigned to fighter training in Bryan, Texas.

Eventually my instructor's fear came home to roost with me. Flying along a few months later in Texas I decided I'd experiment a bit and try for a double Immelmann, which is pretty much a half-loop on top of the first half-loop. I was flying a T-28, a fairly slow plane for a stunt requiring speed, so as was customary, I went into a steep dive to build up speed. I pulled it up and at the top of the first double loop I decided my stunt was a bit sloppy. I decided to try again, forgetting that gravity forces tend to be cumulative and can cause a gray-out, a momentary and unexpected loss of consciousness. The next thing I knew I was awakening as though from a good nap, feeling rested and in the mood to stretch. I was astounded to find myself in a T-28 aimed straight at Texas. I remembered being first puzzled by the fact that there was a propeller in front of me and then realizing I was not only in a plane, I was in a plane and in trouble. I pulled it out with about two thousand feet between me and terra firma. There was no particular sensation of danger, but there was one of amazement. How did I get there? I didn't even remember I had been flying. Later I learned most bold pilots have had the same disorienting sensation and others were less fortunate.

Fighter pilots have a reputation for being rather happy-go-lucky, dashing, and damn-the-risk men. That might have been true in the days of the Jenny, which my father flew, or later with P-40's, but the sophistication of jet aircraft changed all that. Nevertheless, the prospect seemed romantic enough and I was excited to get on with it.

Graduation day at Bryan, my parents arrived from New Jersey to see me receive my wings. As a surprise for my father, I arranged for him to fly with an instructor in one of our T-33 jet training planes. He was still lobbying for me to change to multiengine aircraft and I wanted him to sense some of the independence of fighters. He was pleased with the flight but somewhat unimpressed.

The three months I spent at Bryan were, with the exception of my gray-out, very routine. My social life steadied somewhat when I met a pretty blond stewardess for American Airlines who was good company and susceptible to pilots in general and me in particular.

The serious business of learning to fly the F-80's and F-86's, both fighter intercepter planes then in use in Korea, came next. Sam and I moved on to Nellis Air Force Base near Las Vegas. I lived in the bachelor officer quarters and had no sooner arrived than I discovered that fighter jocks have a sense of humor approaching Grand Guignol. On the bulletin board there was a sign which said, "Farms For Sale. Recent buyers include . . ." along with a list of names. The names were men who had been killed in their planes or, in military parlance, "bought the farm."

The course—classroom studies and actual flying—lasted three months. I also reapplied for a Rhodes scholarship, this time specifying physics. After the interviews I felt I had done better than the first time, but I didn't do well enough. I did not fit into the mold of a Rhodes scholar and again was not accepted. We all knew we were going to Korea and the joke around the bar at Nellis was that Aldrin wouldn't last long in Korea once the Communists found out they had a Rhodes scholar flying around. My disappointment was not nearly as strong as it had been when I was not accepted after West Point.

Because I had applied for the scholarship, my orders to go to Korea were delayed a few weeks for the interviews. As soon as they were completed, I set to work expediting my orders through the service bureaucracy so that I might join my class in Korea. I particularly wanted to be with Sam.

The day after Christmas, 1951, I arrived in Seoul late at night in one of the murderous Korean cold waves. I had been warned in advance and had worn long underwear, but there was simply no way to keep warm. Worse, there was a snafu in the logistics of ground transportation. Instead of boarding buses for the drive to temporary quarters, as was customary, we were told the buses could not be found and were asked to climb up into the backs of trucks —a long cold ride to our quarters. It was two days before I was warm again.

I was assigned to the 51st Fighter Wing, one of two wings flying the F-86, the other being the more glamorous 4th Fighter Wing. The majority of aces in Korea were from the 4th, although the 51st had a good record of its own. It was an Avis to Hertz arrangement, mostly because the 4th had two distinct advantages. It was stationed slightly to the north of us and therefore required less flying time to return from missions—an important consideration, since we were always low on fuel. Also, it was located closer to head-quarters and therefore had pilots assigned to headquarters. Somehow it seemed that the 4th was always getting the better mission assignments.

Most of January 1952 was spent getting checked out and flying training missions. The war was winding down by this time, and though we didn't know it, it would soon be over. One training mission turned into one of the more har-rowing experiences I have ever had in an airplane. Just before turning back to the base—a decision made when you could compute you had little more than just enough fuel left to return—my F-86 kept speeding ahead of my flight leader's. I tried to slow down, but I kept pulling ahead. The main fuel-control system had frozen in the 100 percent power position. Our F-86's were equipped with a button on the left console, an emergency fuel switch that could manually override the main system. But the switch must be hand-held to operate, making radio communication a near impossibility—you need a third arm to operate the radio. I broke off communication and headed for the base. I made it back—just.

I flew my first mission in February, a sortie into enemy territory at a medium altitude. The likelihood that any MIG's would come down as far south as we were was remote. But it did give me a taste of combat missions, of knowing I was flying over enemy territory. If I had any sensation of fear or doubt—and I most likely did—they were suppressed quickly to do the job at hand.

The missions continued to be uneventful and I began to be bored. Between flights, I became intrigued with the business of planning squadron flights and the maintenance of the schedule board. When the officer who had this job was shot down and missing in action, I volunteered to take over and was immediately accepted. Later I was advanced to assistant group operations officer. I continued to fly, mostly with my friends in the Sixteenth Squadron. When my other work was complete, I'd schedule myself in on a mission.

On May 14, I had routinely scheduled myself onto a flight. We took off into a series of low and scattered clouds. We flew in what is called fingertip formation, patterned after four extended fingers with the command order running from the longest to the shortest finger. A National Guard pilot was commander on the flight and I was flying element lead, the position of the ring finger. We were about five miles south of the Yalu River when I spotted two planes flying considerably well below us. We hadn't been informed there would be any friendly aircraft in the area, yet it was unlikely a MIG would be flying so low south of the Yalu. I advised the leader I could see the planes—we called them "bogies"—giving him a chance to spot them too so he could lead the whole flight after them.

He said he didn't see them, so I said, "Number three is taking a bounce," which is how you announced you were going in on an attack. My wingman—in the little-finger position—accompanied me. We dove in and I kept my eyes on them—I don't think I even blinked—because if you took your eyes off a target in the broken clouds, chances were you wouldn't see it again.

The man in the second MIG—the wingman, lagging

slightly behind his leader—kept moving along, taking no diversionary moves. When I was four thousand feet below him, a not very effective range, my itchy fingers started firing. I didn't hit him much so I stopped firing, caught up to him a little more and started firing again.

His engine soon began smoking. I fired again and saw his canopy come off, followed seconds later by the explosive pilot ejection. I watched fascinated as the pilot left the plane in his seat and drifted away from it. It was an unwritten rule that the objective was to get the aircraft, not necessarily the pilot, so I made no attempt to fire at him.

It was a singularly undramatic experience: no dogfight, no maneuvers, no excitement. I simply flew up behind the enemy and shot him down. As for him, I suspect he wasn't paying much attention or was on a training flight. Obviously, he was North Korean or Chinese because the Russian pilots were rarely that easy.

Attached to the trigger is a camera, and I came back with a set of gun camera film of my first MIG. It turned out to be a rather historic set of pictures because they included the ejection sequence, the first pictures of the war to show a pilot bailing out. I didn't think I had gotten pictures of the ejection, but I had. They appeared a week later in *Life* magazine and went on to become one of the more rare photographs of the Korean War.

The Korean War was the first of what historians call the impersonal conflicts. There were no celebrations awaiting me as there would have been in all previous wars. I didn't even get to paint a MIG on the nose of my aircraft—I had no aircraft of my own; I flew whatever was available. That night I bought drinks for several of my friends and that was that.

If my first encounter with a MIG was undramatic, my second more than made up for it. On June 7 we took off immediately behind another flight of four. The first flight's wingman—the little finger on the hand pattern—had engine trouble on the runway and aborted his flight. So did my wingman. As was customary, I radioed ahead and offered to join the flight ahead to give them their full complement. The flight ahead of me, it turned out, was flying the newest F-86F's with no slats on the wings, which were wider and longer to give extra speed and maneuverability. I finally caught up, but not for long.

The mission was important. Fighter bombers were going to bomb the power plants on the south edge of the dam at Suey Ho, a critical power installation. So that we could provide protection we were given permission to fly briefly across the Yalu and into Manchuria, a most unusual situation. Pilots were specifically forbidden to fly across the Yalu and into the MIG traffic patterns at the numerous airfields just inside Manchuria. The intention was to avoid angering Red China into even more participation in the war. Once we had seen the fighter bombers finish their missions we were to patrol our way back. At this time the air war was fairly active.

The whole complicated subject of unauthorized missions behind certain forbidden points exploded into the press during the Vietnam war and curtailed more than a few careers. The same thing occurred in Korea, though on a slightly lesser scale and with little harm to careers. A pilot caught crossing into North Korea above the Yalu or into Manchuria was immediately grounded. Not many were caught, and the matter never received any attention in the press.

I paid no attention to where we were going because I was so busy trying to catch up. I knew that on our way back we would be going through MIG Alley, the place where most MIG's were shot down. It was a pilot's happy hunting ground and I was anxious to get there.

I also didn't know the men I was flying with—a most unusual occurrence caused by their wingman's abort and my moving ahead—but they sure as hell knew where they were going. When I noticed the dam slip by I realized something was up. These guys didn't even circle the dam as we had been told and instead headed straight north to an enemy field about fifty miles north of the Yalu inside Manchuria, all of the time lowering down to pick up all the speed they could get. The penny fell when I saw the enemy field: we were going in on an unauthorized attack well north of the Yalu.

There was no time to think the matter over—and as I deliberated decisions it would have all been over before I'd compiled the pros and cons. What was certain was that I could not leave my flight and couldn't catch up either. As we gained speed the newer F-86F's became little specks ahead of me. The antiaircraft flak started bursting around us as the three of them went in, followed about two thousand feet later by me in my F-86E. I was trying to catch up, a process which now seemed impossible.

I was looking ahead at the three specks I was trying to catch when all of a sudden, coming in from my right, I saw a plane sliding over toward me. I looked up and noticed the high tail. In great astonishment I whispered to myself, "It's a MIG!" He was in a precarious position but he had one advantage: he was flying slower and could maneuver his way behind me more quickly.

I think he saw me at the same time I saw him, because he immediately turned hard into me and I put the speed brakes out and turned steeply. We then fell into what was called a scissors maneuver. If a pair of scissors is broken, the blades will cross in both directions. If you could turn them, hoping to get one blade behind the other, the blade in the rear would have the best position. It may look like an aerial ballet, but it is deadly serious. The maneuver was partly skill and partly luck—the F-86 was easier to maneuver. We did this about three times before I could execute a tight turn, gaining altitude and coming in to his rear. I had the feeling I had a tiger by the tail and couldn't let go.

I started shooting but my sight wasn't working properly.

The tracers fell short of him, so I pushed the throttle full open to catch up a bit and fired again. I started hitting him and seconds later smoke was coming out of his wings and engine and he started a slow descent. His canopy came off and he ejected. I turned steeply to get the good news or the bad news. It was very likely there were more MIG's behind me. I had been unable to catch up to my flight and was alone, which was rare enough, but MIG's were seldom alone. I have no idea what the odds are on such a thing, but when I pulled around I discovered that he was indeed alone. I was drenched with sweat and still full of apprehension—I was twenty miles north of the Yalu and I had over two hundred miles to go to get back home. I turned south and began to climb, hoping to conserve fuel by connecting with the jet stream which ran south along the middle of the country. Within minutes, the flight commander began radioing to find his pilots. I reported back that I was okay and that I got a MIG.

It was customary, even when joining another flight, to report to your own squadron for debriefing. The flight commander soon radioed me and asked me to come to his squadron for debriefing. I didn't know who they were and they didn't know who I was. The only thing they knew for sure was that I might get them in a hell of a lot of trouble. Their leader turned out to be a marine and the others in the flight were a Canadian and an Air Force pilot. The Air Force pilot landed with several 23mm cannon shells lodged in his engine—it was a minor miracle he made it back at all.

They didn't want me to go back to my debriefing in my squadron and blurt out what had happened. I might have gotten into some trouble, but it would be nothing compared to what would happen to them. I kept my silence—I was still shaken when we landed—and went to their debriefing. I took some comfort from the looks on their faces and decided that if they wanted to live with it, they could. I decided I was in no position to turn them in.

By the time the cease-fire was negotiated in July, I had flown sixty-six missions and had just one more encounter with a MIG. Sam Johnson was flying as my wingman when we spotted several MIG's. I went in after them but they were heading north and out of range. I fired several bursts but they were too far away, so I told Sam we'd better head for home. I radioed to Sam and he radioed back, "I'll [*rat-tat-rat-tat*] be right [*rat-tat-tat*] with you, Buzz." Only Sam would conduct a conversation in the middle of a chase. When I had pulled out, Sam, ever eager, continued after the MIG. From the July cease-fire until December, when I left Korea, I flew escort missions up and down the coast scrupulously observing the twelve-mile limit.

My return to Montclair was much anticipated and the outcome totally unexpected. All the time I had flown in Korea I carried with me a picture of a girl named Nancy, who made the best shortcake I'd ever had, and kept the tin boxes of goodies coming almost monthly. She also sent letters and my responses generally went out by return mail. We had met just prior to my going to Korea and, at the time, the attraction was mutual. I went home thinking that this time I'd propose; once before I had met a girl who had come all the way from New Jersey to my flight training school only to find me very noncommittal on matters of permanent relationships.

Nancy had often mentioned the local drama club in her letters, pretty much passing it off as the way she occupied herself evenings. Well, it turned out drama clubs have leading men and Nancy was very much in love—with the leading man. It is one of the wrinkles of war that many relationships are tenuous at best and often continue just to have something going. It was quite obvious to me that she didn't wish to continue the relationship. I pulled my tail between my legs and went to my parents full of melancholy.

I thought I'd never recover. Little did I know how quickly I'd get over it. I had been invited to Long Island for a New Year's Eve party and I needed a date. I got out my little black book and on the first page found the name Joan Archer.

Before going to Korea, while I was in the throes of falling in love, I had accompanied my mother and father to a cocktail party. While there, a tall blond lady named Evelyn Archer insisted I come to dinner and meet her daughter. My mother had an expression to use for such occasions, a look which all but said, "Please do it, dear." My mother gave me the look and I accepted the invitation. The dinner I barely remember: I expected to find a rather homely girl whose mother felt it necessary to haul eligible young men home from time to time. My parents knew the Archers and had described their daughter as attractive, but what did they know? They wanted me married, and the faster the better.

I drove to her home in Ho-Ho-Kus in my dad's Cadillac and nearly ran out of gas. Joan turned out to be fairly tall, willowy, interested in the theater, and more sophisticated than most girls I had known. She also had a master's from Columbia, something rather rare at the time. Her reaction to the dinner, as I remember it, was somewhat regal and amused. She wasn't rising to her mother's bait and neither was I. Besides, I was already in love.

I had forgotten the evening entirely until I opened my book to look for a date for New Year's Eve. I called. I asked her out. She asked to have a day to think it over, and with good reason. Her mother and two of her uncles, returned from a family business meeting in Cleveland, had been killed in a plane crash. Joan wasn't sure she was ready for partying. I suggested going out might be just the thing.

Next day she accepted. The party on Long Island was being given by a pilot I had met in Korea and it proved to be a larger gathering than I expected. I figured it would be a bunch of fighter jocks and their dates sitting around. It turned out to be a rather rich mixture of socialites, businessmen, and a few pilots. Joan fit right in and so did I—after a few drinks. It was a heady evening, all the more so because Joan attracted people left and right. Before I knew it I was listening to theater talk, standing obediently beside my date.

Let's just say the returning war hero was not the star attraction, but he was definitely deciding to make an impression.

We went out twice more before I reported back to Nellis Air Force Base to be a gunnery instructor. She had a way of smiling at me I couldn't figure out. It either meant, "I've got your number, buster," or "Try and catch me." Both, I think now.

I promised to write. She promised to write. She wrote first. I mailed my answer in an hour. Within a month I invited her to come to Las Vegas—if she could work out a way to get there.

She did, and it caused me no small inconvenience. She brought her dad. I arranged for them to stay in a vacationing instructor's quarters. It was terribly hot when they arrived and it was a good bit different from the sophistication of New York. Military life, to make a slight understatement, can be rigorous. I wanted to see if Joan could take it.

Take it she did. All Joan needs is a challenge. She determined to be a good audience for all the flight talk and excelled at it. She even convinced me she was interested. Her dad, Mike, was fascinated. We enjoyed one another's company for a week and the day before she left, I proposed. I don't remember how I proposed but I remember Joan, smiling her smile and saying, "I was hoping you'd ask."

We spent the next day as three grinning idiots. My folks were delighted too. I was concerned about the impact of military life on Joan, but she insisted it would be no trouble at all. And she was right: by the time our military life together—a very busy seventeen years—ended, it was apparent how well she could handle it. Very well indeed.

We set the date. Changed it. Set it again. I had applied to Squadron Officer School, which is at Maxwell Field, just outside of Montgomery, Alabama. It was a good stepping stone for a career officer and I looked forward to it. At about the time I was accepted I got a telephone call from the air force personnel office asking if I'd be interested in becoming aide to the dean of faculty at the Air Force Academy. Would I? The problem was getting my assignment to the academy delayed so that I could go to Squadron Officer School and be married. Eventually the logistics settled.

We were married on December 29, 1954, at the Ho-Ho-Kus Episcopal Church and spent our wedding night at a nearby motel. The first two days of our honeymoon we spent driving to Montgomery, Alabama. The third day we spent trying to fumigate the cockroaches out of the three-room apartment I had rented near Montgomery. The fourth day we went to New Orleans and checked in at the Monteleone Hotel.

I have two distinct memories of our honeymoon. I was running out of money so I asked the hotel to cash a check for $100. They politely declined, all but telling me they didn't cash checks for military men. I was infuriated. I went to the local Standard Oil office, told them who I was and who my father was. Reluctantly, they cashed it. Here I was back from Korea, from defending my country, an officer, and I got the runaround trying to cash a check. It is symptomatic of the attitude many people have toward the military: we move a lot; we are footloose and irresponsible. What never occurs to anyone is that a conscientious military officer isn't about to write a bum check. If the matter ever gets into his record—and it will—it can drastically alter his career. You just don't mess around with such things in the military system.

The other event on our honeymoon I remember was the last morning when Joan complained of an upset stomach. I sympathetically complained of similar feelings and we passed it off as something we ate. We forgot it until well over a month later when Joan became suspicious as her upset stomach recurred from time to time. She went to the doctor and returned with a dazed look. We hoped it would be a boy.

Our routine in Montgomery began at 6:00 A.M. when I jumped out of bed and raced to four different gas heaters to try and light them with one match. If I failed I swore, if I succeeded I jumped into bed until it warmed up. When we got up, Joan's first chore after starting coffee was to spray for cockroaches.

She didn't complain about anything until I came home one day and announced I was going off for six days on a night intruder field exercise. Joan refused to be left alone. She decided to go home for the duration of my trip, but we didn't have enough money for plane fare. She took the train and her dad paid for plane fare back.

Shortly after the field trip we were scheduled to give our major reports. The school was highly competitive and I, as usual, wanted to be quite high in my class.

Delivering my paper—making a speech—was the hardest part of the three-month Squadron Officer School. I dreaded it. To my vast delight, the speech was well received. My elation must have been a bit too obvious because on the last night during a beer-drinking session one of my classmates, a captain I respected a good deal, took me aside and offered some advice. He was older and senior to me—I was a first lieutenant and an eager audience. He said, in effect, that I was too competitive, too insensitive to others, too determined to be the best, and that if I didn't watch it I'd end up with a reputation as a hotshot egotist. He then said he felt I had great talent and potential and that as my friend he didn't want to see me ruin my chances.

To be honest about it, I was so determined to do well in the school that I was at a loss to think of any instance where I might have offended anyone. Yet he must have spoken the truth, because the truth can sometimes hurt and I had tears streaming down my cheeks. I thanked him. It was one thing to point out a man's talents to him—that's easy. It is another to be enough of a friend to point out a man's shortcomings in the hope it might help. The next day I went home and started packing for our move to the Air Force Academy.

I was assigned as aide—semisecretary, flunkie, arranger, pilot, whatever—to General Don Z. Zimmerman and we hit it off beautifully. We had many of the same interests in common, not to mention a passion for football. He had been in Korea as well, so we had much to talk about. He was dean of faculty.

It was a busy time and a happy time. Joan and I both loved Colorado and life at the academy. We had a small pleasant apartment and Joan was busy nesting. She had also become active in a local theater group. They were doing a production of *The Hasty Heart*, and Joan by this time looked not at all in trim as a leading lady. Instead, she directed the play. General Zimmerman was on hand opening night along with his wife.

Within four months of our posting to the academy, General Zimmerman moved on. His departure was personally disappointing and discouraging for what it represented. The general from time to time was contested by a group of faculty members. He tended to experiment and they preferred the traditional ways. He even wanted cadets to read *The New York Times* and absorb its point of view along with the opinions of other papers. The *Times* was—as it often is—at odds with the military at that time, and the general's approach perhaps contributed to his transfer.

His successor was an interim appointee and was not a general. As such he was not entitled to an aide. We groused about his leaving the academy and Joan was apprehensive about moving to another base.

The perfect opportunity appeared quickly. Too quickly. I've always suspected General Zimmerman had a hand in the decision. I was offered a position as a flight instructor for the air training officers, a unique opportunity at the time. There were as yet no upperclassmen at the academy, so their absence was taken up by young first lieutenant pilots. We plunged in, feeling like senior citizens among pilots and their wives five years our junior. I quickly came to like teaching.

We decided to take a vacation in August, the last safe time for Joan to travel. By coincidence, the academy commandant, whom we had gotten to know, also decided to vacation in the East. He invited us along on his plane. We not only got to go home for a very long Labor Day weekend, we didn't have to pay for our transportation. We would be back in Colorado five weeks before the baby was due. On paper, it looked perfect. We spent nearly all of our time at my folks' place on the Jersey shore, lying in the sun, reading, and enjoying the company of both of our families.

One night during Labor Day weekend Joan expressed a hankering for lasagna. By now we were all used to Joan's hankerings and I made a great display out of packing everyone off to an Italian restaurant.

At eleven that night Joan awoke and said she had a terrible stomach ache. She was pale and perspiring as well, so I awoke my mother. We spent the next several hours trying to comfort Joan. Even my father awoke and suggested warm milk. Finally it dawned on us and we called an ambulance.

Three hours later, on September 2, 1955, James Michael Aldrin was born. He was six weeks premature, so he was a tiny little fellow but he looked huge to me. I was all goose pimples and tears as I bent over to kiss Joan in the recovery room. He was early, but he was healthy and lusty. We couldn't have been happier.

Until the next morning, that is, when the sedation wore off Joan. I arrived with an armload of flowers to find Joan sitting up in bed counting on her fingers.

"You're supposed to count his, not yours," I suggested.

"Buzz, how long have we been married?"

I counted it up on my fingers and then said, "Not quite nine months."

Awkward pause. Then, looking pale, Joan said, "Well, we know and to hell with other people."

Such a matter isn't much of a concern in the world as we know it now, but at that time it was somewhat scandalous. Quite scandalous in the kind of enclosed community we came from. Nothing was ever said, although we did take a good ribbing from proud grandparents. They knew, as we did, that it was a physical impossibility. To match his arrival date Mike would have to have been conceived when I was in Las Vegas and Joan was in Ho-Ho-Kus.

The night after Mike was born I went home and had a drink of bourbon with my dad. If I was feeling vaguely immortal as fathers of first sons tend to do, he had his teeth sunk into immortality. It was one of the few times I can remember when my normally stern and disciplined father was literally fidgety with happiness. I had two drinks and caught the exhilaration. I didn't sleep for what was left of the night and in the morning I felt I had slept for twelve hours.

The doctors said that neither Joan nor Mike should travel, so I went back to the Air Force Academy alone and they stayed with our parents.

Because of my work at the academy, I had access to aircraft on the weekends and like most pilots I had a number of hours to put in so that I could remain on flying status. I flew fairly frequently on the weekends—usually in a direct route from Colorado to New Jersey. One early morning, just as the sun was coming up, I was on my way from Westchester County airport to McGuire Air Force Base, and the flight plan took me directly over my folks' home on the Jersey shore. The temptation was too great, so I succumbed and made two simulated bombing runs over the house—just as I had instructed on the Nevada desert, but not quite legal at the New Jersey shore.

The following day as I was returning to Colorado, I took off and flew fairly low along the shore—safely out over the ocean—because I knew the family was at the beach. When they waved I dipped my wings slightly.

It soon developed that a local doctor had been up early that first morning, illegally walking his dog on the beach, and I scared the hell out of him. Meanwhile, someone at the beach was annoyed by my low altitude. I learned all this quite soon because I was grounded for three weeks while an investigation took place.

I, of course, dutifully confessed to my wrongdoing and a reprimand was placed in my file until the next promotion. Three months later I began to be addressed as Captain Aldrin and the reprimand was removed.

Before long we were all back at the academy and I began to think of moving on. My assignment was nearly over and the logical progression obviously was to a tactical flying unit. The best flying was then being done by the 36th Fighter Day Wing in Bitburg, Germany. At that time the squadron flew F-100's, the most sophisticated fighter in the Air Force. I applied and was accepted. In June 1956 we left the academy for a month with our families in New Jersey, and in August I hopped a plane to Germany, leaving Joan and Mike behind until family housing became available on the base or I could find an apartment in town where we would "live on the economy" as the Air Force calls it.

The prospect of finding an apartment was dim and the outlook for on-base quarters was even dimmer. It took me nearly two months of fairly constant searching until I rented a three-room apartment over a beer hall in beautiful downtown Bitburg, a farming town in the middle of Germany's somewhat rolling farm country north of the Black Forest.

Late that fall I drove to Frankfurt looking tan and healthy from several weeks in North Africa learning to fly F-100's. Joan arrived looking exhausted and Mike not much better off. The flight had taken an entire day and Mike hadn't liked it at all. If he disliked the flight, he loathed the drive to Bitburg. He stood in the back seat and cried all the way there, while Joan and I took turns trying to placate him. I was trying a new way to get from Frankfurt to Bitburg which, I had been told, was an hour faster. We kept coming to signs which said UMLEITUNG and had an arrow. We couldn't find Umleitung on the map, so we dutifully followed the arrows. After about ten of them we found ourselves bumping along a dirt road in the middle of nowhere. Three hours later than we should have been, we straggled into Bitburg. Joan had learned her first German word: *Umleitung* is not a town, it is a detour.

Joan had been in Germany four days when I took off for a four-week session at the French fighter base at Cazaux near Bordeaux. I don't believe either of us complained about this sudden separation, which may strike some as unusual. But by now, Joan was as thoroughly accustomed to military life as I was. We were naturally disappointed but we accepted it. Anyhow, I had to get up at five every morning and because of the beer-drinking music, which never ended before one, there was little sleep when I was at home. When I was away, Joan could sleep in. Blessings in those days were decidedly mixed.

The training at Cazaux ended abruptly with the Russian invasion of Hungary. We were placed on immediate alert, stopped briefly at Bitburg, and went on to Fürstenfeldbruck, known as "Fursty," just east of Munich and the closest base to the Iron Curtain. It was there that the murder of the young Israeli Olympians took place in 1972.

This could have been another interruption of our life,

but it turned out to be a blessing. At the Luftwaffe Officers Club at Fursty there were several family quarters—if you can call one large room quarters for a family—available, with first call going to families living on the economy in Bitburg while waiting for on-base quarters. Three days later we moved in, and were together for Thanksgiving.

We had no cooking facilities, so we all ate in the officers dining room. We had no living room, so most of the days the families gathered in the halls, where Mike soon developed great expertise at speeding around the area and dumping the sand out of the big ashtrays. The keepers of the club were not amused, but Mike thought it was hilarious and within days other children joined him. Not long after that, the ashtrays disappeared.

Squadron members were on day alert and off duty promptly thirty minutes after sunset so there was a strong tendency to have parties—any excuse at all would do and we found plenty of them. The most memorable took place for the Army–Navy game shortly after Thanksgiving. West Pointers and Annapolis graduates spent the entire week planning. Together we found a vacant bachelor quarters, took all the furniture out, and built bleachers on two sides of the room. In the middle we drew a football field.

Ed White and I were in charge of the West Point parade, so we borrowed a Volkswagen van and rented ourselves a donkey. When the Annapolis parade committee heard of this, they went off and got a smelly old goat. We painted sheets for costumes and dug out our West Point bathrobes.

Half-time on the big day at Municipal Stadium in Philadelphia, it was evening in Germany. We opened all the windows so it would be properly cold and held our parade in the Luftwaffe Officers Club. The German officers looked on in astonishment as our tipsy band of celebrants paraded through. When the animals appeared their astonishment turned to annoyance.

When the party ended the following afternoon, we not

only all had hangovers, we also had a public relations problem with our German hosts.

The day after Christmas 1956 the alert ended and we returned to Bitburg—this time to on-base housing. I had spent a total of four days in our above-the-beer-hall apartment and Joan had accumulated a total of two and a half weeks there, but we paid rent for four months until I could get back and move our belongings into the base.

We settled quickly into a routine typical of life at Bitburg. Flights went on the alert every four days and I'd go down to the pilots' quarters and wait to be called on a scramble. Sometimes we were on a five-minute alert where we sat around in our antigravity suits so that we could be off the ground five minutes after we were called. Other times we were on fifteen- or thirty-minute alert. There were occasional exercises in which all the squadrons in Europe participated, but we usually had our own. A good bit of the flying had to do with air-to-air combat, which we generally did with the Canadians who flew souped-up versions of the F-86.

Eventually we ceased to be day fighters and became tactical fighter-bomber pilots, a transition which caused a massive shifting of gears and a few psychological jolts. The big adjustment was accommodating ourselves to the fact that we were training in the use of nuclear bombs. It was a fateful and disquieting feeling to go on my first five-minute alert and sit there next to the nuclear weapons anchored to my F-100. I felt considerably reassured when we were told that our targets would be military and not civilian. Still, it was a strange experience the first few times. No one spoke much and we sat there wrapped in a cocoon of silence and apprehension.

The practice missions were considerably more active and the nuclear weapons we carried were only simulations. Because many of our actual targets would be behind the Iron Curtain, we would take off and plan our mission in such a way that if it were the real thing we'd drop our bombs and head for a neutral country. The presumption was that Germany would be either occupied or destroyed by the time we finished our missions.

The practice alerts also involved families. Foodstuffs had to be ready and bags packed for an immediate evacuation. Our cars were kept ready with extra containers of gas. When a drill sounded the families formed convoys which theoretically allowed time to drive to some port of embarkation in France. The irony was that it seemed safer to be in a supersonic aircraft speeding to a neutral country after releasing our nuclear bombs on their target than it did to be on the ground in a complicated convoy heading for a country which would either be occupied or under attack by the time our families arrived.

As the intensity of the practice missions built, so did the fervor to enjoy our days off. There were some wild parties, which we called Mary Ann parties, after the song lyric, "All day, all night, Mary Ann." The parties lasted all day and all night, and as often as not, resulted in occasional marital discord. The parties had themes and an apex of sorts came with the Roman toga party. Rooms were filled with mattresses and guests came in all sorts of costumes made of sheets—and not much else. When one was sufficiently exhausted, there was a special room of mattresses for sleeping. The party lasted thirty-six hours and culminated with a couple of scandals and plenty of very tired celebrants.

We were in Germany for three years and they were especially busy years for Joan. Early in 1957 she became pregnant. We wanted a girl and on August 16, 1957, Janice Rose arrived.

She was barely a month old when the following dialogue took place late one night.

"Buzz, what if I get pregnant?"

"No way. It's too soon—you can't get pregnant this soon again. It's impossible."

"Will you *please* stop at the drugstore tomorrow?"

"Yeah. But there's no way anything can happen this soon."

No Way was born on June 17, 1958, and we named him Andrew John.

Jan and Andy we call our Bitburg babies, because most babies born in Bitburg tend to catch things and both Jan and Andy lived up to the base tradition. They had colds, coughs, and numerous other afflictions, while Mike resisted nearly everything. By the time we had been in Bitburg two years, Joan had been pregnant nearly all of the time.

We had our family and didn't think it would be wise— either for future children or ourselves—to have another. We were also aware by now that Joan was prone to getting pregnant. The various contraceptives we tried were not all that dependable, and it appeared that whenever I was around another Aldrin might subsequently be on the way.

For fifty dollars, I checked into a Wiesbaden clinic one morning and had a vasectomy, a minor surgical procedure still years from notoriety. If anything bothered me, it was the doctor. His credentials were all in order, the flight surgeon had recommended him. But he didn't speak English, something I found out as soon as he got ahold of me where it counts and I joked, "Careful there." He just looked at me blankly, let go, and went to get someone to translate. I asked the translator to hang around a few minutes more —just in case. Other than that, the only discomfort was the ride back to Bitburg. Every time Joan hit a bump in the road I winced.

Whenever it was possible, we traveled. Occasionally we took the kids with us, but most times we left them with Waltraut Sell, our German housekeeper who was like one of the family and quickly became fast friends with Joan.

Usually we headed for warm water, either along the

Riviera or in Spain. On our first visit to Nice I took a scuba-diving course and Joan swam and sunbathed. The combination suited us perfectly. We were then, as we are now, eager travelers.

Joan was pregnant with Andy when we went to Majorca, so I insisted on handling all the luggage. We were traveling by car through Spain and we didn't need all the luggage for the short stay in Majorca. At the airport—late as usual—I carefully checked to see that I had removed all the scuba-diving gear from the car. I had. When we arrived in Majorca, I checked again and the equipment was intact and all of my bags were there. Most of Joan's clothes, however, were in the car parked at the airport in Barcelona.

From then on, pregnant or not, Joan handled the luggage and I served as porter. I have subsequently traveled a great deal, but I have yet to be trusted to properly keep track of all the suitcases. We finally found some clothes and had a great trip, even though Joan collided with an inebriated Irishman during a luau on a sailing yacht and came home with one very black eye.

We visited Paris and Rome, Wiesbaden, and on our final leave, we went to southern Italy. By this time we ate and drank anything without much concern about subsequent problems.

After several days in Naples and Capri we decided one day to climb Mt. Vesuvius. We arrived rather late in the day and hired a guide. We were less than halfway up the mountain when it began to grow dark and the guide suggested we turn back. I was already feeling gypped because I had stopped to inspect one of the so-called volcanic fires and found instead a small wood fire, cleverly set by someone hoping to give the tourists a thrill, so I balked at turning back. Joan prevailed, however, and the guide—probably as much out of guilt as hospitality—insisted we accompany him to his family's wine cellar.

It was a dusty, dirty cave and Joan suspected we were

being kidnaped. The guide poured out two full glasses of wine and a tiny little amount into his own glass. We looked on suspiciously as he explained he hadn't been feeling well and was cutting down. We felt even more suspicious when he handed us our glasses, which looked kind of dusty and cloudy—no doubt from the drugs he was going to use to kidnap us. That, at any rate, was how we told the story once we got back to Bitburg. We drank half a glass each and left, treating it as a rather exotic adventure.

Early in June 1959, after a good deal of decision making, we returned to the United States. Ed White, who had become a close friend and had left Bitburg a year before, had gone to the University of Michigan where he was getting a degree in aeronautics. The word *astronautics* wasn't yet in the vocabulary, but that in essence is what he was studying. I was definitely interested. His infrequent letters were enthusiastic about the virtues of higher education. For me the choice was essentially between graduate school and experimental test pilot school. I had computed that I could get a master's degree and still be below the cutoff age for going through test pilot school. It seemed a perfect combination and I was willing to temporarily postpone my wish to fly experimental aircraft. The school was—and still is—located at Edwards Air Force Base north of Los Angeles. I never did go through the school, but in an ironic twist of fate I would one day become commandant of it.

My dad had received his doctor of science degree at MIT and was still involved in various school affairs. As an undergraduate at Clark University he had also studied under Robert H. Goddard, who went on to become the father of American rocketry and was also heavily involved at MIT.

I applied to MIT and was accepted. In June 1959 we came to New Jersey for a month's vacation at the shore before going on to school in Cambridge.

We were no sooner home than both Joan and I began to feel tired all of the time. Cigarettes, food, and liquor lost their taste. The day my urine turned the color of Coca-Cola, Joan and I drove to the dispensary at Fort Monmouth. After a few hasty tests we received the diagnosis: infectious hepatitis. We were taken immediately to the hospital at Fort Dix and placed in separate isolation quarters. Two days later we came down with jaundice.

The kids were instantly given the first of a series of gamma globulin shots and divided up among their grandparents. Andy and Jan were still infants and went to stay with Joan's father and stepmother. Mike, who was nearly five and more active than either his brother or sister, went to stay with my parents. For him it was a trauma coming at a crucial time of life and we would not know it until we took him to a psychologist in Houston not long after the lunar landing. Jan and Andy, younger and less knowing, came through easily.

Adding up the incubation period and fitting it into our schedule we computed we had been infected by drinking wine in the dusty old cellar in Naples after our abortive hike up Mount Vesuvius.

The days turned to weeks, the weeks into months. We were each in a two-bed room and no amount of begging or pleading could get us assigned to the same two-bed room. I applied and reapplied to the commanding officer with no success. When we saw one another—in wheel chairs and accompanied by nurses who, as usual, were in short supply —we spent the time consoling one another and worrying about our children.

We entered the hospital in mid-June and Joan was the first to be released. In August she went home but would be back in a hospital within a few weeks. I remained until nearly Thanksgiving.

It was without a doubt the most depressing time we had ever experienced. As the fall term approached and Joan prepared to leave the hospital I nearly climbed the walls. I applied to be taken to the Chelsea Naval Hospital, the military hospital nearest to MIT. I was flown there in an Air Evac hospital plane and as soon as I was in the hospital I arranged for my books and lessons to be sent in. This occurred during the week Joan was at home and she took advantage of the time to find an apartment in Boston and, with my dad's help, moved in. The move was too much. She was in the hospital at Chelsea with me for the first three months in Boston and the kids stayed with their grand-parents.

From time to time I was allowed to get out of bed and walk around the hospital. Usually, after three days of this restrictive freedom, my liver would act up again and I'd be confined once more to my bed. It had been the same with Joan, although she recovered more steadily than I did. At one point I became so thoroughly depressed that when I was told to try walking again I refused to get out of bed. The prospect of another setback was too much to bear. Finally, I got up, and eventually I stayed up.

I had nothing to do but study. It paid off because when the first-semester grades were posted in December, I was first in our class of Air Force officers.

We settled into a comfortable routine once we were a family again and our life was only vaguely connected with the Air Force. To maintain my flying status I spent eight hours a month in a T-33 and Joan returned to the military only long enough to take advantage of one of our few fringe benefits by doing her shopping on-base.

Academic life appealed to us and before long we were contemplating staying on so that I could get a doctor of science degree—at least another year and a half of study.

Still, if I continued on to a doctorate I would graduate too old for test pilot school, which was mandatory for becoming an astronaut. At that time all of the seven Mercury astronauts had attended the school and it was a requirement for application as an astronaut.

A requirement, I suspected, that would not last. Academic

work would eventually become more important and my grades were very high. Adding to my suspicion was the fact that the number of experimental aircraft available for testing was rapidly diminishing.

I decided to stay in school and methodically set about choosing a subject for my thesis. I wanted to choose a subject which would have a practical application to the Air Force—after all, they were paying for my education—but which might also apply to astronautics. There were three areas to be considered. First, there was the reentry of manned space vehicles, a specialized interest of aerodynamicists, of which there were already too many. No. Second, how to land a manned spacecraft on the moon. Besides being rather awesome and futuristic, such study had no application for the Air Force. No again. Rendezvous, the joining together of two vehicles in space. The subject had military application and NASA application, and was already being discussed. There were as yet no experts dealing with the problem from the pilots' viewpoint.

I zeroed in on the idea of man controlling rendezvous with space vehicles. I knew there were computers and other sophisticated means of rendezvous being planned but what if they failed at the last minute? Success would depend on the amount of knowledge the astronaut had about man-controlled rendezvous.

This particular interest was rather unusual at MIT, where students usually selected a thesis subject related to an adviser's pet project. The alternative and more difficult way was to find an original idea and somehow convince the adviser of its merit. It also struck me that many students were digging specialized academic holes and crawling into them, with the resultant thesis having little practical application. I wanted to avoid this if at all possible.

The title of my thesis eventually became "Line of Sight Guidance Techniques for Manned Orbital Rendezvous." It is some of the most tedious reading on record but it fulfilled its purpose because it subsequently proved its practical application in space. That I happened to be the astronaut in space at the moment the theory needed to be tested was a stroke of divine good luck.

At the time I started my doctorate, I also applied to NASA to be a member of the second group of astronauts, asking that the requirement of attendance at test flight school be waived. The waiver was denied. Ed White, who had also applied and was just finishing test school, was accepted. Nevertheless, I believed when my thesis was well underway my chances would improve.

As soon as we knew we were staying at MIT a while longer, we bought our first house. It was on the south shore and a typically suburban home with four bedrooms and a good-size yard for our kids. The yard was full of dandelions when we bought the house and I worked two full weekends to clear them out. They reappeared within days and the war was on. I'd be in my study working on my thesis and I had only to look out the window and I'd be out in the yard digging. I put up a good fight, but the dandelions were still there when we sold the house.

Andy had a favorite toy, a battered little red wagon, which he would push up and down the street for hours. One day he was crossing the street when a man on a motorscooter came around the corner and lost control. Andy, barely three, came out of the collision with bruises on his head and a broken leg. Undaunted, Andy was back on the street within days, only this time his cast-bound leg was in the wagon and he used his good leg to propel himself up and down the street.

The day the cast was to be changed I took him to the hospital and waited for the X-rays to be developed. When I saw them I noticed that his break was not perfectly joined. I became enraged. Why wasn't it joined perfectly? Why, when I was studying to join together two objects in space in absolute precision, could doctors not notice his bones weren't healing perfectly? Finally, no fewer than three doctors assured me that the break would heal and that it was necessary only to connect the bones roughly at one point—a perfect joining was not necessary. I allowed them to convince me, but from then on I kept a close eye on Andy to look for a limp or any other clue of error. It turned out that the doctors were right. I know, because I made Joan take the X-rays to an orthopedic specialist.

Jan was a chubby little girl who walked around most of the time with a bar between her feet to keep her legs apart. Her hip socket hadn't been completely formed when she was born, and by the time she was two we could remove the bar.

This was no sooner done than we noticed something rather strange. I looked at her one night and when she looked back, her gaze split apart. I forget the technical term, but what mattered was that about 20 percent of the time she appeared to be walleyed. We took her to a navy specialist who prescribed an operation. Her recovery was fast and perfect.

Andy, just recovering from his broken leg, developed the same problem, only his was there just 10 percent of the time. We took Andy to the same doctor. He had the same operation and when we took off the bandages, Joan and I looked on in horror. His eyes were now crossed. The operation had been on the outside muscles of his eyes, and after a proper interval the process was repeated. Nothing changed.

A third operation was performed, this time on the inside muscles and by now his eyes crossed only 80 percent of the time. We were advised against additional operations and, instead, exercises were prescribed for him.

It was not until nearly a year later—we were already in Houston but I was not yet in the space program—when we heard of a specialist who had had great success with treating problems like Andy's. We went immediately, and he suggested another operation. He told us that Andy's chance to recovery was less now because of the previous operations. He was confident he could straighten his eyes, but he wasn't sure Andy's vision would fuse. The operation was a success and we waited, all of us taking turns working with him on his exercises. Within months, his depth perception and ability to accommodate began to improve and now it is perfect. He is the most accident- and wound-prone of our family.

Joan remained healthy and so did I, except for a bothersome case of hemorrhoids brought on by bouncing through the Boston traffic in my little Sprite. They were treated and from time to time recurred. When I made my Gemini flight, the low-residue diet, the two-day launch postponement, and my reluctance to defecate in orbit—a reluctance I shared with most of the other astronauts—caused me big trouble. After the flight we were on the aircraft carrier *Wasp* and I decided to make a long visit to the head. I even took along some newspapers. When I finally finished, I was in agony. After the brief public appearances following the flight I checked into the hospital for a hemorrhoidectomy. A friend had said it would be painful and it was.

MIT is a very theoretical and computerized institution, and I fit in well. My emphasis on the ability of man often got me into impassioned discussions with my thesis advisers, but they respected my research and let me proceed.

Passing the doctoral examination was no piece of cake. I took the written examination twice before doing it well enough to suit my advisers and the oral exam was nearly my Waterloo. Deliberative, precise, and theoretical Aldrin was not exactly quick on the verbal uptake, but one day I emerged drenched with sweat—and victorious.

The actual writing on the thesis was nearly complete by December 1962, and we, of course, were looking around for the best thing to do next. The rules requiring test pilot school for astronaut volunteers had not been changed, although by now there was no shortage of hints the rules would be changed. For one thing, too few men were now going to test flight school to fill the astronaut ranks. I dedicated my thesis to "The men in the astronaut program," adding, "Oh, that I were one of them."

I was offered a job with the Air Force working at the Space Systems Division in Los Angeles for a couple of months with the option of working into the Department of Defense experiments being planned for the Gemini flights. The offer suited me perfectly. At the same time, I reapplied to become an astronaut.

By January, I was in Los Angeles working and Joan was agonizingly trying to sell our house. It took several months, but she finally unloaded it for a good bit less than we originally paid. When she left Boston, she departed owing our real estate broker $8 and we lost all of our equity.

While Joan was selling, I was in a short but heated argument with my Air Force supervisors. The stay in Los Angeles was to be short, and I was scheduled to move on to Houston to work on the Defense Department experiments in cooperation with NASA. I was ideally suited to the job, but suddenly the Air Force balked. For my part, I readily admitted to my superiors that I had applied to become an astronaut. That, of course, was a tactical error. Someone, some Air Force bureaucrat, said, in effect: "Why should we pay to move him and his family to Houston when he's going to become an astronaut."

I had long ago discovered the best method for fighting this bureaucratic mentality: fight back—loud. I asked them to please show me someone else as qualified to start work on the Defense experiments. They couldn't. I told them I'd end up in Houston one way or another. They finally moved me to Houston.

Joan, the kids, and our furniture arrived in Houston shortly after I did. I plunged immediately into my work, eager to prove I was not wasting Air Force money.

Early in the spring, just a few months after I had made

my application, my hunch proved true. NASA officially announced that candidates need not have attended test flight school. Not only that, but I sensed a trend toward pilot-academicians.

This was my second application to NASA and I wanted it to work. The physical would be first. I knew I was in good physical condition, but just to make sure I began jogging a mile or so each day. I passed the physical easily.

Then came the psychological testing. Mine was conducted by an amiable Air Force psychiatrist named Dr. Don Flinn at the Brooks Air Force Hospital in San Antonio. We went through the whole battery of tests, numbers, readbacks, puzzles, Rorschach inkblots, symbols, and everything else they could think of to test our mettle.

That was July 1963, and I passed the tests easily. I was rock-solid stable. I'd be back in San Antonio to take the same tests nine years later under very different circumstances, following a preadmission interview by the same Dr. Flinn.

During the physical exams the doctors noticed I had an elevated liver function because of the long siege of hepatitis. Jim Lovell, who had entered the program in the second group of astronauts, also had a similar liver disorder. He was taken by a flight surgeon to a specialist in Atlanta, and after extensive testing, was cleared for NASA. I first learned of Jim's problem when I was told that my liver function elevation was higher than his had been. With no small amount of apprehension, I too was taken to Atlanta to the specialist. I made it—just.

We returned to Houston to be interviewed by various NASA officials, including Deke Slayton. At the onset I would estimate five hundred of us applied to be in the third group and by the time we reported for our physicals and psychological testing we were down to forty.

Thirty-four of us were left when we arrived for our interviews at NASA. During the week-long process, as much to ease the strain as to see how we performed socially, there were various social activities. At the official cocktail party for the group of us, I was the only candidate to be accompanied by his wife, and Joan was at her disarming best. None of the other guys lived in Houston and their wives were not invited.

During the week, a number of the men I had known at various points confided that they thought, of all of us, I had it wired the best. I was the most obvious choice, or certainly one of the more obvious choices.

Nevertheless, when the week ended I was a bundle of nerves. We were told that only thirteen to fifteen of us would be selected and that we'd be informed within the next three weeks. I suppose I should have felt more self-confidence, but the fact is that I vacillated between two wishes: that the results never be announced or that they be announced instantly. I had become so oriented to the goal of becoming an astronaut that I felt being refused would bring about destruction, deep disappointment from which I might never recover.

Early in September, I was hunched over my desk studying some technical document for the fortieth time when my secretary walked in and said that Deke Slayton was on the telephone.

I held my breath for a full minute—a duration of about ten seconds—and picked up the phone.

Deke, in a matter-of-fact voice, issued a friendly invitation to become an astronaut. He hoped, he said, I would accept.

"Shoot, Deke, I'd be delighted to accept."

He went on to say that the selection would be announced in October and that we'd enter the program early in January. Meanwhile, the selection was to be kept as secret as possible but I should let my family know.

"Shoot"? I don't think I've used that word twice in my life—or at least not more than twice since adolescence. Delighted? I was out of my head with excitement would be more accurate. I have since come to look upon my casual and polite acceptance as characteristic of the time. I was determined to look casual and self-assured and from somewhere deep in my conditioning, that attitude materialized at that very important moment for me. My response was at best phlegmatic. Violently phlegmatic.

I didn't tell a soul for the next two hours. Instead, I sat alone in my office with my feet on my desk and daydreamed. I didn't even call Joan. I wanted to tell her in person so I could see her reaction.

When I walked out of the office, I didn't even notice that my commanding officer and a few other people were standing around trying to look busy, nor that our secretary, Bobbie Wright, an efficient civil service secretary whose loyalty I had acquired shortly after arriving in Houston, was faking it too. She looked up at me and immediately saw through what I thought was an everyday look of composure.

"Congratulations, Major," and all around the room hands appeared to be shaken and smiles broke out.

"Sssssh. It's a secret." Like hell it was, but they kept it anyway.

I had planned to drop my information as a tidbit during dinner, but I blew that too. Joan took one look at me when I walked in the house and that did it.

On October 17, 1963, the fourteen of us gathered together for a press conference at which the official announcement was made.

6

The social pecking order among the astronauts and their wives ran roughly by group. At the top were the seven astronauts originally selected for the Mercury space program. Next came the nine named toward the end of the Mercury program shortly before the Gemini program began. We were members of what was called the Third Group, the fourteen astronauts selected to man some of the *Gemini* flights and to participate in the Apollo moon-landing program.

As in any community, a further division came by neighborhood and schools. Nonastronaut families lived in the various neighborhoods, most of them space program employees or employees of contractors supplying NASA. There were also occasional families with no involvement with the space program. We were a middle-class community predominantly Wasp. All of Clear Lake, Texas, grew roughly in proportion to the impersonal but utilitarian buildings being constructed on the northwest side of NASA Road 1, the Manned Spacecraft Center. The site, about three-quarters of an hour's drive from Houston, was selected at the behest of a Texan then serving as vice-president and as chairman of the space program, Lyndon Baines Johnson.

In October 1964, shortly after my appointment to the Astronaut Corps, we built our dream house. Ours cost $55,-000, a sum well beyond our means. But we figured on staying awhile, so why not? It became a two-story, English-country-style home on a cul-de-sac in Nassau Bay, the residential community immediately across the highway from the Manned Spacecraft Center. Joan and I designed it and Joan spent hours deliriously planning her kitchen. The house had a family room, dining room, living room, study, and a bedroom for everybody. Our bedroom had a fireplace in it, a luxury to which we both became addicted. The backyard was narrow and long—it connected with seven other homes, several of them occupied by astronauts—with ample room for a tree house, dutifully erected soon after we moved in, and a swimming pool. At first the pool was the delight of the kids, but within two years they began to use it less and less. It was quite a change from the cramped quarters we had grown accustomed to in the service, and light years away from the two-room apartment over the beer hall in Bitburg, Germany.

There wasn't much socializing at the beginning. We were new and the word was work. The wives had monthly coffee and cake gatherings and Joan dutifully accepted her first invitation. She arrived home to say they were poorly attended and that she had made her first friend. A heart murmur, which some years later would go away, had taken Deke Slayton out of the original seven astronauts and landed him the job as chief of Flight Crew Operations. It wasn't a particularly enviable job, but he did it well. His wife, an attractive and sociable woman, took on the even less enviable, unofficial task of being chief of wives, and did it equally well. Marge and Joan met at that first coffee and cake gathering and have remained friends since.

The children, meanwhile, settled in easily. They were accustomed to moving about and rightly sensed that we would be staying a good while, so one by one they put tentative roots into the rich Texas soil and came to like it a great deal. They still refer to Texas as home, although, fortunately, they never developed accents. The communities around the space center spoke in a most un-Texan manner because we were nearly all imported.

I went to work on the Gemini program, following my

natural bent and doctoral thesis studies on manned rendezvous. I completely accepted the complicated and arcane theories of rendezvous by computer and radar, but my belief was that if man was going to be on board the spacecraft, he would do well to know how to perform the rendezvous too. I would, hereafter, pursue the human involvement.

The Gemini program had been conceived early during the first manned flights of the Mercury program. Originally, NASA officials had hoped information on manned spaceflight would accumulate rapidly enough for going directly into the Apollo program with its goal of a lunar landing. This soon proved an impossibility. The Gemini spacecraft, an exceedingly cramped two-man capsule, was evolved to perch atop a Titan rocket. Later on in the program, the combination would be complemented by the Agena rocket and docking vehicle for the first rendezvous exercises.

Generally, the Gemini program had four major goals: to subject two men and their attendant equipment to long-duration flights; to rendezvous and dock with other orbiting vehicles and to maneuver the two together; to perfect as well as possible methods of reentry and landing at a preselected point; and to gain additional information on the effect of weightlessness on man inside and outside the spacecraft.

Ideally, we hoped to work in the purely scientific manner, taking each step logically and with great care. This was impossible to do because world opinion inevitably influenced the planning. Space-walking, originally scheduled to appear later in the Gemini program, was hastily moved up to Gemini 4, the second manned Gemini flight. This occurred when the Russian cosmonaut, Leonov, performed the first space walk from his Voskhod spacecraft; this placed sufficient governmental pressure on NASA to schedule the first American walk much earlier than planned.

Looking back on the Gemini program, this decision obviously affected its success. By and large, the entire program succeeded, but the space walks did not accomplish their goals until the very end of the flights. We weren't ready, we didn't know enough, and though the danger was minimized, it seems obvious we walked in space too soon for too little.

From the astronauts' point of view, certain flights held a distinct appeal over others. At the start, the favored flights were *Gemini 3*, because it was the first manned flight, and *Gemini 6*, the first rendezvous mission. At the onset, the first space walk held only minimal interest and when it was announced for *Gemini 4*, the crew had already been selected; so there was no maneuvering to get on the flight. Maneuvering is a euphemistic phrase used among astronauts for politicking, or lobbying, for certain flights.

It is difficult for me to explain the maneuvering process because I don't think I ever really caught on to it. I do know it involved a great deal of subtle moving about and hinting, qualities that I don't possess. I am a very direct person: when I have a goal, it is stated. When I want something, I am not afraid to make my wishes known. This quality did not always serve me well, since the presumption seemed to be that people who made their wishes known weren't observing the unwritten rules. I am by nature competitive and I hadn't gone this far only to sit back and let things happen —or not happen—to me. I wanted to fly, it was as simple as that. Pete Conrad, probably the most gregarious of the astronauts and a born survivor if ever there was one, also had this same problem. One day the two of us sat down and attempted to discuss the subtle intricacies of the selection of crews. I figured I could learn from Pete because he was—and still is—doing well at getting himself into space.

"I have no idea how it works," he said. "I never knew anything about how crews are selected. Some day, all of a sudden, somebody comes up behind you and says, 'Hey, how'd you like to fly with so and so?' I say, 'Sure, I'd like to.' It's beyond me."

It was beyond me too. I wanted to work at what I did

best and let the diplomacy take care of itself. There was one method of determining when you might fly. If you were assigned on a back-up crew to any flight, you'd wait through two subsequent flights and then be the prime crew on the third. Theoretically, the back-up crew on *Gemini 4* would then become the prime crew on *Gemini 7*. It was early in the program and I figured my chances were at least equal, if not slightly better, than the others in our group waiting their turn. After all, the major Gemini goal was rendezvous —my specialty.

Within the Astronaut Corps we divided essentially by areas of expertise. There were groups specializing in space suits, cockpits, orbital mechanics, booster propulsion, fuel cells, electrical systems, guidance and control, and all the various major categories of spacecraft operations. If you held no particular expertise, you worked to have one.

Taking its title to be a literal definition of its function, I became a member of the panel on rendezvous and reentry, chaired by a rather opinionated Canadian named Dick Carley. It soon turned out that the important rendezvous work was being done by the trajectories and orbits panel. The rendezvous and reentry panel concerned itself more with testing equipment as opposed to, from my view, the more important operational aspects.

My great tactical error was to point out the absurdity of this arrangement. Dick Carley was not at all delighted by this, and continued to ignore my suggestions. I shifted the bulk of my attention over to the trajectories and orbits panel.

The chairman of this panel was a jovial and talented man named Bill Tindall who had the respect of all the astronauts and the friendship of most of them. He clearly and obviously understood what it was he had to do and the panels he chaired literally beat their subjects to death, until there wasn't one unknown left. Tindall's memos of the minutes from each meeting were a joy to read: clear, precise, and informative. They became known as Tindallgrams.

Our job, basically, was to examine every possibility within our appointed area: every contingency and detail of the computer, the gearing up of ground support for the whole operation, or any other matter which might alter our expectancies. It was an essential job and it was gratifying.

As our preliminary work became completed, the panel on trajectories and orbits was discontinued and the workload shifted. However, when our work on rendezvous and reentry was nearly complete, we returned to trajectory and orbit studies. The first Tindallgram to be issued as we resumed the work of the trajectory and orbit panel was titled "T & O Rides Again!" The title this time was accurate.

The philosophy for scheduling crews remained unclear, but certain decisions were obvious. The command position was generally filled by one of the *Mercury* astronauts, with his pilot partner coming from the second group. As soon as possible, the second-group astonaut moved up to a command position and a member of my third group was chosen to be pilot. By simple mathematical computation it became obvious that some—but not all—of the third group would participate in the Gemini missions.

By the time the crew of *Gemini 5* was announced, I was in St. Louis working at the McDonnell facility developing still more rendezvous techniques. When I got back to Houston, I asked to have a talk with Deke Slayton.

I told him I felt the rendezvous techniques being developed in Gemini were important—in fact, they were crucial —to the Apollo program. I detailed as well as I could my studies in the process. I believed the techniques I was developing would fit in very nicely. I understood the rendezvous business as well if not better than any of the others and I wanted to make my interest known. I also told him that I had no idea at all how the selections were made, but that I felt it was honest to at least state that I had some pretty good qualifications.

When I finished, there was a moment of awkward silence before Deke politely said he'd take the matter under consideration. What I had done, in my characteristic directness, was break an unstated ethic. I had been brash. I don't think of it as a brash thing to do, but apparently that is how it was greeted by the NASA hierarchy.

A few months later, the assignments came out on the crews through *Gemini 10*. My heart sank. I was assigned to the back-up crew on *Gemini 10*. Under prevailing custom I would skip two flights and be on the prime crew of *Gemini 13*. This was fine with me, except that the *Gemini* program ended with *Gemini 12*. I would not fly in the *Gemini* spacecraft.

I comforted myself with the knowledge that the Apollo program held considerable possibilities for me, though they were somewhat diminished because I would not fly in the Gemini program. I still believed I had a contribution to make on rendezvous and felt that though I had been excluded from the actual flying, it was my duty nevertheless to assist wherever possible.

Joan, meanwhile, had plunged into working with a local theater group and was recovering from her first encounter with the ways and workings of the unspoken in the astronaut business. Her disappointing experience had started so innocently: as she settled into the community, she had become known for her talent in the theater, which was not surprising, since she tends to put her knowledge to work. One day, she arrived home brimming with excitement: a local radio station had asked her to host a twice-weekly afternoon talk show. She could choose the subject and her guests. She had decided not to involve the space program at all and, if necessary, would use her maiden name, Archer, to avoid any identification with the program.

Obviously, she wanted to do it very much. I proceeded with what we considered the formality of asking permission from Field Enterprises and my fellow astronauts. This was because the astronauts, their wives, and families were under contract to Field Enterprises and *Life* magazine, which gave them first shot at our personal stories. The contract itself had caused somewhat of a controversy and had generated a disapproving editorial in *The New York Times*. By the time the third group of astronauts entered the program, the matter had been settled and we all dutifully signed and thereby diluted the shares of the original two groups. The problems and blessings of the contract I'll discuss in another place. Suffice it to say, whatever decisions we were asked to make regarding other media, we made under the terms of the Field Enterprises and *Life* contract and by a consultation with the other astronauts.

We considered our permission request to be only a formality because a precedent had already been set. Rene Carpenter, the wife of Scott Carpenter, had been given permission to have a newspaper column in which she concentrated with wit and style on her personal philosophy, wisely leaving the space program to other writers.

Imagine our surprise, then, when the Field people said that though it wasn't specifically in the contract, they would nevertheless consider it politic of us to drop the radio show idea. This was followed closely by an even more surprising message: my fellow astronauts didn't really approve of Rene Carpenter's column and would be similarly displeased by any attention Joan might receive from the radio show.

Joan withdrew from the radio show and attempted to be gracious about it, but a seed of bitterness had been planted. It took root a few weeks later when we learned that Rene Carpenter's newspaper column was being sold by those lovable folks from Field Enterprises.

It was even more difficult to accept the feeling of the Astronaut Corps that our collective flanks needed to be protected even to the extent of a local radio talk show. What we really wondered was whether it was their collective flanks or collective egos that were being protected.

162

Joan plunged back into her little theater across Clear Lake in League City. It thrives on today and has extended its season. Years later, after our lives had changed radically, Joan confessed to me one night that when she was working to overcome her anger about the radio show and I was slipping into a deeper and deeper despair over my standing in the Gemini program, she had been tempted to suggest for the first time in our life together that we get the hell out of town. She decided not to, she said, because she felt she couldn't ask me to leave until I had flown at least once.

Tom Stafford, a bald and fatherly-looking man who is in fact about as gentle and easygoing as people can be, was the pilot, or second in command, of *Gemini 6*, the first rendezvous mission. The commander was Wally Schirra. My offer of assistance was accepted immediately and I set to work helping them prepare for this important mission. Tom and I became a most agreeable work team and friends as well. We were both enthusiastic and our work went well. Tom was a ready and willing listener to my theories and before long I became aware that certain changes were underway. There is no tangible method for measuring such a thing, but my stock was clearly going up. I found out much later that Tom had undertaken to champion my theories.

We had become friendly with a family whose backyard connected with ours. Charlie and Jeannie Bassett lived a life much like ours. Their children were often with ours, Jeannie and Joan became friends, and Charlie and I had the astronaut business in common. Charlie was scheduled to be on the prime crew of *Gemini 9*, and because it included a rendezvous, we had much to talk about. Our two families were together often.

Early in the morning on February 28, 1966, Charlie and Elliott See, the *Gemini 9* crew, took off for St. Louis in a T-38 to inspect their space capsule. Elliott was piloting the plane and Charlie was in the back seat. On their approach to St. Louis the weather began worsening with snow showers, so they circled the field once and on their final approach realized their rate of descent was too rapid. They fired the afterburner to go around again, but it was too late. The plane hit the roof of the building where their space capsule was being assembled and both men were killed instantly.

I was in my office that morning when the news came in. I telephoned Joan, who hurried through the gate we had installed between our two backyards to be with Jeannie. I raced the short distance home and across the two yards. Al and Sue Bean, another of the families we lived close to, arrived at the same time. Jeannie was nowhere to be found. We frantically called various places, praying she wouldn't hear the news on the radio or from a stranger. It turned out later she was at Ellington Air Force Base doing her grocery shopping.

We were joined by the minister of the Presbyterian church we attended, and silently sat waiting. Jeannie eventually arrived home. She walked into the house, took one look at all of us, and with a courage and bearing I shall never forget, instinctively understood why we were there, summoned all her strength, squared her shoulders, swallowed twice, and said, "Thank you for coming to me," then went into her bedroom, followed by her minister.

For the next several days, one or another of us was present in the Bassett household. It is an old and effective—not to mention comforting—military tradition to foregather and insulate at the time of death. We were no longer strictly in the military, of course, but in the untried and unfamiliar world of space travel, and the specter of death hung uneasily about us all. There was always the possibility, however remote, of death in space. Thus we became even more insular and protective.

Joan later said that she realized, shortly after Charlie's death, that Jeannie was really no longer one of us, although the two of them have become even closer friends and Jeannie often stays with us in Los Angeles. Jeannie never expressed any bitterness about this to me, but Joan—I think correctly—sensed it. She explained it to me in the following way: "When Charlie was killed it was as though she wasn't a part of us anymore. I considered her one of us, but she didn't. I could understand, because when you're out of town and traveling, no one tells me anything. Our job is to keep house, take care of children, and not ask questions. Magnify my feelings by Jeannie's realization that Charlie is never again coming home to tell her anything, and you can see how she feels. You cannot turn your back on what has been your husband's life. You still care about what's going on, but no one can tell you exactly the way your husband can. When he's gone, your sense of participation is taken away from you."

We set out to find some way of making Jeannie feel a part of all that was going on. I regularly gave her reports of various activities Charlie had been interested in, but it simply didn't work. The church raised money for furnishing a library in Charlie's memory. When she finished decorating the library, Jeannie sold their home and moved with their children to California. She left a year after Charlie's death. It was not until her most recent visit with us that we realized Jeannie was at last beginning to have a life very much her own, with virtually no involvement with her past. She has not remarried, but we hope she soon will. I'll bet anything that when she does remarry, it will be to a man who has no involvement in either aviation or aerospace.

Within weeks of Charlie's death, one of life's terrible ironies took place. When he and Elliott were killed, their back-up crew automatically became the prime crew. A series of shifts began to unfold in which, roughly, every crew moved forward one flight. Jim Lovell and I shifted from back-up *Gemini 10* to back-up on the flight before it. Because of the shifts, there was no prime crew for *Gemini 12,* the last flight in the program. Under the existing procedures the choice was obvious. Jim and I would skip two flights and be assigned as the prime crew on the last flight. I was back in the Gemini program. I would fly after all, because of a tragedy.

That night after dinner, my courage fortified by several stiff drinks, Joan and I went to tell Jeannie what had happened. It was one of the most uncomfortable moments in my life. Jeannie reacted in a way that made me want to weep. "Charlie felt you should have been in it all along. I know he'd be pleased," she told us. Tears were out of the question. They weren't part of our image even in the privacy of a close friend's living room.

Our flight, the last of Gemini before the shift into the considerably more complicated Apollo program, involved a rendezvous. It also involved a space walk, the one major bugaboo of the program. They just never worked out right. I plunged into the intricacies of space-walking. The first thing I discovered was that unlike rendezvous, where theory was fairly well agreed upon by that time, space-walking was awash in conflicting theories and there was but one area of agreement: this last attempt had to work.

Throughout most of the Gemini program, the space walks either had been less than successful or canceled by other problems during the flights. Ed White did the first walk on *Gemini 4*, a twenty-minute trip outside the spacecraft which made the whole procedure look like a piece of cake. He propelled himself with a maneuvering gun and because of his success the astronaut maneuvering gun acquired no small number of proponents.

The other system given much credence—all in theory, since it had not flown—was called the astronaut maneuvering unit. A large, bulky second body, it contained the works—propellants, batteries, radio, and other necessary life-support systems. It was anchored to the spacecraft by a tether, and at first it seemed this system would be much better than the maneuvering gun if only it weren't so complicated for the astronaut to get it on.

I simply couldn't decide which method was the most effective, but as did many others, I knew for sure which one had the greatest potential. If we could make it work, the astronaut maneuvering unit compared in possibilities to the maneuvering gun like a Ferrari to a Hudson. The Air Force was also vitally interested in it—a man with a maneuvering unit could leave a spaceship and go to a satellite to perform maintenance and repair work. For possible mobility it couldn't be beat. It also made its user potentially able to function separately from the spacecraft; no support lines or tethers were needed. We spent hours testing the two methods in the air force's version of a 707 which, when put into a series of climbs and dives, afforded us roughly thirty seconds of weightlessness.

The second space walk in the Gemini program was scheduled for *Gemini 8* and would be conducted by David Scott, perhaps the strongest and most vocal of the astronauts favoring the maneuvering gun. He had already done an exceedingly thorough and successful job at working out a number of complications with the life-support back pack.

Dave and Neil Armstrong lifted off from Cape Kennedy on March 16, 1966, with two highly important missions. They would rendezvous with the Agena and, for the first time, actually dock with another vehicle in space. The second important mission was Dave's walk. The rendezvous and docking went off splendidly. On their seventh earth orbit the spacecraft began to tumble, necessitating an undocking in the interest of safety. Unexpectedly, after the undocking the tumbling became worse. A faulty thruster engine was discovered and *Gemini 8* was brought down near Okinawa, providing a valuable but obviously unwanted test of emergency landing procedures. The important walk didn't take place. Less than eleven hours after the crew left Cape Kennedy, they were rolling in the distant Pacific Ocean, sick from the sea and despair.

Gemini 9 also included a space walk, this time by Eugene

Cernan, for whom I served as back-up. The pilot of the flight was Tom Stafford, by now the acknowledged veteran of rendezvous. We literally spent hours on end in simulators for the astronaut maneuvering unit, testing various ideas. We were determined that this expensive and complex machine would prove once and for all which was the best way for a man to maneuver in space.

The flight plan called for Gene to open the hatch for a couple of experiments, then move out up toward the nose of the spacecraft, then travel to the back of the spacecraft where his maneuvering unit was stored. His job was to check the unit out, put it on, and perform various maneuvering tests.

The two of us had a secret hope. If we could make it work really well, we would have built up a good case for abandoning the 100-foot tether that attached him to the spacecraft. On a subsequent flight the space-walker could move free of any physical attachment to the spacecraft, free of a messy 100 feet of tether floating around in space inviting entanglement.

Gene was an agreeable man who sometimes said surprising things. One day, frustrated at every turn on some relatively minor problem, we were walking to our cars when he said he felt it would really be simpler than either of us thought—it was just a matter of plain brute force. I argued that in the vacuum of space, force meant nothing at all. We left the situation unresolved—the answer was in space, not there in the parking lot on a hot, humid Texas afternoon. One thing we agreed on: the mission would accomplish as many space-walking activities as possible.

I have since learned that some astronauts felt later that Gene and I had been a bit too ambitious in the amount of activity we wanted to accomplish. We had crossed one of those invisible boundaries shared by a number of astronauts who believed in having missions as simple as is possible so as to avoid any failures. The world, after all, was watching, and the flight must appear to be a great success. Don't overcomplicate things. I happen to think they have a point, but I'm much more interested in establishing a happy medium: get the maximum out of a mission even if the world looks on as one or another activity doesn't work perfectly. You can make it right the next time.

On June 4, 1966, nearly five hours into the mission, Gene opened the hatch for his space walk while I stood anxiously by at Mission Control. I had good reason for my concern.

Tom Stafford had earlier performed the rendezvous with the docking vehicle only to discover that its shroud had not come off properly. He described it as looking "like an angry alligator."

We were summoned quickly to a meeting, hoping in some way to salvage that part of the mission. We wanted to explore every possibility, including the unusual.

Dr. Robert Gilruth, the head of the program, attended the meeting and when it came my turn to speak, I directed a suggestion to him. If it were possible for Gene to remove the shroud, the action would have once and for all proven the value of a man in space. What about beginning the EVA (Extravehicular Activity), as the space walk was called, early? Have Gene take a pair of wire cutters out and pull the shroud off. Both Dr. Gilruth and Chris Craft, the flight director, seemed aghast at such a suggestion. It was treated with silence and the meeting continued. It would be six years later on a troubled Skylab mission that an unplanned EVA would once and for all establish man's value in space operations.

Well, leave it to Aldrin to open his mouth. The shroud was not man-proof—it was not tested for contact with man in space and was therefore to be considered dangerous. It was possible that while cutting the various wires to move the cone-shaped shroud which was only half-open, Gene's spacesuit could have been punctured. Okay, I was tired, it was late at night. But I sure as hell had no intention of suggesting feats of daring for Buck Rogers, I only wanted to know if the possibility had been considered. The angry alligator was allowed to drift off.

I could see Dr. Gilruth sitting down the aisle from me in Mission Control as the walk began. The space walk was his nemesis as well as mine.

The preparation went exactly as we had expected it would. Gene installed a small, rear-view mirror in front of the open hatch at the nose of the spacecraft and had some small difficulty with it. He moved on back to the adapter where his maneuvering unit was stored. He began to encounter difficulties. It was, more than anything else, much harder work than any of us had anticipated. His feet kept floating away from him, causing valuable minutes to be wasted getting his feet and body back into position. He began to perspire. He was breathing heavily. His visor began to fog up. The schedule fell further and further behind. While the spacecraft traveled through the night side of the earth for forty minutes, he'd rest a bit, then return to work as they reached daylight.

It was a shambles. Gene never even got the unit on, never got its unwieldy arm rests under his own arms, the oxygen system connected, or any of the other things we were all so curious to evaluate. It was by no means Gene's fault. He was the victim of the unknown. We had walked in space too soon and now we were finding out we didn't know much about it at all. The space walk was discontinued ahead of schedule and Gene, discouraged beyond patience, returned to the spacecraft.

In less than a week, Deke Slayton came rushing into my office and said, "What in hell did you say to Gilruth? He's all pissed off at you. Said he had had great confidence in you and now he wants you taken off *Gemini 12*."

After I explained the whole conversation to Deke, he told me to wait in my office—he'd be back, hopefully before the afternoon was over. I waited by walking up and down my office, which was four steps wide and five steps long. I paced them off for three hours before Deke returned.

"I told him that whatever might have happened, I had great confidence in you and that I honestly felt you should remain on your flight. Everything's cool, you're on," he smiled. "But listen, Buzz, why don't you use me as your translator from now on?"

I laughed—much more relieved than amused—by Deke's attempt at humor.

The next space walk was scheduled for *Gemini 10*, to be performed by the unflappable Mike Collins, while John Young remained in the spaceship. Once again we were plunged into frenetic preparation and in little more than a month after Gene Cernan's venture had ended in frustration, *Gemini 10* was off the launching pad. And for that whole month I was the very model of quiet diplomacy whenever anyone from the executive suite was around.

After the rendezvous with Neil's old *Gemini 8* Agena, Mike's main job was to propel himself over to the Agena with the maneuvering gun and strip an expensive metallic gizmo off the Agena, part of an experiment to see if there were any microbes or unusual particles in space. In taking the exposed experiment surface off to stow it in the *Gemini* spacecraft for eventual study back on earth, Mike experienced some difficulty maneuvering. In the process, his camera got loose and promptly drifted away. No EVA pictures on this one.

The gun didn't work as well as expected, we lost a camera, but by and large Mike's EVA was the second success in an otherwise disastrous series of space walks—the second success, that is, if one includes Ed White getting out there and dangling for twenty minutes so that America could say they'd done it too.

The tasks were simple and there was one unexpected problem: both Mike and John Young experienced painful burning in their eyes, caused by a substance which Mike claimed smelled like lithium hydroxide, a chemical used to control the environment inside the spacecraft by removing carbon dioxide.

Gemini 11 planned the most ambitious space walk thus far. Dick Gordon had a number of experiments to conduct, and the emphasis was on testing the maneuvering unit—there wasn't much time left. I was especially interested in seeing them succeed because two months after their flight I would be elaborating on all that was done thus far.

On September 12, 1966, they were off, Pete Conrad at the controls and Dick Gordon primed to do the experiments. Their flight went fine through the rendezvous and other experiments, and then Dick Gordon prepared to open the hatch. By this time, he was receiving cooling from his chest pack, not from the spacecraft's oxygen system. When he reached up to pull down his EVA visor—a tinted shield designed to function rather like sunglasses in the glare of space—it stuck. He struggled and struggled. Because of the cooling system working less well inside the spacecraft than it did outside, he was drenched with sweat by the time he opened the hatch. And he had lost some valuable time. His first experiment was expected to take a good deal less than five minutes. He was to climb to the Agena docking vehicle and tie it to the *Gemini* spacecraft with 100 feet of coiled tether. To do this he was to straddle the Agena as though it were a horse. It turned out to be one hell of an elusive horse. Dick kept floating away and could not keep his straddle position for more than a few seconds. It took him twenty minutes to complete the tethering.

He returned to the spacecraft, exhausted and out of time. He never got back to the adapter and was not able to do any of the crucial maneuvering unit tests. He never even got it on. His EVA was, in a word, a failure. It wasn't his fault, but *Gemini 11* sealed the fate of the maneuvering unit on our *Gemini 12* flight. It was dropped.

My feeling is that the unit still could have been tested and that one of the reasons it was dropped had to do with interagency politics. I became aware of these overtones when I first came to Houston in the Air Force to work with the NASA people on rendezvous. It was never stated outright, but it was nevertheless generally conceded that NASA wanted to do it alone and didn't particularly welcome any collaboration from the Air Force. I went one day to a rendezvous meeting to explain some of the theories from my thesis and midspeech I realized my NASA audience wasn't listening. Such things are, I am told, familiar occurrences within other government agencies, but I nevertheless find such behavior stupid, annoying, and usually self-defeating.

If the Air Force was interested in the maneuvering unit and had spent considerable time and money in helping to develop it, and if we didn't try it as scheduled, they would never know if it would work. NASA needed—desperately needed—a successful space walk. And they had only one chance left.

My extravehicular activity was just two months away and it would be the last, taking place as it did on the final *Gemini* flight. I was determined to make it work well, and, in the process, clear up my yawning credibility gap with Dr. Gilruth.

I literally and figuratively submerged myself in preparations. A few months before, when Dick Gordon made his try, I was underwater when *Gemini 11* lifted off. The idea of underwater tests didn't originate with me, but I was the one who pulled all the various elements together and got it going full speed ahead. Months earlier, two enterprising men, partners in a small aerospace research firm outside of Baltimore, convinced the various agencies concerned to foot the bill for a little bit of underwater experimentation to see how it might help in solving the problems of moving around in space. They conducted their experiments in a swimming pool they rented from a boys' school outside of Baltimore.

We had all been aware that water held good possibilities for training in zero gravity, but its theories and applications in space-walking hadn't been investigated a great deal.

I went under. The two partners and I had theories that dovetailed perfectly and we soon started our experiments. One by one, the other astronauts who had been in space came to town to test our theories against their actual experience. We were on the right track—most of them said that the underwater effect of moving steadily and slowly rather than jerking or reaching quickly was quite accurate. Gene Cernan, who had trouble with floating feet, was a particularly enthusiastic convert.

My chores for the space walk were actually nothing more than the average suburban handyman might perform in his garage on a Saturday afternoon. I had hooks to hook, connectors to connect to their fittings, a torque wrench to investigate engineering techniques in space, and numerous other equally small projects.

Also, to keep my feet from floating free, I had suggested a pair of stirrups be tried out on Gene's flight. They had worked, but not terribly well. For my flight, a pair of step-in, gold half-shoes, functioning like ski bindings, in which you can place your foot, then turn to lock it in, were designed by the McDonnell people in St. Louis. We called them golden slippers.

I was in a spacesuit especially adapted for underwater use, so I had no feelings of discomfort during the long periods in the deep end of the pool, working at the mock-up of the back end of the spacecraft. The other guys photographing and working with me usually looked like prunes at the end of the day.

One day, Gene and I were underwater clipping, connecting, screwing, torquing, and otherwise following the routine when I suddenly felt absolutely ridiculous. The monkey I had bought for Joan could have performed these jobs, probably not underwater, but at least out in the garage. I let out a high-pitched staccato screech. When a startled Gene looked up and asked what was wrong I glared at him and said, "Shut up and pass me a banana." The joke spread and whenever I was back in Houston, parties unknown to me kept a supply of bananas in my office.

Things went well as the fall season wore on and before long it was time for the big test. As the day approached, none other than Dr. Gilruth stopped by to say how terribly pleased he was about our work and how enthusiastic he was to learn the outcome of it. Gene, whom I'd backed up on his flight, was now my back-up man and was just as curious. As for me, I couldn't wait to try it.

Jim Lovell, the commander on the flight, grew curious and stopped in Baltimore for a look. Jim and I got along well; our relationship was based in trust: he knew his job and expected me to know mine. Jim set a record for the number of flights by one astronaut, and I'm certain his innate abilities along with his extreme dependability and a good bit of luck, have had a lot to do with his success. All of us were what is now called "workaholics"—we had to be, even in our social life. Those days Joan and I saw a good deal of Marilyn and Jim Lovell.

Our four-day flight was scheduled to lift off November 9, 1966, and Joan and I decided it would be best if she didn't come to the Cape for the lift-off. She would actually see more of it on television and, besides, the kids were still very young and we agreed she should be with them in case anything went wrong. She was also apprehensive about leaving them; she seldom left them for more than an overnight trip.

I prevailed upon her to hire a sitter, a lady known for her ability to handle rambunctious children, for three days prior to the flight so that she could at least come to Cape Kennedy and see what was going on. Her father and step-mother also came. I allegedly lived at the crew quarters, a requirement, and the family stayed at the Holiday Inn.

Joan proved an enthusiastic audience. I took her to the simulator near the launch site and she stood by fascinated as I acted out—for what must have been the 300,000th time —my extravehicular activity. She compared it afterward to play rehearsals—move here, move there, cross here, move left. She said I was lucky because I would not have any furniture to bump into.

I asked for and received permission to take her to the White Room on one of my routine trips there. The White Room is just that: a small, enclosed white room in the center of which sat our spacecraft. It was such a compact room that the sensation of being high off the ground beside a massive piece of rocketry was lost. She said it all seemed cozy and familiar.

The White Room was operated under the Teutonic exactness of Gunter Wendt and his famous White Room crew. Gunter was one of the most popular men in the space program and his work was of crucial importance. He was responsible for the safety and maintenance of the spacecraft until the moment of lift-off and he was the guy on hand for the final sealing of the astronauts into their capsule.

He wore glasses as thick as his accent and his inflexibility during various stages of preflight preparations evolved into a game. While the rocket was being fueled—a hazardous situation—the astronauts and White Room crew would leave the spacecraft and move to a safe place. The game was to beat Gunter back to the spacecraft from the blockhouse. No one ever did until Jim and I got very lucky one day.

His strict adherence to safety procedures, though we all teased him about it, was understandable. Gunter was on hand for all of the *Mercury* and *Gemini* flights as an employee of the McDonnell Aircraft Corporation, manufacturers of the space capsules. With the advent of *Apollo,* a shift in manufacturers took place and Gunter was not on the job during preparations for the first three-man flight. Disaster struck. Roger Chaffee, Ed White, and Gus Grissom died in a fire during a standard preflight check. I don't mean to say the accident would not have happened if Gunter had been on the job; it's just that we were a lot more confident with him there. I don't know who made the official suggestion or even if one was made, but North American, the manufacturers for *Apollo,* subsequently hired Gunter and we all breathed easier. There is no underestimating the importance of this man.

The day before the scheduled launch of *Gemini 12,* Joan flew home. I was in the simulator, clumping my way through the EVA when word came that the flight would be delayed two days because of a malfunction on a back-up autopilot.

The ordinary human reaction to such a situation would be, I think, one of extreme disappointment mixed with the ongoing apprehension over something yet to happen. Also, one might be likely to think of it as a clue: if this little autopilot is screwing up, the message is that the whole thing is destined to end in some sort of disaster.

Any such feelings I suppressed. I permitted myself only a momentary discouragement, then went back to work. Both Jim and I spent the two days working in our simulator.

On launch day, we slept in until 10:00 A.M. and ate the sort of breakfast I could eat every day: filet mignon, eggs, toast, juice, and coffee. For several days prior to a flight we were on a special diet stressing foods which would keep our bowels minimally active. With weightlessness and all its attendant problems, the prevailing theory was that if you didn't really have to, then don't. I telephoned home. Neither of us can now recall the conversation except that we discussed the fact that the Aldrin brood had been packed off to school until an hour before lift-off and that Joan was apprehensive about the members of the press gathering on our lawn. She had, however, taken sympathy on them and moved them into the garage when it began raining.

As we suited up, a process involving at least two hours of zipping and snapping, a cooling tube in my left sleeve refused to work. The suit was partially dismantled, costing us valuable time, and the tube was repaired.

The last thing Jim and I did after we finished suiting up was to attach the two signs we had made to our backs. Jim would precede me walking to the capsule. His sign said THE and mine said END.

At 2:00 P.M. we were inserted in the spacecraft and eight minutes later the Agena docking vehicle roared to life as its Atlas hoisted it into space to wait for us. It was a letter-perfect launch, and its orbit was good.

Minutes before lift-off, the White Room opened up and moved away from us, disrupting some inhabitants we hadn't known about. A hive of bees, furious that their quarters had suddenly disappeared, settled down on the nose and windows of the Gemini capsule. Both of us laughed—the bees were in for one hell of a surprise.

At 3:46 P.M., November 11, 1966, within half a second of schedule, we were on our way.

Although I'd been told exactly what to expect, I was nevertheless struck by the lack of sound or immediate motion. I did not know we had ignition until I heard the launch director say, "We have ignition," and I did not feel any lift until seconds after I had heard him say, "We have lift-off." The coast of Florida slowly moved away. The more speed we gained, the harder we were pressed back into our seats by the forces of acceleration. As our speed built up, the forces of acceleration pushed against us with mounting momentum. When the first stage shut down we waited for the second stage to ignite. It did, smoothly, and right on schedule. The second-stage acceleration became so rapid we were being slammed by a force seven times our normal earth weight and the Gemini capsule was rattling from the pressure. Suddenly it stopped. After a short burst from our thrusters to separate us from the second-stage rocket, we were in orbit and weightless.

Again, I knew what to expect, but I was momentarily

betrayed by my conditioning back on earth. A simulation of zero gravity on earth had never lasted more than thirty seconds; here it would last until our reentry four days later. My body reacted as though it had only thirty seconds to do its work with a surge of activity, followed by the realization it would be lasting a good bit longer this time.

The Gemini flights were busy, perhaps the busiest of all. Immediately after insertion into orbit and without so much as two minutes to adapt to the peculiar sensation of weightlessness, we were furiously at work. I took off my helmet and stuffed it between my legs and then removed the pair of gloves and stuffed them in the area between my thighs and the edge of the seat. We had rehearsed this thousands of times and it went exactly as planned except that a minute later one of my gloves came floating up and behind it another.

A word about Velcro, a minor miracle of adhesive engineering. We have all had some encounter with it—I have a pair of swimming trunks on which the fly can be secured shut by sticking the two pieces of Velcro material together. It is gradually gaining wide usage on earth and in space it is a blessing. Everything, from our toothbrushes to meal packets, had Velcro stuck on it, and there were patches of the material located on the panels of the space capsule. For some reason there was no Velcro on my gloves, and I made a note to ask why as I wedged them into the space between my ejection seat armrest and the cockpit wall.

The surge of activity at the start of the flight was to thoroughly check and double-check our navigational and guidance systems. Within forty minutes we were done and had successfully fired a thruster to accomplish a slight change in course so that we would be able to rendezvous accurately.

For me, the rendezvous and docking made years of study suddenly worth while. Our on-board computer was programmed to store computations we received from earth;

when we needed them for rendezvous, they could be retrieved. They could be, that is, providing the radar lock—an electronic connection, really—wasn't broken.

I, of course, was interested in proving man's usefulness in space. For months, working on my thesis at MIT, and later in helping the crew prepare for the first rendezvous on *Gemini 6*, I had slaved over the design of a series of charts. The charts would enable an astronaut to arrive at the correct conclusions for rendezvous should the radar lock be broken.

Ours was the only flight on which the radar lock broke. We eventually discovered it was caused by a small mechanical irregularity over which we had no control. What a great piece of luck. I pulled out my charts and was able to provide the computer with the correct information. The computer then provided the correct answers. We were back in business. The rendezvous and docking went off perfectly and I had proven a major point. Man, working from the computer on his spacecraft with a series of cryptic charts, could do as effective a job as the hundreds of men and hundreds of computers back on earth.

During the first twenty-four hours, I did several of my extravehicular activities. They were stand-up EVA's, the easiest part of the schedule. It required my opening the hatch, standing up and taking pictures: ultraviolet pictures of various constellations for some astronomy studies and standard home pictures for the folks back on earth. The astronomy studies were being done at the behest of a professor named Karl Henize. He was a consultant to the space program and the sponsor of the infrared studies. I had met him and found him most interesting; a scientist was a welcome change in a corps consisting mostly of pilots. Karl was one of the first astronaut-scientists appointed to the program some time later and he and his family moved in next door to us in Houston. He usually plays host to visiting scientists and invites them to his house. I have spent some very stimulating evenings listening to scientists talk, and I am still curious to know what Karl will observe if he ever gets to space. It isn't likely he'll go now, though he's still in the program. A pity really, but Karl is forty-two, and he still hasn't flown. It's getting late. He undoubtedly would make a worthy contribution.

The second day was the big test: a two-hour-and-eight-minute excursion that had to succeed.

I felt virtually the same as I had underwater in Baltimore. The golden slippers held my feet in place, making hand and body movement very earthlike. The pair of restraining straps we had designed and modified, with the help of anyone who had any suggestions to give, worked perfectly. They were, in effect, little different from the straps window washers use when working on high-rise buildings. On the Agena, after I had used the handrail to work my way easily between it and the spacecraft, I reached in and pulled out my little surprise for Jim. The Lovells were passionate football fans and Jim had graduated from the Naval Academy. The annual Army–Navy game was a few weeks away. I had a pennant which said, GO ARMY, BEAT NAVY.

From the Agena I inched my way back to the Gemini spacecraft and on in to the adapter behind it where I would do all my racheting, bolting, and screwing chores. Everything was there as planned with one exception: a bright-yellow paper Chiquita banana was wedged in with the tools.

While working in the adapter secured in the golden slippers, I was to take a couple of rest periods to avoid the exhaustion that had plagued the previous space walks: two naps during two night passes around the earth.

I couldn't. Here I was in my own dream world, a world removed from the world as I knew it. My heart rate was slow and I was not at all tired. For me, rest was a waste. I felt that if I went to sleep or even closed my eyes for longer than a blink I might wake up and it would be over.

I have no particular fear of heights, but I was nevertheless surprised to see that 160 miles above the surface of the earth there was no awareness of height at all. I was secure and comfortable—though encumbered—in the spacesuit. I felt enclosed and safe. The golden slippers and restraining strap functioned as anchoring devices. The view was spectacular, the colors of the earth—a benign combination of blue, brown, and green with white and gray clouds formed above—the colors of life.

I have a habit of rubbing my thumb against the tip of my index finger whenever my hands are idle. During a night pass in which I was resting I looked down at my hand and noticed that my unconscious rubbing generated a glow on the surface of my gloves.

During the next rest, I caused the glow to reappear by deliberate rubbing. It was soft and small and I have no idea what caused it. It was exotic but not at all dangerous. Friction obviously is different in space than it is on earth. It did not feel warm—I was not building a fire as a boy scout might, but it did seem strange. I reported on the phenomenon during our debriefing and it was the subject of much speculation, which so far as I know has never been completely resolved.

The only disappointment in the whole adventure was that the movie camera I had back in the adapter to photograph my activity wouldn't work. The frustration was considerably more than the sort you feel when you've got the entire family lined up at the Christmas tree and the flash won't go off.

Had we lifted off on the day originally scheduled, my EVA would have taken place on Veterans Day. I had brought along a Veterans Day pennant and, in memory of the men who had lost their lives in the service of their country, planned to cast it into space. It was, I thought, an appropriate gesture. The few brief words I muttered as I cast it into space were, I knew, being broadcast directly from Houston to the entire world.

My heart rate had remained normal throughout the entire flight, but it went up suddenly when I made my offering. That gesture was the one time in the entire flight when I felt any apprehension at all.

My sense of jubilation when the major section of the EVA was complete was shared back on earth. The nemesis of the Gemini flights had been met once again, and this time conquered. In subsequent conversations, people involved in the space program—the general public was not fully informed of the difficulties since NASA chose to deemphasize the matter—would refer to it as the only successful EVA in the Gemini program. I disagree. Mike Collins had also had a success for as long as his excursion lasted. He succeeded in accomplishing much of the work set out for him.

The third day, cameras in hand, I opened the hatch and stood for another 51 minutes. When I had finished I had set a record for duration of extravehicular activity—a total of 5 hours and 26 minutes. Jim, meanwhile, set a record for the most time in space—425 hours, 10 minutes, and 2 seconds. His hours are considerably longer now.

A word about records. Every flight contained a first of sorts. Some were planned, others were not. I have a first no one else will ever beat, but that doesn't come until later. The purpose behind setting records was public relations. Immediately upon setting whatever record one was to set, the accomplishment was announced with great seriousness and dutifully spread throughout the world by the press. It gave the general public a measure of our success and though it may have been unimportant in reality it was nevertheless reassuring. Some of the "firsts" were contrived. When Pete Conrad found himself faced with the prospect of a recordless—though scientifically important—flight on Gemini 11, he held some hurried consultations with the authorities concerned. As a result of this, several minor variations were introduced into his fuel load and Gemini 11 soared on up to set the existing altitude record.

Among ourselves, we decided to decorate and honor the first guy who had an erection while in orbit.

While we were reentering the earth's atmosphere I took pictures of the flames searing past the windows. It wasn't easy. Because of the changes in acceleration forces, the camera at moments weighed four times its normal weight and was impossible to hold. Once I let go and it slammed into my chest. The view was very sparkly as the used sections of the heat shield came off and drifted past the windows.

On September 15, our fourth day, we splashed down in the Atlantic, just 3.8 miles from the target area.

We hit the hard Atlantic with an impact rougher than most other Gemini flights. Within minutes we discovered water had seeped into the capsule. It got quite hot moments after we landed and the heat shield reacted much like a frying pan put under a cold water faucet.

Our reentry and landing was the second to be automatically computer-controlled. It was an unqualified success. So, in fact, was the entire mission.

We were picked up by the carrier *Wasp* within an hour. Not much later we were back at Cape Kennedy. It was over, my first flight and the entire Gemini program. There was a feeling of finality about it, an emphasis on what was still to come in the Apollo program. If I had one regret it was that Jim and I were at that time two astronauts who were not in deep training for Apollo flights.

After each flight, custom called for a splashdown party. Ours was rather anticlimactic and was less whoopee than a sigh of relief that it had all worked out so well. What made the evening memorable for me was what Dr. Gilruth said to Joan. He told her how very pleased he was about both my charts for rendezvous and the success of my space walk. Those were the very words I needed to hear, and I appreciated his telling Joan, who knew very well what I went through.

Joan found the experience most agreeable. She knew the Gemini program well and knew it was safe. She claimed to have no apprehension at all. Her only problem had been the daily press conferences. Because of the *Life* contract, our personal stories were reserved in advance. The daily conferences, held on the front lawn, were a bit of a problem. She was obliged to withhold her more personal feelings, but still had to say enough to satisfy the remainder of the press corps. Also, she never knew what to expect from the children who were asked questions too. Unlike a number of other astronaut children, and very much unlike their normal selves, ours turned blessedly monosyllabic at the press conferences. Within fifteen minutes after our return to Cape Kennedy, Joan looked out the front window and discovered the press had gone.

"It was easy," she said. "The minute it was over everyone was gone. It was nothing like I expected. The kids want to know when you're going again."

How we had deceived ourselves, and the deception continued.

Our first official function was to stop off at the LBJ ranch over the long Thanksgiving weekend. If we were at all apprehensive about it, our worries were immediately dissolved. The Johnsons were charming hosts. Our next stop was in New York where several events were planned. Jim, Marilyn, Joan, and I went to a performance of *Mame*, with Angela Lansbury, and afterward the four of us had a small celebration at one of New York's endless number of good Chinese restaurants.

The following day we were given a midmorning reception at the United Nations. We gave no speeches, but instead shook hands with a large number of delegates. I found it all a little unreal, but not particularly bothersome.

Arthur Goldberg, who at that time was the American Ambassador to the United Nations, gave a lavish luncheon in his apartment in the Waldorf Towers. We walked in and took our places at two round tables. This was the first time Joan was seated at a separate table from me, a customary arrangement which eventually would become a sore point with her. She sat at Ambassador Goldberg's right at one table and I sat at Mrs. Goldberg's left at the other.

Gastronomically, the meal was a hit with me and a disaster for Joan. When she had tonsillitis as a child, Joan was told by her grandmother that the best thing to eat was a raw oyster because it would just slide right down. It stuck, and from that day on Joan would not touch oysters. As for me, I had them whenever I saw them on a menu.

There they were, lavish plates of oysters on the half shell, sitting in front of us. Joan didn't even have a chance to respectfully decline to a waiter. She shot me a terrified look and poised her fork for battle. This was followed by a meat pie and a rich dessert.

Following the lunch we were all to go to a Boy Scout convention and Joan had planned to accompany us. Instead, explaining that she didn't feel well and that she was not accustomed to anything but a peanut butter sandwich at lunch, we dropped her off at our hotel. When I returned two hours later, Joan was still in the bathroom throwing up.

We had stashed the children with Joan's father and stepmother, Mike and Rosiland Archer, in Ho-Ho-Kus. We joined them late that afternoon, Joan a little bit the worse for wear.

The next day was my first official homecoming in Montclair and I have virtually no memories of the day because it was subsequently superseded by another, much larger, homecoming. I do remember agreeing to serve as the chairman of the YWCA Building Fund Drive and a short parade. My most vivid recollection involves one Andrew Aldrin, age eight, who disappeared while we were having drinks at the home of old friends. We found him out on the front lawn signing autographs and offering, for a price, to secure mine.

On the plane back to Houston we discussed the last couple of weeks. Neither Joan nor I could quite figure out what it was the others complained about. The public part of life after a space flight wasn't all that difficult. Some of it had even been enjoyable.

"Maybe we liked it because we came at the very end," Joan suggested, with no clear concept of how very right she was. Life quickly returned to the familiar and normal.

I went to Cape Kennedy for a party ending the Gemini program, then went to Baltimore once again to go underwater and make a few more alterations there so that the training could be even more as if it were being done in space. I was also anxious to thank my co-workers in Baltimore personally for their work. What we had done there had secured the success of a space walk. It developed that the technique would not apply on the moon landing because the gravity on the moon is one-sixth that of the earth instead of zero. It would, however, once again become very useful. The underwater training has since been reactivated for the Skylab manned orbiting laboratories. That day in Baltimore we were all full of a sense of accomplishment and pride.

Joan, meanwhile, had returned to her peanut butter lunches and preparations for Christmas. One night, after my trip to Baltimore, I was sitting at the television, watching nothing in particular, when I felt an almost overwhelming sense of fatigue mixed with a vague sadness. I yearned for sleep so strongly, I considered nodding off right there and not going to bed. I made it to bed and stayed there for five days.

We both attributed it to what we considered a justifiable exhaustion. The five days were unpleasant and eventually they passed. What we did not know then—and did not realize until we were poring over our calendars trying to figure out what happened after the flight—now becomes clear. My nervous system was sending out a distant early warning, and it was completely lost on both of us. Four years later it would reactivate itself and once again we wouldn't catch on until all my defenses seemed to be penetrated and I had to say it: I'm sick and I need help. It was an admission I could never at any time have conceived I might one day make.

I finally struggled out of bed to do my part in the annual charity function the astronaut families supported. Not far away was a boys' home, underfinanced and overloaded with youngsters who were either unwanted or troubled. Joan was on one of the committees in charge of blackmailing merchants out of things little boys like and she was also on the entertainment committee, not at all an unusual committee for her. She nominated me to be Santa Claus. I didn't like the idea of it at all until I was passing out the presents and got into the spirit of the evening. Then I liked it a lot.

I had a similarly enjoyable but somewhat more inebriated time at my "pin party," a name which may sound like a sorority function but which for us was a special occasion. A pin party took place shortly after each space flight.

When we became astronauts we were given small silver pins on which is an ellipse and a star with three shafts pointing up toward the star. It was an adaptation from the Air Force symbol added to the usual pilot wings and presented to those who had flown above fifty miles, the arbitrary division between standard pilots and a pilot-astronaut.

The first time an astronaut traveled into space he was given a gold pin of the same symbol at his pin party. The parties took place whether or not there were pins to be presented. The entertainment was handled by the back-up crew of the particular flight and, as is customary with any sort of intramural party, the entertainment had to be more lavish than the party before. Other astronauts helped choose the location and the food. The wives appreciated the parties because they had nothing to do with planning them. We used them as an opportunity to let our hair down. If you imagine a lot of military men with close-cropped hair trying to let their hair down, you'll understand two things: the parties weren't especially high in quality but were great fun.

I don't remember any special event at my first pin party except that there was a great deal of joking about my bananas. I do remember my second. Tom Stafford, John Young, and Gene Cernan had flown on *Apollo 10,* and because of the enormous activity and concentration required to get *Apollo 11* off to the moon, their party was postponed. When a lull in our activities after the flight permitted a free evening, the crews of *Apollo 10* and *11* were given their gold pins.

The highlight of the evening was a film showing Fred Haise, my back-up on the flight to the moon, stumbling around on the surface of the moon until, in desperation, he retreated to the lunar lander which, the moment he stepped on the ladder, tumbled into pieces around him.

Fred, whom we all called Fredo, also had a special presentation for me. It was a plaque on which was mounted a purple rock and the following inscription: "To Buzz Aldrin for keen observation and exceptional judgment in furthering geology while milling around the lunar surface on July 20, 1969: 'I never saw a purple rock, I never thought I'd see one, but when I reached the moon, I did, I did, I saw one.'" It was signed "Fredo."

Weeks before we had started on our journey the exasperating question, "What do you expect to find on the moon?" was asked just once too often. I shot back, "A purple rock," and walked off. Word of my action spread and later, on the lunar surface, in the shade behind the *Eagle* lander, I noticed a slight hue of color in the otherwise colorless lunar surface. "Hey, you know what? Would you believe there's a purple rock up here?" I said back to earth. No great feat of humor, but it did relax everyone on earth, or at least those who knew what I was talking about.

The gold pins were always presented by Deke Slayton, and by a secret vote of the entire group of astronauts, we had a surprise planned. Deke was still troubled by a slight heart murmur in those days and was grounded; the one original Mercury astronaut who had never flown. We also sensed that no one really said thanks often enough for his essentially thankless job. We presented a gold pin to Deke. In his acceptance, he gave a brief but highly emotional speech. He was truly moved, and that pleased me no small amount.

I think everybody had great respect for Deke's honesty and integrity. They might have argued that he ran our complicated offices with a flair for dictatorship more like the fighter jock he was than as a diplomatic executive. Probably the most comforting and confidence-building thing Deke ever did involving me—besides standing up for me before an angry Dr. Gilruth—took place shortly before the announcement of exactly which Apollo flight would make the lunar landing.

The speculation on which it would be was, to say the least, endless. So was the gossiping, maneuvering, and other quirks of human nature under pressure. Speculation finally exploded and the pressure simply got to be too much even for Deke.

He summoned the crew members and back-up men for the three flights being readied, *Apollo* 7, 8, and 9—eighteen of us returned to Houston from our various training activities around the country. I attended as the back-up for 8.

In carefully and thoughtfully chosen words he told a collection of nervous and edgy astronauts that the crew for the lunar-landing mission would be drawn from only those in the room, but that the decision on who the guys were hadn't yet been made. The decision would be made in the normal fashion within the NASA hierarchy with Deke's suggestions being perfunctorily accepted. As far as he was concerned, he told us, each and every one of us was equally qualified. No internal pressures would be involved in the final selection. The selection would be made by the normal rotation system.

That session quieted things down a good bit for the next couple of weeks. It also did much to alleviate certain misgivings I was having about the possibility of being on the first lunar landing crew. I never discussed this with any of the others who attended that meeting, but I for one wasn't at all certain I wanted to be on the first flight to land. Instincts send messages just as computers do, but the trouble with instinct is that we either ignore or challenge it instead of investigating it. My instinct was murmuring quietly that my own scientific interests might be better served by one of the longer, more adventurous missions later on and, if I went on the first flight, it might turn out a bit difficult to get back into the swing of the astronaut business again. My instinct eventually proved to be guilty of a major understatement.

The long lull between the end of the Gemini program and the beginning of the Apollo flights was punctuated by boredom and finally by disaster when Roger Chaffee, Ed White, and Gus Grissom died preparing for the first manned Apollo flight. In the long tunnel of gloom of those days, Marge Slayton decided something had to be done to cheer people up. One day she telephoned Joan with an idea and Joan agreed. Marge rounded up several other wives and they went to work. What we all needed, they decided, was a good party. A lavish party that didn't cost much at all.

Mother-hen Marge and Joan were the finance committee along with Pat Collins. They devised an ingenious budget: there would be an open bar following the dinner. It would be held at the Kings Inn, not exactly the most inexpensive restaurant around Nassau Bay. They computed the average number of drinks the average person consumed at a party, added a little bit extra just in case, totaled in the cost of the dinner and arrived at the final figure. I forget what it was.

It sure as hell wasn't enough. After the dinner and drinks,

as the restaurant was closing, the indomitable finance committee handed over their money to the restaurant. And checked their math. Double-checked it. They were over two hundred dollars short.

The moral here, besides the obvious one that astronauts drink a good bit more than the average person, was that both Deke and Marge Slayton took their jobs seriously. That night, a very tipsy and very annoyed Deke whipped out his checkbook and rescued our wives from debtors' prison.

The party served its purpose. It generated enough arguments and gossip to get everybody going once again.

7

One of the major activities after our appointment to the astronaut corps was survival training and field trips. All American manned space missions fly between 32 degrees north and south of the equator, a portion of the earth covered mostly by deserts and jungles.

There was a tendency among most of us, myself included, to regard the training rather disdainfully, like going to camp. It didn't take long, however, before I was a willing convert, especially to the many geology field trips.

The desert survival training took place at Stead Air Force Base outside of Reno. We had along our Gemini survival kits and, later, the Apollo kits. They weren't very much, but what they included was handy: a .22 rifle, flares, a machete, and various other pieces of equipment. We learned how best to use our parachutes to construct a shelter, what animals and snakes are edible, and what other indigenous growth could be eaten. I became an expert at attacking a palm tree for the heart of the palm. I have always liked hearts of palm, and the fresh kind was even better. They are also nourishing and a hell of a lot of work to uncover. The heat was always intense, but not quite as bothersome as going without food—which happened from time to time on the trips.

Dick Gordon and I found ourselves partners for a jungle survival exercise in Panama. First, we set out to catch fish, but we saw neither fish nor fowl for two days. Finally we caught some fish, which Dick promptly burned on our makeshift fire. Moments later we spotted an iguana, and gritting our teeth, watched our instructor demonstrate what to do. The theory was practical but uncomfortable. The idea is to catch an iguana and, rather than kill it immediately and carry a smelly body around, to immobilize it until you're ready to eat it. Their two front claws have nails, and if you can reach in and pull quite hard on the nail, it will pull loose and hang by a tendon. Thereby you have a live, incapacitated iguana and its tendons can be tied behind its head for easy portage. We were told it didn't hurt the iguana, but it certainly looked like it did.

On the trip to Panama we were presented with a group of eight monkeys, tiny marmosets with long hair and loving faces. Both Dick and I chose pets. The monkeys were shipped to Houston and I quickly installed Popo, later to be known as Popo the First, in a cage in the kitchen. Dick's monkey and mine lived the longest. His died when one of his children knelt on the little animal. Within weeks, Popo died of a human virus and I vowed he would have a successor who had been bred in captivity.

Thus, on Christmas Day 1966 Joan unwrapped her presents and found a stuffed monkey in one of them. The children liked my first monkey, but Joan was not, to say the least, a fan. She looked at the toy monkey and said, "Oh, no, you don't."

"Oh, but I already have," was my answer. The second Popo moved into our house fit and healthy, and proceeded to take over not only our house but as much of the neighborhood as he could. The new Popo, a squirrel monkey, was much better adapted to civilization.

Within a few weeks he was so tame we kept his cage door open and he would rest awhile, then go exploring. He seemed to like the family room best, so from the round wood chandelier I strung a piece of rope not quite to the floor. Popo would take a running leap for the rope and then swing all over the room.

He didn't like water, but he could swim and proved it

whenever he fell into the pool. One day when I was away Joan found Popo sitting in a tree in our front yard, chattering nervously. He had never climbed a tree before, so Joan panicked a couple of hours later and called the fire department. The firemen dutifully arrived and put up a ladder as Joan stood by anxiously. The long ladder was all the way up the tree, with the fireman halfway up the ladder, when Popo came scampering down by himself, much to Joan's embarrassment.

Our cats immediately departed whenever Popo arrived, and only Missy, our dog of doubtful pedigree, adjusted to him. It tended to astonish people driving down the street, but it was not at all unusual to see Missy strolling along with a monkey on her back.

Popo, especially during the intensity of the Apollo program, was a welcome relief. Other pastimes and hobbies I had chosen provided nowhere near the diversion Popo offered, for both me and my family. Joan realized this and tolerated him accordingly. She even trained him to go to his cage and stay there while she was cooking.

In cooperation with the scientific community, NASA undertook to give us all an education in geology, a subject that many thought would be valuable when the lunar exploration began. The trips proved fascinating.

Geology opened my eyes to the immensity of time when one day I found myself standing at the bottom of the Grand Canyon paying rapt attention as the instructor talked about things that took place eons before man existed on this earth.

Geology also tested the imagination. We would find rock formations similar to those we expected might be on the moon, and it was up to the observer to look past all the growing things on the earth and to pretend that particular spot was on the lunar surface.

Interesting or boring, the field trips were a unifying force. Working on various committees or assisting with a particular flight, either on a panel of some sort, or with a back-up crew, the astronaut corps was spread far and wide. On the field trips we went by group, and if there was camaraderie among us, it came from these trips.

The initial goal of the Apollo program was a manned lunar landing. President Kennedy had wanted this accomplished before the end of the decade that would close on December 31, 1969.

The schedule was fairly well maintained until the fire that killed Ed White, Gus Grissom, and Roger Chaffee. The inquiry boards and their subsequent recommendations for redesigning the Apollo capsule caused nearly a year's delay for the first manned flight.

If the revised manned flight went according to schedule and the vast, complicated machinery, both in space and on the earth, performed as hoped—a possibility most of us considered remote in view of the various problems with the Gemini flights—the fifth manned Apollo flight would make the lunar landing.

To accomplish this, the preceding flights had to perform a great many successful demonstration exercises, primarily in rendezvous techniques, and complete satisfactory test flights of the ungainly and spindly Lunar Module, which we called LM.

The logistics for all of this were incredible. Thousands of people had to be coordinated, as did the hundreds of manufacturers involved. The pressure was intense. The first LM was still in the manufacturing and testing stages when the initial manned Apollo flight orbited the earth to see how the space capsule would endure during the length of time it was estimated that a trip to the moon would require. It appeared that *Apollo 11* might make the first lunar landing, but the more likely candidate was *Apollo 12*.

For crew assignment in the Apollo program, as in Gemini, the general rule was to back up one flight, skip two flights and then be assigned as prime crew on the subsequent flight. There was, of course, maneuvering to be assigned to one flight or another, but the final decisions were made by Deke Slayton, and I know of no instance where his recommendations were altered by any higher authorities.

I was off participating in altitude-chamber testing of spacecraft when word came I had been assigned to the back-up crew of *Apollo* 9 along with Neil Armstrong and Jim Lovell. The flight was scheduled to make a number of navigational experiments and perform some complicated rendezvous. The prime crew was Frank Borman, Mike Collins, and Bill Anders. My doctorate, interests, and single-minded pursuit of rendezvous techniques had by this time earned me the sobriquet of Dr. Rendezvous.

Compared with the Gemini program, the Apollo project seemed enormous. There were so many more people involved than in Gemini that once one of us had an idea for some technique or application, it could develop into quite a chore to find out just whom to take your idea to. Added to that, we had to literally sell our ideas to many people. As usual, I was my customary self: direct and outspoken. This habit was looked upon agreeably by some—usually those with the same characteristics—humorously by others, and much less tolerantly by some. Frank Borman, for one, became quite annoyed by my suggestions for his *Apollo* 9 flight. During one of the many pre-flight conferences I made a suggestion. Frank shot back that he didn't need any suggestions from me that would screw up his flight. There was an awkward silence, and then the conference continued. Oddly, Frank's remark—probably made more out of nervousness about the impending flight than anything else—caused a sudden surge of support for my theories. Frank was known to be very cautious and, I thought, not particularly inclined to expand the flight beyond the flight plan. For several days after the conference people came up to me to offer their support and even asked to propose questions for me. I liberally passed my ideas around.

Mike, scheduled to be the command module pilot on the

flight of *Apollo 9*, developed neck problems in the early months of training. When surgery was required he was taken off the flight. Jim Lovell, Mike's back-up counterpart, was the logical man to move into his place, and this was done. Fred Haise was then put on the back-up crew. This minor game of moving people about, almost as is done in chess, was not at all unusual. However much we were the ultimate in technology and science, the human element was also a consideration. Thus, if custom was maintained—and I stayed healthy—I would eventually be on the prime crew of *Apollo 11*, which in those early days seemed a much too optimistic candidate for the first lunar landing.

Apollo 8, with Jim McDivitt, was critically important in that it would be the first flight to go with an LM. As the flight approached it became obvious that the LM simply wouldn't be ready in time.

During planning stages, and within the program itself, we did not call a flight by a numeral. It was, of course, much more complicated than that. Highly simplified, here is what happened: after a discussion of epic proportions it was decided that the flight which would have been *Apollo 9*—the second earth-orbit rendezvous and navigational test flight which would be repeated as many times as was necessary to perfect the systems—would become *Apollo 8*, without an LM, while the flight of what would have been the original 8—the first test of the LM—would become *Apollo 9*.

Later, it was decided that *Apollo 8*, with Frank Borman in command, and myself on the back-up crew, would be the first flight to orbit the moon. To me, these were crucially important decisions which subsequently put the entire program back on schedule to land on the moon before the end of the decade.

I set to work on the navigation experiments, the purpose of which in essence was to find some way to adjust man's natural inclination to navigate from reference points on earth to some system of exact navigation in space. There had been a number of experiments, but the prospect of traveling from one planet to another made navigational techniques critically important. Ideally, they had to be as precise as was humanly possible. The computers on board the spacecraft performed a great deal of work.

It was essential for the pilot to understand what the computers were doing and to make sure the computer made no errors that went unnoticed—that is, the pilot should know how to guide the computer to the correct conclusions. To do this you needed to know, as precisely as possible, where you were. Looking through the spacecraft windows with star charts accomplished this. Up to *Apollo* 8 we used what is called celestial equator oriented navigation, assisted by star charts.

I became convinced that on subsequent flights we needed to orient the star chart with respect to the most useful plane. The plane most obvious was the ecliptic plane, the plane in space containing the sun and the orbital path of the earth; the moon's orbit is within five degrees of this plane.

In the early 1960s, when the Apollo program was not yet in existence, Dr. Richard Batten, a professor of astronautics at MIT, and one of my thesis advisers, presented some theories on travel in space. These were recalled years later and reapplied to the Apollo program. A plan was developed whereby we could make measurements between a star and a landmark on earth—or the horizon of the earth—and as you measured this one angle over and over again and fed the information to the computer along with many other star sightings, a nearly exact knowledge of the spacecraft's course could be maintained. The readings were done by taking sextant sightings. This system gained much credence in the Apollo program, and I was pleased to be part of it.

Neil and I, because we had backed-up *Apollo* 8, were by now quite certain we would fly *Apollo* 11, but we did not know who the third man would be. Fred Haise would probably be rotated out of our flight, and Mike's bad neck had left him in a kind of assignment-limbo. Neil and I agreed that we wanted Mike on our flight. Mike said he wanted it, too. Neil made an appropriate hint to Deke Slayton, and we were pleased when his decision matched our desires.

I recall no great anxiety about the possibility—and it was still only a possibility—of making the first lunar landing. There existed at all times the uncertainty of not knowing.

Joan, too, quickly sensed the uncertainty. What time we had alone together was passed in discussion. If we were chosen for the first landing, it would be an enormous honor. To be sure, the end result would be a great deal different from my return on *Gemini 12*, but just how different we were unable to guess. Our speculation in no way approximated what would happen. The one conclusion we arrived at we kept to ourselves: if I had had a choice, I would have preferred to go on a later lunar flight. Not only would there be considerably less public attention, but the flight would be more complicated, more adventurous, and a far greater test of my abilities than the first landing. Joan agreed.

We kept this secret simply because in my business such an idea is tantamount to sacrilege. No one had ever refused a flight. If I, as one individual, refused, both Mike and Neil would likely be taken off the flight. And if I did such a thing, I would so impair my position that I'd probably never be assigned to a subsequent flight. The subject was never directly approached by either Mike or Neil as the months wore on, but I rather suspected that at times they, too, might have had reservations.

On Christmas Eve 1968 we turned on our television set as did millions of other families, and heard Frank Borman read from the Book of Genesis while in lunar orbit. The next day, when *Apollo 8* rounded the dark side of the moon, reestablishing contact with earth, and started home on a perfect course, my destiny—if the next two flights went well—seemed sealed. By now the whole thing seemed so unreal that it was not even discussed as we packed up and took off for a week in Acapulco.

On Monday, January 6, I went back to my office. Joan drove me because my car was in the shop. I asked her to pick me up at 5:00 P.M. I figured it would be a day like any other, or rather, I suspect I *hoped* it would be a day like any other.

As with so many dramatic moments in one's life, this particular event took place in very ordinary surroundings. We were simply called into Deke's office and told: "You're it." We responded accordingly, trying to maintain a façade of business-as-usual while adrenaline sped through our bodies. Maintaining the façade, I telephoned Joan early and asked her to come and pick me up.

She saw nothing unusual in my request. She was in the middle of a typical housewife's problem; we had returned from Acapulco with bales of dirty clothes, and true to its perverse nature, the washing machine broke down. She picked me up and together we went to the laundromat. Thus, driving home in a car jammed full of wet laundry, I told my wife I was going to land on the moon. By the time she had worked her way from the broken washing machine to the news I had just presented her with, she was half hysterical, partly out of pride, but mostly out of fear.

That night, perhaps overstating it a bit, Joan made the following entry in the diary she sporadically kept:

> Buzz went to work this morning without a job and came home tonight LM pilot on Apollo 11, the first lunar landing. So it is really happening and I am scared.

The next day she wrote again in her diary:

> I have a marvelous faculty for putting out of my mind those things I don't want to face up to, but it no longer

works. It was a day, the first of many, I'll bet, of walking on eggs, or normalcy tinged with hysteria. I wish Buzz were a truck driver, a carpenter, a scientist—anything but what he is. I want him to do what he wants, but I don't want him to. He is such a curious mixture of magnificent confidence bordering on conceit and humility, this man I married.

On Thursday, January 9, the news was made official and public. The sense of unreality lifted a bit because what was going to happen was blinking at us out of our television set and could be read in the newspapers. Joan's brief entries in her diary tell best the story of the next several weeks.

On Friday, January 10:

Buzz spent much time explaining to me the various methods planned for obtaining rocks from the moon. Seems it's not just a matter of picking them up and dumping them in a sack. That's about as far as I understood. Ah, the complications of the space age!

On Thursday, January 16:

Broke out with blotches last night, which still persist today. I'm covered with pancake makeup and jumpy. Nerves. If I'm like this now, what will I be like when it really happens?

Though the real thing was still a bit behind schedule, the training version of the LM had been built and could be flown on earth in a fairly reasonable approximation of the effect it would have in the airless lunar gravity. The earth-bound LM was even more improbable-looking than the actual LM itself. It looked like a big brass bed frame without a mattress, and proved to be rather hazardous to fly. It could stay in the air—tentatively and noisily—long enough to fly the length of the runway. One day Neil was flying it when he noticed something wrong in the rate of descent. Neil, who once said he reserved his God-given right to be wishy-washy, was instantly decisive. It was well he was, for a second or two later it would have been too late. He ejected, and the craft, which flew at extremely low altitudes, crashed near the runway and exploded. Seconds later Neil came down by parachute.

Among the more difficult projects in the Apollo program was deciding just which computer programs were essential and which were expendable—a subject that could bring on hours of debate. The computers were capable of handling just so much information, and our dependence on them was such that they were continually being given more and more to do.

When it came time to sort out the various programs, NASA would conduct what became known as a Black Friday. The navigation engineers from MIT, where much of the programming was planned, would come to Houston and we'd all sit down and go to work.

As the programs expanded and the confidence in earthbound tracking grew, the subject of on-board navigation sightings fed into the computer became the topic for a Black Friday meeting. Previously a computer program automatically instructed the astronauts on how to leave a lunar orbit for a return to earth in the absence of earthbound tracking data. Should communication with the earth be permanently halted, the computer on board the spacecraft would take over and compute the maneuver in case of such an emergency. The program itself was complicated and tended to crowd the computer's bank of information. Additionally, the various systems of communication were now developed to a point where the on-board computation of the maneuver might not be necessary. Aboard the spacecraft were special pads of paper called maneuver pads, onto which we could copy the many computer entries needed to make the departure from lunar orbit. These entries were sent to us by voice from earth well in advance of any possibility of the need for using them. One Black Friday this computer program was thrown out. It was called "Return to Earth." If the eventuality ever arose, man could do the job based on the information on his maneuver pads.

All our telescope sightings, crucial to navigation, had to be made in the dark. The star charts which had been used in the Gemini program were on white cards with black printing. Anyone who has walked out of a dark theater into the bright sunlight knows the change from darkness to sudden light necessitates an uncomfortable and momentarily confusing adjustment of vision. The opposite is also true. Much the same sort of problem existed between making celestial sightings and referring to the white star charts.

In a burst of do-it-yourself handicrafting, I decided to correct this problem so that we could see the star charts in the near dark without destroying night vision. I built a small light box which was illuminated by the flashlight we all carried. I designed it so that it would fit easily on the spacecraft panel just below the sextant, then I redesigned the star charts on black plastic sheets, with only the chart specifics in white. I changed the size of the charts so that they were easily slid through the box.

One day I proudly displayed my small invention and was intrigued with the reaction. Most readily accepted it, obviously grasping its practicality. There was a great deal of this sort of improvisation, and from time to time it caused difficulties, not so much in a technical sense but rather with egos. An acronym we adopted pretty much said it all; some reacted to my light box as though it was NIH (not invented here). A few were openly skeptical, while several others proceeded to prepare their version of a light box. Black star charts have been standard ever since.

The crucially important first flight of the LM was scheduled for *Apollo* 9 early in the spring of 1969. It was also the first of two remaining markers which would tell for sure whether Neil, Mike, and I would go to the moon. I stood in Mission Control for the final LM rendezvous and docking, silently listening to the progress of the flight. It worked perfectly and I knew at that moment that *Apollo 10*, the dress rehearsal for our landing, would go just as perfectly. We would be the crew to attempt the first lunar landing.

In the meantime I was having my own problems. Throughout the short history of the space program, beginning with Ed White's space walk and continuing on all subsequent flights, the commander of the flight remained in the spacecraft while his partner did the moving around. I had never given it much thought and had presumed that I would leave the LM and step onto the moon ahead of Neil.

Through that most deplorable system known as the grapevine, I heard the contrary. I don't recall being angry or disappointed, but I do remember being puzzled.

Finally I did become angry when the grapevine reported Neil was going to make the first step on the moon because he was a civilian. Such a move, I thought, was an insult to the service. I understood that my country wanted to make this moment look like a triumph for all mankind in the cause of peace, but the implication was that the military service, by being denied the right to be first, was some sort of war-monger. As to any differences between Neil and myself, there simply were none. Neil had learned to fly in the service, just as I had. Well before he was chosen for the astronaut corps, he had left the service and become a civilian. When I was selected I had just completed my doctoral studies at MIT. My salary was paid by the Air Force, but it had been ten years since I had served in any capacity other than maintaining my flying hours.

After I had mulled it over a few days, I decided that the subject was potentially too explosive for even the subtlest maneuvering and that it would be best to be honest and direct about it. I went to Neil.

Neil, who can be enigmatic if he wishes, was just that. Clearly, the matter was weighing on him as well, but I thought by now we knew and liked each other enough to discuss the matter candidly. Neil equivocated a minute or so, then with a coolness I had not known he possessed he said that the decision was quite historical and he didn't want to rule out the possibility of going first.

I was more surprised by the manner of his reply than by what he said, for what he said did have logic. I kept my silence several more days, all the time struggling not to be angry with Neil. After all, he was the commander and, as such, the boss. I also suspected—correctly, as it turned out —that the decision was not Neil's alone to make.

Deke Slayton finally dropped by to say that it probably would be Neil, but Deke at least had a more acceptable reason: Neil was a member of the second group of astronauts, the group ahead of the group to which I belonged. As such, it was only right that he step onto the moon first, as Columbus and other historical expedition commanders had done.

I mentioned this to my father on the telephone one night. He was instantly angry and said he intended to do something about it. It took a great deal of persuasion, but I finally got him to promise he'd stay out of it.

Whether or not I was going to be the first to step onto the moon was personally no great issue. From a technical standpoint, the great achievement was making the first lunar landing, and two of us would be doing that. We all expected the actual surface activities to be relatively easy, a deduction based on detailed study and the space walks of the Gemini program. It would probably be even simpler than the Gemini space walks because they were made in zero gravity and the lunar surface has one-sixth the earth's gravity. It might even seem a bit familiar.

Yet the larger share of acclaim and attention would go to whichever of us actually made the step. Considering my reaction to acclaim, it was fine with me if it was to be Neil. What I did resent was that the decision was stalled and stalled, until finally it was the subject of gossip, speculation, and awkward encounters.

I went finally to George Low, director of the Apollo program office, and explained what I had heard. I said I believed I understood their need for careful consideration, and added I'd happily go along with whatever was decided. It was no huge problem for me personally, but it would be in the best interest of both morale and training if their decision would be made as soon as possible.

Meanwhile Neil relaxed somewhat and we began to speculate together. Our conclusion was that the decision as to who would be first would be determined by the allocation of tasks on the lunar surface and by our physical positions in the LM itself. Unless something changed, as LM pilot I'd be on the right, a pilot's usual position, and Neil would be on the left next to the hatch opening. It was not practical, and it was an added complication to change positions with Neil after landing.

And that, to the best of my knowledge, is how the matter was finally decided. With a great lifting of pressure we all quickly and simply accepted the decision. All, that is, except my father.

Apollo 10, the dress rehearsal for our lunar landing, lifted off May 18, 1969. Tom Stafford, Gene Cernan, and John Young flew a perfect flight. The only difficulty involved certain repercussions when Gene, in lunar orbit, discovered an error had been made and radioed back, for all to hear, "Son of a bitch!" Tom then set another precedent when a camera balked by saying, "Ah, shit." Besides preparing the way for our flight, Tom and Gene were also establishing the reality of astronauts—we were, after all, human.

We were it. With the decision made, the commitment

made, the work intensified. From early in the year through our scheduled launch in July, the amount of work seemed endless and, at times, practically insurmountable. The three of us, along with our back-up crew. Jim Lovell, Ken Mattingly, and Fred Haise, were literally spread all over the country. Once again Neil and I shared many common causes and attended many meetings to determine what kind of orbit would be best for the rendezvous with the command module after leaving the lunar surface. Bill Tindall, the likable expediter of meetings in the Gemini program, was again his thorough and decisive self. The deliberations soon settled onto the established and proven step-by-step rendezvous theories of the Gemini program, which relied as much on ourselves as pilots as on the vast fund of information available from the computers at Ground Control in Houston. While all this was going on, Mike was off working in the simulators of the command module and preparing to command our reentry into the earth's atmosphere. We each spent over four hundred hours working in simulators.

Neil and I prepared to go to the moon. As Neil said at one of our press conferences, our flight would not truly be a flight into the unknown.

The moon had been measured, compared with other planets, and poked at. One by one the old misconceptions about it had died. In the seventeenth century, scientists believed there were creatures on the moon. A modern scientist stated his theory that the lunar soil, roasted by the heat of the sun and the frigidity of space, was in such chemical imbalance that man's footsteps might trigger a monstrous fire. More widely held was the suspicion that the moon's surface was covered with dust so thick it would swallow a man or a spaceship like quicksand.

These theories had been disproved one by one until only the concern about the dust remained. The unmanned Surveyor landings indicated a well-compacted surface which would more than adequately support the weight of the LM.

So this, too, was a relatively minor concern. No one would know for sure, of course, until we were there.

Actually more of a small planet than a moon, the moon is the largest of the thirty-two moons shadowing the nine planets in the solar system. It is less dense than the earth and its gravity is one-sixth as strong as earth's gravity. A 150-pound man would weigh only 25 pounds on the lunar surface. The moon measures 2,160 miles in diameter and 6,790 miles around the middle. Its days are 28 earth days long. One side of it always faces the earth, while the other side cannot be observed from the earth.

As man actually prepared to explore the moon larger questions persisted. How did the moon begin? How was it created? There were three main theories: the moon literally erupted out of the earth and, in its momentum, spun into its present position; another held that both the earth and the moon formed at the same time—forged out of the primordial gases of creation; still another held that the moon was a gypsy planet captured by earth's gravity. Finding the answers to these questions was part of the reason for going—that and the desire to be the first nation to fulfill the dreams of mankind throughout history.

Late in June I began to feel I was catching a cold. I immediately began taking vitamin C and tried to put the worry out of my mind. Popo, our monkey, was a prime source of what entertainment there was during infrequent periods of leisure. I was no sooner swallowing vitamin C than Popo began to grow listless. Occasionally I could urge him into playing, but he was clearly not feeling well. He grew steadily worse until one day, my heart in my throat, I carried the miserable little animal to the NASA medical department. They confirmed that he was dying, so I asked them to put him to sleep and spare him the misery of a slow death. The doctor caught me completely unawares when he said there had better be an autopsy to make certain I didn't have whatever virus he might have had. Two nervous days went by until I learned Popo had indeed died of a virus, but to my vast relief, it was one which never appeared in men and only infrequently in pregnant women.

Dee O'Hara was the nurse for the astronauts; she had established her own tradition of occupying the same hotel room at Cape Kennedy prior to launchings. We all had our small superstitions, and having the same hotel room for every launch was Dee's.

Dee, who has left the space program, was the rare sort of person who can attack a monumental work load with great good humor. As *Apollo 11* neared, we were all so busy operating by the numbers that Dee suddenly looked at our gigantic bureaucracy and must have found it very amusing. She prepared the following memo regarding efficiency in the bathroom and duly circulated it:

TO: All Personnel
SUBJECT: Rest Rooms
PURPOSE: To Define Policies and Procedures
           Governing the Use of Rest Rooms
OBJECTIVE: To Provide Control of the Use of Rest
           Rooms by Employees in order to Eliminate
           Abuse of this Service

It has been observed that certain employees are using the rest room for other than the intended purpose. This observation pertains mainly to the use of the enclosed stalls. It is suspected that these stalls are being used to read novels, newspapers, to perpetuate amateur artwork, etc. In order to eliminate this abuse of privilege, the following procedures will be initiated:

1. Employees will be issued a new IBM key-punched I.D. Card. This card will have employee's badge number coded into it.

2. In order to use the enclosed stall, the employee must insert his I.D. card into the slot provided on the stall

door. This unlocks the door and records "time in" and badge number on magnetic tape.

3. Employee shall complete his mission with all haste. *REMEMBER HASTE MAKES WASTE.*

4. In order to leave the enclosed stall, the employee must insert his I.D. card in the slot provided on the inside of the door. This unlocks the door and records "time out" on magnetic tape. *IMPORTANT:* employee is cautioned not to misplace his I.D. card. If card is lost, call Lock and Key at 3,6203.

5. At the end of each week, the magnetic tapes will be processed by our IBM 360/75 computer. A "Rest Room Status Report" (UCH 4985 A) will be reviewed by division management.

To the three of us fell the duty of naming both the command ship and the lunar lander. Neil and I asked Mike to choose a name for the command ship. He replied instantly; he'd done his thinking in advance and had chosen "Columbia." Neil and I considered a long list of possibilities for naming our LM and settled on "Eagle," the symbol of America.

We then held lengthy discussions about some sort of universal symbol for our flight emblem and patch, something to show that our landing on the moon was in the best interests of mankind throughout the world. We were stymied. We settled for an eagle, but we felt something more was needed. Then, standing beside the simulator one day, Tom Wilson, a friendly and very capable computer instructor, overheard us.

"Why not have the eagle carry an olive branch?" he asked.

Why not? Into the design of our patch we incorporated an olive branch, the universal symbol of peace. We placed it in the eagle's beak.

Collectors of the vast amount of memorabilia on our flight quickly noticed the difference, but few outside of the space program are aware of a small change in our symbol. With a quick shift, on the first patches and symbols the olive branch in the eagle's mouth slipped down and reappeared one day—with no official explanation—in his claws. Dr. Gilruth reacted strongly against the branch in the eagle's beak. We countered by moving the branch from his mouth to his claws, making the eagle appear more benign. In fact, we disagreed with his objection, but by this time we were past arguing such a matter.

There was also a slight change in the plaque we were to leave on the moon—a change made by President Nixon. The original read, "We come in peace for all mankind." Mr. Nixon changed "come" to "came," a decision we all supported.

Neil and I had another decision to make: what to call —for communication purposes—the exact place on the moon where we would land. It would be somewhat similar to a radio call sign, but we wanted to give it added significance. Moon One? Base Camp? Moon Base? When we made our choice, we told only Charlie Duke, who would be our Capsule Communicator back in Houston, and who we felt should know the exact name in case transmission was garbled. I cannot remember which of us originated the selection, but once we had thought it over it was an obvious choice. We were landing in an area known as the Sea of Tranquility; we would call our landing site Tranquility Base.

There were delays—some of them critical. The LM simulator did not become operative for our mission until late in March, leaving us little time for the myriad experiments and training tests we needed to conduct. As various stages of the training fell further and further behind, several NASA managers became concerned.

Not long before our flight, Deke queried us about this growing concern. He happened to pick a day when nothing seemed to be going right. Tired, slightly discouraged and worried we might not be ready, we intimated we would not object to a delay of one month. The final decision, however, was to go as scheduled, in July. Personally, I didn't think I wanted to wait any longer, so I acquiesced quickly.

On the long July 4th weekend I spent my last days at home. There was no Popo to amuse me and the kids were all involved in projects of their own, so I spent the weekend completely dismantling and reassembling our dishwasher, which had never worked properly. When I returned to Cape Kennedy it was working perfectly. But it didn't last long, for when I returned from the flight I saw that Joan had bought a new washer.

Joan had decided not to attend the lift-off. She reasoned, quite correctly, that the crowds would be gigantic and she didn't especially relish the thought of all the attention she'd get by being on hand. Also, by this time the pressure on our children was quite intense, and she wanted neither to subject them to more by taking them to the Cape, nor to leave them alone.

People, mostly prominent ones, from all over the world attend launches, and ours was the most eagerly awaited. The three of us were allowed to invite a number of guests. I invited many relatives, Clary Anderson (my football coach in high school), and two of my old classmates. Tom Manison, a close friend in Houston, whose summer camp was a source of much pleasure to my family, was also invited, along with Dean Woodruff, our preacher. The total came to twenty-five.

There were also several people who had helped us in various training matters and the like that the three of us wanted to invite. Certain social customs had to be observed, one of them being the tradition of inviting John King, an enormously wealthy Colorado businessman and the host of most launch parties. A number of the astronauts were beholden to him for various favors, and a few had business dealings with him. Basically, favors were bestowed on astronauts for two reasons: to be generous or to take advantage. I personally felt King's motive was the latter, and so apparently did Neil and Mike, because when his name came up we all agreed that he not be invited. There were certain people who objected. (King is no longer much in evidence. I've read there were some problems in a Swiss investment firm in which he was prominent. He no longer has as much clout as he once had, at least among astronauts.)

We also prepared our personal preference kits, the small packets of personal belongings we would take with us to the moon. Mike had been approached by the Houston Manned Spacecraft Center Stamp Club with an offer of as many commemorative envelopes as we might like, at cost. We took several hundred with us and left about as many behind with our signatures. The envelopes we left behind would be canceled on the day of lift-off and kept as a sort of insurance policy for our families in the event of a disaster. The signing of the envelopes we left behind is something I don't believe had been done up to that time.

This, of course, was long before stamps and envelopes carried by astronauts became such an issue. In those days the three of us—and the NASA hierarchy—were a good deal more naïve. NASA had requested we furnish them with a list of everything we were taking, and we quickly obliged. It was of such small import that NASA's official compilation of what I took was not even deemed worthy of being typed up. The confirming list they gave me back was handwritten and complete.

We were taking a flag to put on the moon, and the process of its selection indicated that NASA did have an understanding of certain commercial realities. George Low and his colleagues in high places within NASA were justifiably concerned that the manufacturer of this flag would use it for advertising purposes. So the unlucky man in charge of getting the flag was instructed to buy one flag from every manufacturer he could find. The flags were then jumbled together and placed in a room. Labels, if any, were removed.

A secretary was brought in and ordered to enter the room and come out with just one flag. That was the one we took with us.

Other precautions were taken, some of them bordering on the ludicrous. Chuck Berry, "the astronauts' doctor," appeared on the day of our last press conference before lift-off and told us to wear special masks, and not to remove them except when we were sitting in front of the special plastic shield facing the audience. A special fan would then blow the air from behind us into the audience. He didn't want us to come in contact with any germs the press might be carrying. The idea struck the three of us as ridiculous, but we complied. For their part, the press reacted with great good humor, most of them holding handkerchiefs to their faces. Immediately upon leaving we were told we could remove the masks, even though we were standing in the same hallway the press had entered through moments before. Berry's assumption must have been that the press had germs while the dozens of NASA people we saw each day had none at all.

This concern for health was carried to a further, more embarrassing extreme for the dinner before lift-off. President Nixon had indicated his interest in attending, and someone—whoever did it never admitted it to any of us, but rumors homed in on Chuck Berry—informed the White House that it might not be a good idea for health reasons. Frank Borman, whose line to the White House was direct, was enraged and said so to anyone who would listen. Was it possible the President had some germ the thirteen other people at the dinner didn't have? The whole thing now strikes me as slightly crazy, but at the time the three of us passed it off with only minor puzzlement. Our concentration on what lay ahead was total. We saw ourselves as the objects of a gigantic, intense effort, and not at all as individuals.

When NASA began to build its sprawling complex called Cape Canaveral, which would later be renamed Cape Kennedy, Merritt Island in Florida was a sparsely populated hunk of open land. The few residences were along the coast and several were refurbished to serve as cottages for the astronauts to use for relaxation. Most of the time we lived in special crew quarters.

As was customary, we had the last day before launch to ourselves at a cottage. Our cook was an avid coin collector who had recently purchased a magnetic detector built somewhat on the same principle as a mine detector. By scanning along the ground, a dial would move when it sensed metal. I had expressed an interest in the detector, and the cook brought it to the cottage. I carefully combed the beach with the detector looking for hidden treasures or, if nothing else, some loose change. I found absolutely nothing, but I had a good time anyway. Mike, Neil, and I swam and relaxed.

Special telephone lines leading directly to Houston were installed. I called home just before dinner for a final talk with my family. Neither Joan nor I have any exact recollection of the conversation, nor do our children. Joan and I do remember that it was the first time I mentioned what to do in case of any major catastrophe, and there was a brief, uncomfortable discussion of mortality. We talked less than half an hour.

The next morning would be July 16, 1969, a day that would go down in history. Actually, it was a day already noted in history, though few remember it or knew of it at the time. On July 16, 1945, on a barren and secret piece of land in New Mexico the first atomic bomb was detonated.

8

At breakfast early on the morning of the launch, Dr. Thomas Paine, the administrator of NASA, told us that concern for our own safety must govern all our actions, and if anything looked wrong we were to abort the mission. He then made a most surprising and unprecedented statement: if we were forced to abort, we would be immediately recycled and assigned to the next landing attempt. What he said and how he said it was very reassuring.

We were up early, ate, and began to suit up—a rather laborious and detailed procedure involving many people, which we would repeat once again, alone, before entering the LM for our lunar landing.

Biological needs came first. We rubbed our behinds with a special salve and pulled on what were euphemistically called fecal-containment garments. Had we, say, a major emergency after leaving the earth's orbit or some problem docking in space, the cabin could possibly lose pressurization. It would be some five or six days before we were back floating in the Pacific and, in spite of our low residue diets, a bowel movement while in the pressurized spacesuits was likely. The fecal-containment garment was designed to do what its name implies—also to keep the odor from making both the culprit and his buddies sick.

In order to urinate, we were fitted with a prophylactic-like devices from which a connector led to a bikini-like sack secured around our hips. It was almost inevitable we would use these, since five to six hours elapsed from the time we put the spacesuits on until we took them off. The rubbers must fit snugly in order to work without leaking; consequently they were a subject of much joking. Our legs weren't the only things with a tendency to atrophy in space.

In less critical stages of the flight we stripped down to our regular underwear and put on two-piece constant-wear garments which made urinating much easier. A second set of underwear was reserved for the trip home. Urine was vented out of the spacecraft, where it formed bright crystals and disappeared. Other waste was stowed in special containers.

The rest of suiting up is a comfortable, almost restful procedure. It is also fairly routine, and once the cool air began running through the suit I leaned back and relaxed. My only anxious moment came when I noticed my grandfather's 32nd-degree Masonic ring was missing. I had been wearing it for over a year and considered it part of me. Several minutes went by as I indulged in a curious—and uncharacteristic—surge of superstition. After all, I had planned to take the ring to the moon and back, and now it had disappeared. I figured it must have come off when I washed the fecal-containment salve off my hands. A doctor volunteered to run down the hall and search in the bathroom. Within five minutes he was back with the ring.

The *Apollo* capsule is not the most commodious means of travel, and even less so while its crew is being inserted. A member of the back-up crew is on hand, and in the capsule, checking things out. Gunter Wendt and his meticulous and safety-conscious crew are also on hand. We were traveling tourist, three abreast and prone on tightly and closely packed couches. As the man in the middle, I was the last to go in.

While Mike and Neil were going through the complicated business of being strapped in and connected to the spacecraft's life-support system, I waited near the elevator on the floor below. I waited alone for fifteen minutes in a sort of serene limbo. As far as I could see there were peo-

Going to the moon was easy compared with speaking to a joint session of Congress. I came to look back on this brief speech—over which I had slaved for hours—as the moment I realized that my life would never again be the same and that somehow I was unequipped for what would come.

From the left: Pat Collins, Jan Armstrong and Joan during the Buenos Aires stop on our world tour. Our wives got along beautifully, even though by this time Mike, Neil and I were drifting apart. I missed the stop in Buenos Aires because I was summoned—as a favor to the President, I was told—to speak at the AFL-CIO convention in Atlantic City.

When Russian cosmonauts Andrian Nikolayev and Vitaly Sevastynov visited the United States, I was appointed their host. The three of us got along beautifully and the trip was both a technical and political success. It was also my last public act as an astronaut: I had decided it was best to leave NASA. By this time I was also receiving special medical care.

At age four, I was wiry, energetic and short for my age. My older sister, Madeline, was a good bit more tolerant of my antics than my sister Fay, who could—and did—give as good as she got. Mom, meanwhile, tended to look on in helpless dismay as her only son created havoc in a home dominated by women. Dad, who was often away, didn't say much about it—he saved his involvement for a good bit later.

For seven summers I went to Trout Lake Camp, where the emphasis was on competition and the winners got all the attention. My dad would visit from time to time, attracting attention in his officer's uniform and constantly urging me on to more victories.

In high school, football was my passion and homework my nemesis. Finally my father intervened and I gave up football for academics, but not before I was knocked senseless one Saturday afternoon in a game. I finally chose pole-vaulting because of the skill it required and because it was a solitary sport.

At brace *(left)*, my first year at West Point. Walking was not permitted, so at all times we ran at brace and we even ate at brace. Even today I sometimes find myself on a podium giving a speech at rigid and tense attention.

In Korea, I had my first—and only—taste of actual combat. The first MIG I shot down provided the first photographs of the pilot actually bailing out of his crippled plane. Many of my missions were flown with my good friend Sam Johnson, who later spent almost seven years as a POW in Hanoi.

Joan and I were married on December 29, 1954, at the Episcopal Church in Ho Ho Kus, New Jersey. I had already tested her reaction to the rigors of military life and discovered she only needed a challenge. Three days later she was fumigating the cockroaches out of the three-room apartment we rented in Montgomery, Alabama. I don't think she's been idle since.

The purpose of the zero-gravity flights was to conduct various experiments and to determine the effect of weightlessness on astronauts. Only once did I feel nausea—and that was most likely caused by the martinis from the night before. That's my good friend Charlie Bassett's behind. His tragic death had a profound effect on my involvement in the Gemini program.

The training was endless, and my son Andy was always an eager audience. Of our three children, Andy is the most like me. Mike, like his mother, is interested in the theater, Jan loves music—and her horse Nova—while Andy much prefers spare parts from the motorcycle shop.

Eating iguana on survival training.

My strongest memory of those few hours as the first men on the lunar surface was the constant worry that we'd never accomplish all the experiments we were scheduled to do. Philosophy and emotion were not included and, in fact, were discouraged. NASA

TRAVEL VOUCHER
MEMORANDUM

DEPARTMENT, BUREAU, OR ESTABLISHMENT	VOUCHER NO.
NASA - Manned Spacecraft Center	014501

PAYEE'S NAME	SCHEDULE NO.
Col. Edwin E. Aldrin 00018	

MAILING ADDRESS **PLEASE MAKE CHECK PAYABLE TO:**	PAID BY
Nassau Bay National Bank P.O. Box 58008 Houston, Texas 77032 Account #1-0348-9	

OFFICIAL DUTY STATION	RESIDENCE
Houston, Texas	

FOR TRAVEL AND OTHER EXPENSES		TRAVEL ADVANCE	CHECK NO.
FROM (DATE)	TO (DATE)	Outstanding $	
7-7-69	7-27-69		CASH PAYMENT OF $
APPLICABLE TRAVEL AUTHORIZATION(S)		Amount to be applied	RECEIVED (DATE)
NO.	DATE	Balance to remain	
X-22002	6/18/69	outstanding $	

TRANSPORTATION REQUESTS ISSUED

TRANSPORTATION REQUEST NUMBER	AGENT'S VALUATION OF TICKET	INITIALS OF CARRIER ISSUING TICKET	MODE, CLASS OF SERVICE, AND ACCOMMODATIONS*	DATE ISSUED	POINTS OF TRAVEL	
					FROM—	TO—
Gov. Air					Houston, Texas	Cape Kennedy, Fla. Moon Pacific Ocean (USN Hornett) Hawaii and return to Houston, Texas

		AMOUNT CLAIMED →	Dollars	Cts
8-4-69			33	31

APPROVED (Supervisory and other approvals when required)	DIFFERENCES:		
NEXT PREVIOUS VOUCHER PAID UNDER SAME TRAVEL AUTHORITY	Total verified correct for charge to appropriation(s) (initials)	33	31
VOUCHER NO.	D.O. SYMBOL	DATE (MONTH-YEAR)	Applied to travel advance (appropriation symbol)		
AUG 2 6 1969 C. W. Bird Authorized Certifying Officer	NET TO TRAVELER →	33	31

ACCOUNTING CLASSIFICATION
039-00-00-00-EA-2031-CB11

* Abbreviations for Pullman accommodations: MR, master room; DR, drawing room; CP, compartment; BR, bedroom; DSR, duplex single room; RM, roomette; DRM, duplex roomette; SOS, single occupancy section; LB, lower berth; UB, upper berth; LB-UB, lower and upper berth; S, seat.

e U.S. government com-
nsates all its employees
o travel at its request. This
s my compensation.

SCHEDULE OF EXPENSES AND AMOUNTS CLAIMED

PREVIOUS TEMPORARY DUTY (Complete these blocks only if in travel status immediately prior to period covered by this voucher and if administratively required.)

DEPARTURE FROM OFFICIAL STATION (DATE) (HOUR)	TEMPORARY DUTY STATION LAST DAY OF PRECEDING VOUCHER PERIOD (LOCATION) (DATE OF ARRIVAL)

DATE 1969	NATURE OF EXPENSE*			AUTHORIZED MILEAGE RATE ___¢		AMOUNT CLAIMED		
				SPEEDOMETER READINGS	NO. OF MILES	MILEAGE	SUBSISTENCE	OTHER
7-7	LV:	Residence	0445	POV		8		56	
7-7	AR:	EAFB	0500						
7-7	LV:	EAFB	0530	Gov. Air					
7-7	AR:	Cape Kennedy, Fla.	0800						
7-16	LV:	Cape Kennedy, Fla.	0832	Gov. Spacecraft					
7-19	AR:	Moon	1325						
7-21	LV:	Moon	2400	Gov. Spacecraft					
7-24	AR:	Pacific Ocean	0600						
7-24	LV:	Pacific Ocean	0800	USN Hornett					
7-26	AR:	Hawaii	0900						
7-26	LV:	Hawaii	1200	USAF Plane					
7-27	AR:	EAFB	0100						
7-27	LV:	EAFB	0215	Gov. Veh.					
7-27	AR:	LRL	0300						
	Government meals and quarters furnished for all the above dates.								
	POV was used for 100 miles official vicinity travel at Cape Kennedy, Fla.								10.00
	POV authorized for official vicinity travel at Cape Kennedy, Fla. in lieu of rental car.								
	Thomas P. Stafford								

| Grand total to face of voucher → (Subtotals to be carried forward if necessary) | | | | | | 33 31 | 56 | 225 1000 |

*If per diem allowances for members of employee's immediate family are included, give members' names, their relationship to employee, and ages and marital status of children (unless this information is shown on the travel authorization).

The Aldrins, summer of 1973.

ple and cars lining the beaches and highways. The surf was just beginning to rise out of an azure-blue ocean. I could see the massiveness of the Saturn 5 rocket below and the magnificent precision of the Apollo capsule above. I savored the wait and marked the minutes in my mind as something I would always want to remember.

Fred Haise was the member of our back-up crew who was inside the capsule with us. He helped the suit technicians hook up the shoulder straps and the seat belts; he adjusted the armrest, turned various switches and valves, and attached each of us to the spacecraft's oxygen system. My recollection of this procedure is a mass of hands reaching and tugging from several directions. Mike, Neil, and I were fairly helpless by this time—three totally battened-down people waiting for the ride to start.

At 9:32 A.M. Eastern daylight time we lifted off on schedule. As it had been in the Gemini program, we didn't sense the movement of the lift-off until it was confirmed a second or so later by the voice of launch control.

For the thousands of people watching along the beaches of Florida and the millions who watched on television, our lift-off was ear-shattering. For us there was a slight increase in the amount of background noise, not at all unlike the sort one notices taking off in a commercial airliner, and in less than a minute we were traveling ahead of the speed of sound.

It's seldom mentioned, but the first twelve seconds or so of any flight are, from a safety standpoint, the most dangerous. For those seconds, the rocket is rising alongside the launch tower. If anything should go wrong in the automatic guidance system—some minute change in the angle of the rocket—there might be contact with the tower. The entire Saturn 5, loaded with highly explosive propellants, could turn into a gigantic fireball. When launch control comes over the speaker with "Tower clear" the danger is over, and there is a sense of relief stretching from Houston to

Cape Kennedy to us. At this point, flight control shifts from the Cape to Houston.

During the initial seconds—up to about a minute—there is a feedback computation at work in the guidance system. The resulting effect for us was rather like the motion one feels in a train, a kind of sway and swing as the rocket settled on rails of its own. We hadn't expected this, for none of the other Apollo crews had mentioned it during their debriefings. The motion, however, was noticed on flights subsequent to ours.

A busy eleven minutes later and we were in earth orbit moving about very cautiously. There had been numerous instances of nausea during the early stages of the Apollo flights and we hoped to avoid it. One of the methods was moving carefully and deliberately at the onset. Neil, who had had just six hours in space, was even more cautious than Mike and I. I was less concerned, not only because of my long extravehicular activity on Gemini 12, but also because two days before the flight I had made a weightless test in an Air Force version of the Boeing 707 in which I did everything I possibly could to induce nausea. Nothing had happened. None of the three of us experienced any nausea during the flight, much to our relief. In fact, we ended up the healthiest crew of any Apollo flight to date— we never once opened our medical kits.

While we were in orbit, the earth didn't look much different from the way it had during my first flight, yet I kept looking at it. From space it has an almost benign quality. Intellectually one could realize there were wars underway on earth, but emotionally it was impossible to understand such things. The thought occurred and reoccurred that wars are generally fought for territory or are disputes over borders; from space the arbitrary borders established on earth cannot be seen.

Mike, as command module pilot, was the busiest at this time, and would continue to be busy. While he was checking the inertial platform alignment with the sextant, Neil and I had various chores, but most of the time we spent adjusting to being weightless and securing various odds and ends floating within the light-gray cabin walls. We had hoped to have time to send back television pictures before we left earth orbit to head for the moon. We had the time, but Houston was unable to configure the communications network to receive our unexpected signal. After one and a half earth orbits a pre-programmed sequence fired the Saturn 5 briefly to send us out of earth orbit and on our way to the moon.

Mike's next major task, with Neil and me assisting, was to separate our command module *Columbia* from the Saturn third stage, turn around and connect with the lunar module *Eagle*, which was stored in third stage. *Eagle*, by now, was exposed; its four enclosing panels had automatically come off and were drifting away. This, of course, was a critical maneuver in the flight plan. If the separation and docking did not work, we would return to earth. There was also the possibility of an in-space collision and the subsequent decompression of our cabin, so we were still in our space-suits as Mike separated us from the Saturn third stage. Critical as the maneuver is, I felt no apprehension about it, and if there was the slightest inkling of concern it disappeared quickly as the entire separation and docking proceeded perfectly to completion. The nose of *Columbia* was now connected to the top of the *Eagle* and heading for the moon as we watched the Saturn third-stage venting, a propulsive maneuver causing it to move slowly away from us.

As soon as all the work and communication related to the separation and docking was completed, the three of us took turns stripping down and pulling on the considerably more comfortable two-piece flight suits. Stowing the space-suits brought about a good deal of confusion, with parts and pieces floating about the cabin as we tried to keep logistics under control.

After some complicated procedures the spacecraft was continually rotating very slowly about its axis. This process kept us perpendicular to both the sun and the earth. This maintained an even temperature around the outside of the spacecraft, and provided continuous communication with the earth. This practical spin produced an incredible panorama every two minutes as the sun, moon, and earth appeared in our windows one at a time.

We were departing the earth at ever-decreasing speeds, initially some twenty-five thousand miles per hour, but we could not immediately detect the fact that the earth was shrinking as we sped away from it. The sensation was rather like watching the hand on a clock move. You know it is moving, but watching it you cannot see it move. Only after looking elsewhere for a time, then returning to the minute hand, can one realize it actually did move. The earth would eventually be so small I could blot it out of the universe simply by holding my thumb up to it.

It was also intriguing to get as close a look as possible back at the earth. We had with us our version of a tourist's viewing device called a monocular, and that's exactly what it was: half of a set of binoculars. It served as a magnifying glass, which put us visually closer to what we were looking at. With it I improvised a method of getting a fairly clear and steady look at the earth. It was an intriguing process: in order to minimize any manual disturbances and compensate for the vibrations we could feel, I'd very carefully remove my hand from the monocular and leave it floating, weightless, in front of the window. I'd then look through it, and for the several seconds before it drifted away from pointing at the earth we had a greatly improved view. Neil joined me in doing this while Mike finished his chores.

When we finished looking at the panorama we settled down to eat. It wasn't long before I developed my first affinity for food in space: the shrimp cocktails. The shrimp were chosen one by one to be sure they would be tiny enough to squeeze out of the food packet, and they were delicious. There was some fairly good soup and some cheese and meat spreads for crackers, but most of the rest of the food was bland. Much of it required water from the hot- or cold-water guns. It wasn't long before we discovered that the little device designed at the last minute to ventilate hydrogen from the water, as it passed from the gun to the food bag, was not always the success its designers had hoped. Frequently the hydrogen tended to do what it had done on previous flights: it stayed in the water and was swallowed by us. The result was stomach gas. At one point on the trip back to earth it got so bad it was suggested we shut down our altitude-control thrusters and do the job ourselves.

The important thing, of course, was to consume the proper amount of water and calories—whether or not the food was an epicurean delight wasn't particularly important. As anyone who watches television knows, the people who manufacture Tang make a big thing out of the fact that astronauts drink it for breakfast while they're traveling in space. I can't speak for the other flights, but before ours, the three of us dutifully sampled the orange drink, supposedly Tang, and instead chose a grapefruit-orange mixture as our citrus drink. If Tang was on our flight I was unaware of it.

The first night we started our rotation for watch. Two of us slept anchored in hammocks beneath the left and right couches while the third floated above the left couch connected by earphones. The center couch had been folded down and put out of the way, and it covered our space-suits. We rotated positions from night to night. The first night we slept less than five and a half hours. We were still adjusting to space travel and our adrenaline level was still fairly high from the excitement of lift-off and translunar injection. If my adrenaline level was high, my heart rate remained unchanged and slightly below normal during the lift-off and the initial hours in space. Mike speculated I

223

might lose my title as Dr. Rendezvous and become Dr. Cool instead.

In the middle of one evening, Houston time, I found myself idly staring out the window of the *Columbia* and saw something that looked a bit unusual. It appeared brighter than any star and not quite the pinpoints of light that stars are. I pointed this out to Mike and Neil, and the three of us were beset with curiosity. With the help of the monocular we guessed that whatever it was, it was only a hundred miles or so away. Looking at it through our sextant we found it occasionally formed a cylinder, but when the sextant's focus was adjusted it had a sort of illuminated "L" look to it. It had the shape of some sort—we all agreed on that—but exactly what it was we couldn't pin down. We asked Houston some casual questions: "How far away is the Saturn third stage?" The response was in the vicinity of six thousand miles. That wasn't it.

It could possibly have been one of the panels of the Saturn third stage which fly off to expose the LM and cannot be traced from earth. We could see it for about forty-five seconds at a time as the ship rotated, and we watched it off and on for about an hour. We debated whether or not to tell the ground we had spotted something, and decided against it. Our reason was simple: The UFO people would descend on the message in hordes, setting off another rash of UFO spottings back on earth. We concluded it was most likely one of the panels. Its course appeared in no way to conflict with ours, and it presented no danger. We dropped the matter there.

The flight plan to the moon had several blank pages, periods in which we had nothing to do. I have no recollection at all of being idle. I don't think any of us was. Nor do I remember any idle conversation. We might have been physically idle at times, but mentally we were continually anticipating what would come next.

One of the first things that struck us—and kept us busy on

and off the entire voyage—was the mostly unanticipated number of housekeeping chores necessary for three men traveling through space. This is even more improbable in view of the fact that the *Columbia* was about as big as the inside of a small station wagon. Everything had to be stowed or sealed away or anchored to one of the many panels by Velcro. We each had little cloth pouches—forerunners of the purses some men would begin to carry a few years later —in which we kept various frequently used items, such as pens, sunglasses and, for me, a slide rule. As often as not, one or two of us would be scrambling around on the floor searching for a missing pair of sunglasses, the monocular, a film pack, or a toothbrush.

We had a tape recorder and cartridges of music to listen to during rest periods. Before the flight I felt I was much too busy to be bothered with selecting music and deferred to Neil and Mike, who chose mostly easy listening music.

Also during rest periods we did our televising back to earth: short entertainments prepared, we hoped, to show the television audiences back on earth the activities within the spacecraft. We went to great lengths to make the telecasts seem improvised, and we apparently were successful; we received compliments on them when the flight ended. The fact is that they were carefully planned in advance and for me the exact words were written down on little cards stuck onto the panel in front of us. Spontaneous I was not.

The second day en route—the day before we were scheduled to begin lunar orbit—I scrambled through the hatch back into the LM *Eagle* to begin preparing it for separation from *Columbia*.

It was probably the oddest sensation of the entire voyage as I crawled from the floor to the top of *Columbia* and entered the *Eagle*, only to find myself descending head first from its ceiling. The two were docked with the ceiling of the *Eagle* connected to the nose—or what seemed to be the top—of *Columbia*. Though slightly disorienting, it was intriguing to move about my chores, knowing all the time that just a few feet away everyone else was, by my reckoning, upside down.

In our preliminary flight plan I wasn't scheduled to go into the LM until the next day in lunar orbit, but I had lobbied successfully to go earlier. There were a number of things I wanted to move around; I also wanted to remove the big bag covering the instrument panel, along with the things stored in the bag. My strongest argument for going in early was that I'd have ample time to make sure the frail LM and its equipment had suffered no damage during the launch and long trip. By that time neither Neil nor I had been in the LM for about two weeks. The last weeks before the flight were spent mostly in the simulator brushing up on earth launch and chores, separation and docking, and the lunar landing and lift-off.

I took the movie camera and television camera along, and much to the distress of the television networks, who hadn't scheduled the time, I sent back to Houston the unexpected first pictures from the LM. This performance was spontaneous, and to my surprise, turned out rather well.

There was a fascinating and unusual view as we neared the moon because we were flying through its shadow. The moon was eclipsing the sun and it appeared weirdly three-dimensional. It was lit from the back—a huge dark object shadowing the brilliant beams of light from the sun. We took numerous pictures of the effect, but the lighting was such that the pictures were mostly unsuccessful.

The morning after our third night traveling we made the five-minute 59.9 second burn, which placed us into lunar orbit. The burn was called LOI-1 (Lunar Orbit Insertion one), the first of two such burns. It went perfectly.

The second burn to place us in closer circular orbit of the moon, the orbit from which Neil and I would separate from the *Columbia* and continue on to the moon, was critically important. It had to be made in exactly the right place and for exactly the correct length of time. If we overburned for as little as two seconds we'd be on an impact course with the other side of the moon. Through a complicated and detailed system of checks and balances, both in Houston and in lunar orbit, plus star checks and detailed platform alignments, two hours after our first lunar orbit we made our second burn in an atmosphere of nervous and intense concentration. It, too, worked perfectly.

Before we began to make a more complete check of the LM, we received data from earth for what is called the trans-earth injection, a burn to get us out of lunar orbit and on our way back to earth. There were fifteen to twenty such possibilities, and one by one as they came up from Houston we copied them down and checked them, and the data was then ready for insertion into our computer in case of any emergency. This system replaced the Return to Earth computer program we had decided to discard a year earlier.

We began preparing the LM. Powering it up and preparing it was scheduled to take three hours, but because I had already started the checkout, we were completed a half hour ahead of schedule. By the time we had completed the long list of LM communication checks and had set a number of switches, the *Eagle* was ready to go. So were we. We were confident we were going to fly the *Eagle* to its first lunar landing. In fact, we were impatient to do so.

Reluctantly we returned to the *Columbia* as planned. Our fourth night we were to sleep in lunar orbit. Although it was not in the flight plan, before covering the windows and dousing the lights, Neil and I carefully prepared all the equipment and clothing we would need in the morning, and mentally ran through the many procedures we would follow. I was so anxiously anticipating the next few days' events, I completely forgot to look for the odd flashes I had seen the two previous nights en route to the moon. I slept fitfully.

The next morning we got up ahead of schedule and set to work. The activity of three men in space must, of necessity, be a cooperative venture. By now we had worked out various routines for living together, but in our excitement this particular morning the system came unglued. For eating we had a system where one guy pulled the food out, another snipped the packages open while the third liquefied his food and passed the water gun to the man waiting. The rhythm got slightly out of whack this last morning, and once we finally got it going properly, we all three bemoaned the fact that the simple act of eating was something there was no training for. It was one of those things we had to learn by doing.

We then began undressing and getting back into our spacesuits, beginning once again with the fecal-containment garment and the urine-collection bag. I got as far as my liquid-cooled underwear and left to make some initial checks in the LM while Neil took my place in the navigation bay to begin changing. There is only room for one man to change clothes, with another standing by to help pull the long crotch-to-shoulder zipper closed. Both Neil and I were determined to put on our suits as perfectly and comfortably as possible—we were going to be in them for quite some time.

Mike, meanwhile, would suit up for our separation and landing, then return to his in-flight coveralls until we were ready to lift off and rendezvous with the *Columbia*.

When Neil was completely suited up he took my place in the LM while I returned to finish suiting up in the navigation bay. I then crawled back into the LM, and Neil and I sealed the hatch between the two ships. After powering up many more systems we deployed the LM's spiderlike landing gear. Seconds later Houston confirmed its deployment.

After several more communication checks we undocked and separated to inspect one another visually. Mike had made a special trip to the Grumman factory to see what the LM looked like with its landing gear deployed so that his check in space would be accurate. He checked the five-foot touchdown sensor prongs extending from the left, right, and rear footpads. He also made sure the footpad in the front gear was in proper position. Neil and I had asked that the landing sensor be removed from the front leg which had the ladder we would use to descend to the lunar surface. The sensors would break off or be completely bent on touchdown and we were worried we might trip over the one nearest the ladder. NASA agreed.

We were still sixty miles above the surface of the backside of the moon when we made our first burn of 28.5 seconds to begin our coasting descent to the front side of the moon. Neil and I were harnessed into the LM in a standing position. We proceeded with a detailed range rate check which would enable us to return to the *Columbia* should our computer navigation have failed us. This process and other navigational checks were part of our check-and-balance systems and, as such, were more reassuring.

At precisely the right moment the engine ignited to begin the twelve-minute powered descent. Strapped in by the system of belts and cables not at all unlike shock absorbers, neither of us felt the initial motion. We looked quickly at the computer to make sure we were actually functioning as planned. After twenty-six seconds the engine went to full throttle and the motion became noticeable. Neil watched his instruments for proper readings while I looked at our primary computer and compared it with our second computer, which was part of the abort guidance system, to make sure they were reading properly by checking their figures against those on a group of cards Neil and I had between us.

I then began a computer read-out sequence to Neil which was also being transmitted to Houston. I had helped develop it. It sounded as though I was chattering like a magpie. It also sounded as though I was doing all the work. During training we had discussed the possibility of making the communication only between Neil and myself, but Mission Control liked the idea of hearing our communications with each other. Neil had referred to it once as "that damned open mike of yours," and I tried to make as little of an issue of it as possible.

At six thousand feet above the lunar surface a yellow caution light came on and we encountered one of the few potentially serious problems in the entire flight, a problem which might have caused us to abort, had it not been for a man on the ground who really knew his job.

When the yellow program alarm light came on we routinely asked the computer to define its problem. The coded answer it gave was that the machine was overloaded; it was being asked to do too much in too little time. It turned out that the men at MIT, who had designed the landing computer program which interrogates the landing radar had never talked to the men who designed the rendezvous radar program. The combination overloaded our on-board computer. The problem had never come up in the simulators because we were using special-purpose computers.

Back in Houston, not to mention on board the *Eagle*, hearts shot up into throats while we waited to learn what would happen.

We had received two of the caution lights when Steve Bales, the flight controller responsible for LM computer activity, perceived the problem and told us to proceed through Charlie Duke, the capsule communicator. We received three or four more warnings but kept on going. When Mike, Neil, and I were presented with Medals of Freedom by President Nixon, Steve also received one. He certainly deserved it, because without him we might not have landed.

At an altitude of five hundred feet, Neil took over manually, and together we began our final descent. We immediately saw that the area of the moon where our computer intended to land was rather more strewn with rocks than we had anticipated. The area beyond it, however, was quite clear. Neil extended our trajectory and thereby changed our touchdown point. Because of weight, fuel was computed precisely. The slight course change caused our flight to last quite a few seconds longer and used a great deal more fuel. I remember hearing the Ground advise us we had sixty seconds of fuel left.

At an altitude of fifty feet we entered what was accurately referred to as the dead-man zone. In this zone, if anything had gone wrong—if, for example, the engine had failed—it would probably have been too late to do anything about it before we impacted with the moon. There were no fail-safe abort systems available until landing or impact with the moon. I felt no apprehension at all during this short time. Rather, I felt a kind of arrogance—an arrogance inspired by knowing that so many people had worked on this landing, people possessing the greatest scientific talents in the world.

"Thirty seconds," Charlie Duke at Mission Control said regarding our remaining fuel.

At ten seconds we touched down on the lunar surface. The landing was so smooth I had to check the landing lights from the touchdown sensors to make sure the slight bump I felt was indeed the landing. It was.

"Contact light. OK, engine stopped," I communicated back to Houston, quickly launching into the post-engine procedures in preparation for the possibility of an immediate abort lift-off. We had trained to do exactly this and I was surprised when Neil interrupted to say, "Houston, Tranquility Base here. The *Eagle* has landed."

I had known what he was going to say, but he had never told me when he was going to say it. When he was through I continued with the postlanding procedures. We landed at 4:17:42 P.M. Eastern daylight time on July 20, 1969. From now until we left the moon we would be called Tranquility Base.

We gave in to our excitement long enough to pat each other on the shoulder, then we plunged into frantic activity. Before beginning preparations to go out onto the lunar surface we were planning for the first of several emergency lift-off times to rejoin the *Columbia*. The first came less than one minute after touchdown and was followed less than two minutes later by the second such ideal time for rendezvous. Preparation mounted to a simulated countdown. Capcom told us we were "stay" for both times. The next opportunity wouldn't be until Mike completed another lunar orbit.

If there was any emotional reaction to the lunar landing it was so quickly suppressed that I have no recollection of it. We had so much to do, and so little time in which to do it, that we no sooner landed than we were preparing to leave, in the event of an emergency. I'm surprised, in retrospect, that we even took time to slap each other on the shoulders.

The first two hours on the lunar surface were, for me, the busiest part of the flight. I had to make all sorts of measurements and alignments with stars for navigational purposes. This all had to be communicated back to earth and rechecked by voice—a process that is as long as it is boring to listen to. Neil used the few minutes I was not communicating to make his brief descriptions of the lunar surface. After Mike passed overhead we ceased our simulated countdown. It was obvious now that we were going to stay awhile.

According to the flight plan, this sequence was followed by an eating period and a four-hour rest period before we were scheduled to start the involved preparations to walk on the lunar surface. It was called a rest period, but it was also a built-in time pad in case we had to make an extra lunar orbit before landing, or if there was any kind of difficulty which might delay the landing. Since we landed on schedule and weren't overly tired, as we had thought we might be, we opted to skip the four-hour rest period. We were too excited to sleep anyway.

During the first idle moment in the LM before eating our snack, I reached into my personal preference kit and pulled out two small packages which had been specially prepared at my request. One contained a small amount of wine, the other a small wafer. With them and a small chalice from the kit, I took communion on the moon, reading to myself from a small card I carried on which I had written the portion of the Book of John used in the traditional communion ceremony. I had intended to read my communion passage back to earth, but at the last minute Deke Slayton had requested that I not do this. NASA was already embroiled in a legal battle with Madelyn Murray O'Hare, the celebrated opponent of religion, over the *Apollo* 8 crew reading from Genesis while orbiting the moon at Christmas. I agreed reluctantly, and instead I took my communion after first saying, "Houston, this is the LM pilot speaking. I would like to request a few moments of silence. I would like to invite each person listening in, wherever or whoever he may be, to contemplate for a moment the events of the last few hours and to give thanks in his own individual way."

After eating, we told Houston we estimated it would be another three and a half hours before we opened the hatch. We had housekeeping chores to perform—food packages, flight plans and the like that we needed to stow. It took longer than anticipated to depressurize the *Eagle* and to get the cooling units in our back-packs operating.

It was very cramped in the *Eagle*. We felt like two full-backs trying to change positions inside a cub scout pup tent. We also had to be careful of our movements. Weight in the LM was an even more critical factor than in the *Columbia*. The LM structure was so thin one of us could have taken a pencil and jammed it through the side of the ship. It was thin and fragile, but it was also a reassuring and familiar place set down in unfamiliar surroundings. We used up the estimated time and then some. By the time Neil swung open the hatch to step onto the surface, it was an hour later than we had estimated.

On the way to the moon Mike and I had asked Neil what he was going to say when he stepped out on the moon. He had replied that he was still thinking it over. He has since told people that he didn't decide exactly what to say until we were nearly there. His remarks are hard to dispute; nevertheless there are those who have disputed them. There was, in fact, widespread discussion prior to our flight about what he should say. When it reached epidemic proportions, Julian Sheer wrote a terse memo to the NASA heads saying in effect: Did Queen Isabella tell Christopher Columbus what to say? There were also rumors—unconfirmed—that Neil was advised what to say by Simon Bourgin, a United States Information Agency official who was in frequent contact with astronauts, and who accompanied us around the world later. He was also the rumored source of Frank Borman's reading from Genesis. For his part, Neil declined to comment on any of these rumors to anyone, including Mike and myself.

We opened the hatch, and Neil, with me as his navigator, began backing out of the tiny opening. We were so busy that neither of us noticed that Neil had momentarily forgotten to pull the small handle he passed on the small porch of the LM. The handle deploys the side of the LM where all the equipment we needed on the lunar surface was stored, and it also activated the television camera that was going to televise back to earth his step onto the lunar surface. The ground noticed the omission and reminded Neil, who moved back a bit and pulled the deployment handle.

It seemed like a small eternity before I heard Neil say, at 10:56 P.M., "That's one small step for man . . . ah . . . one

234

giant leap for mankind." No matter who thought it up, it was a neatly appropriate expression.

In less than fifteen minutes I was backing awkwardly out of the hatch and onto the surface to join Neil, who, in the tradition of all tourists, had his camera ready to photograph my arrival.

I felt buoyant and was full of goose pimples when I stepped down on the surface. I immediately looked down at my feet and became intrigued with the peculiar properties of the lunar dust. If one kicks sand on a beach, it scatters in numerous directions with some grains traveling farther than others. On the moon the dust travels exactly and precisely as it goes in various directions, and every grain of it lands very nearly the same distance away.

The second thing I did was record my own first on the moon, a first that became known to only a select few. My kidneys, which have never been of the strongest, sent me a message of distress. Neil might have been the first man to step on the moon, but I was the first to pee in his pants on the moon. I was, of course, linked up with the urine-collection device, but it was a unique feeling. The whole world was watching, but I was the only one who knew what they were really witnessing.

I quickly discovered that I felt balanced—comfortably upright—only when I was tilted slightly forward. I also felt a bit disoriented: on the earth when one looks at the horizon, it appears flat; on the moon, so much smaller than the earth and quite without high terrain, the horizon in all directions visibly curved down away from us.

As we had planned, I took off jogging to test my maneuverability on the surface. The exercise gave me an odd sensation and looked even more odd when I later saw films of it. With the bulky suits on, we appeared to be moving in slow motion. I noticed immediately that my inertia seemed much greater on the moon than it was on earth. Earthbound, I would have stopped my run in just one step —an abrupt halt. I immediately sensed that if I did this on the moon, I'd be face down in lunar dust; I had to use three or four steps to sort of wind down. The same applied to turning around. Earthbound, it is a very direct motion; on the moon it is done in stages. My earth weight, with the big back-pack and heavy suit, was 360 pounds. On the moon, in one-sixth of the earth's gravity, I weighed only 60 pounds.

At one point I paused, looked around, and remarked that the surface was "Beautiful. Beautiful. Magnificent desolation." I was particularly struck by the contrast between the starkness of the shadows and the desertlike barrenness of the rest of the surface. It ranged from dusty gray to light tan and was unchanging except for one startling sight: our LM sitting there with its black, silver, and bright yellow-orange thermal coating shining brightly in the otherwise colorless landscape. I had seen Neil in his suit thousands of times before, but on the moon the unnatural whiteness of it seemed unusually brilliant, a contrasting white like no white I had ever seen before.

We could also look around and see the earth, which, though much larger than the moon the earth was seeing, seemed small—a beckoning oasis shining far away in the sky. We had hoped to take a picture which would include the earth, the LM, and one of us. In order to do so, however, one of us would have had to lie down on his belly to get the proper angle, and getting back up would likely have been quite an effort. But I did manage to take a picture of the LM and the earth. It turned out to be a disappointment.

As the sequence of lunar operations evolved, Neil had the camera most of the time, and the majority of the pictures taken on the moon that include an astronaut are of me. It wasn't until we were back on earth and in the Lunar Receiving Laboratory looking over the pictures that we realized there were few pictures of Neil. My fault perhaps, but we had never simulated this in our training.

We had a number of experiments to conduct and precious little time to do them. Because of the large variety of unknowns involved on this first trip, our surface activity was limited to two hours and forty minutes, and every minute was busy. Solar wind experiments had to be assembled; experiments to test the seismic characteristics of the moon had to be set out; a laser reflector had to be deployed; and after all this was done, rock samples had to be gathered.

At some point we also had to set up the American flag we had brought and uncover the commemorative plaque attached to the front leg of the LM. We had trained to do everything in minute detail, but there had been no training for these ceremonies.

During a pause in experiments, Neil suggested we proceed with the flag. It took both of us to set it up and it was nearly a disaster. Public Relations obviously needs practice just as everything else does. A small telescoping arm was attached to the flagpole to keep the flag extended and perpendicular in the still lunar atmosphere. We locked the arm in its 90 degree position, but as hard as we tried, the telescope wouldn't fully extend. Thus the flag, which should have been flat, had its own unique permanent wave. Then, to our dismay, the staff of the pole at first wouldn't go far enough into the lunar surface to support itself in an upright position. After much struggling, we finally coaxed it to remain upright, but in a most precarious position. I dreaded the possibility of the American flag collapsing into the lunar dust in front of the television camera.

Neil took a picture of me next to and saluting the flag. As we were about to change positions so that I could take his picture, Houston announced that President Nixon would like to talk to us. My heart rate, which had been low throughout the entire flight, suddenly jumped. Later Neil said he had known the President might be speaking with us while we were on the moon, but no one had told me. I hadn't even considered the possibility. The conversation was short and, for me, awkward. I felt it somehow incumbent on me to make some profound statement, for which I had made no preparation whatsoever. I took the handiest possible refuge. Neil was the commander of the flight, so I let him do the responding. I conveniently concluded that any observation I might make would look as though I was butting into the conversation, so I kept silent.

We were all very proud of the commemorative plaque we next uncovered on the front strut of the LM. It displayed the west and east hemispheres of the earth; the words, "Here men from the planet Earth first set foot on the Moon. We came in peace for all mankind. July 1969 A.D.," were followed by the signatures and names of the three of us and the President. (This was one place where I felt signing "Buzz" was too informal.) I have often wondered when human eyes will next read the words on the plaque.

Next, I unloaded a complicated experiment from the rear of the LM, and together Neil and I deployed what was called the laser reflector and set up the passive seismometer experiments. My last experiment was to take a specially designed core tube, drive it into the lunar surface and retrieve a core sample.

Considering all the people who believed the surface would be soft—some had even believed we'd sink in the dust—it proved surprisingly solid. I worked and worked to get the core tube down, and I finally began pounding the shaft of the tube. Eventually I got the sample, but it came from a much shallower depth, about six inches, than we had hoped.

While I pounded for the core sample, Neil was moving around, gathering rocks and putting them in a bag. We were so busy rushing to get as much done as possible that I was halfway up the ladder before Neil asked me if I had remembered to leave the mementos we had brought along.

I had completely forgotten. What we had hoped to make into a brief ceremony, had there been time, ended almost as an afterthought. I reached into my shoulder pocket, pulled the packet out and tossed it onto the surface. It

contained two medallions for each of the Russian cosmonauts who had been killed and a patch from the *Apollo 1*
crew, who died in the fire at the Cape. There was also a
small gold olive branch, one of four I had had made. The
other three were for each of our wives and were also carried
on the flight.

We had a pulley system to load on the boxes of rocks and
the various things we were going to take back with us.
With Neil on the surface and me in the LM, we went to
work and found the process more time-consuming and dust-
scattering than had been anticipated.

After all the gear and both of us were inside, our first
chore was to pressurize the LM cabin and to begin stowing
the rock boxes, film magazines and anything else we
wouldn't need until we were connected again with the *Columbia*. Following that, we removed our boots and the big
back-packs, opened the LM hatch and threw these items
onto the lunar surface, along with a bagful of empty food
packages and the LM urine bags. The exact moment we
tossed everything out was measured back on earth—the
seismometer we had put out was even more sensitive than
we had expected.

We had a seven-hour rest period before beginning the
final lift-off procedures and settled down for our fitful rest.
I eased myself onto the small amount of available floor
space while Neil leaned against the rear of the cabin and
placed his feet in a small strap. We didn't sleep much at
all. Among other things, we were elated—and also cold.
Neil, who looked quite comfortable, found that his line of
vision was directly into the telescope pointed at the earth,
whose brightness made it difficult to sleep.

Lift-off from the moon, after a stay totaling twenty-one
hours, was exactly on schedule and fairly uneventful. The
ascent stage of the LM separated from the descent stage
with its chunky body and spindly legs, sending out a shower

of brilliant insulation particles which had been ripped off from the thrust of the ascent engine.

There was no time to sightsee. I was concentrating intently on the computers, and Neil was studying the attitude indicator, but I looked up long enough to see the flag fall over. Seconds after lift-off, the LM pitched forward about 45 degrees, and though we had anticipated it would be an abrupt and maybe even a frightening maneuver, the straps and springs securing us in the LM cushioned the tilt so much and the acceleration was so great it was barely noticeable.

Three hours and ten minutes later we were connected once again with the *Columbia*. The intervening time had been consumed by long and detailed series of rendezvous procedures and navigational and back-up checks. Three hours may seem a long time, but we were too busy to notice. The last two miles before rendezvous we controlled manually, and our intercept trajectory was nearly perfect. Our various calculations for maneuvers agreed very closely with Mike's and those from the earth.

Rendezvous had come a long way since I first started contemplating it at MIT. Looking back on it now, I honestly believe that the contributions I made to the space program in the development of pilot rendezvous techniques surpass even my part in *Apollo 11*.

Once docked to the *Columbia*, Neil and I extracted a small vacuum cleaner head from its storage place and proceeded to vacuum the moon dust off our suits. When we were told we should do this we thought the idea a bit silly, but we had agreed to do it. Now we found out just how ineffectual it was. The vacuum didn't take off much of the moon dust at all. We got more off by dusting each other by hand, but even that didn't do the job. Still dusty, we crawled back into the familiar and roomy *Columbia* and a much relieved Mike. Once we had transferred the rock boxes from the LM to the *Columbia*, we began to prepare to jettison the LM and begin the voyage back to earth.

The LM was sent on its way. It is still orbiting the moon, a reminder of man's first visit. Another reminder is the considerable amount of debris we left behind. The LMs used on subsequent trips have all been impacted on the moon after the men's return to the Apollo capsule.

The burn which took us out of lunar orbit and sent us off on our way home went exactly as planned. The three of us relaxed.

As we sped away from the moon it rapidly grew smaller. Unlike the busy departure from earth, we now had ample time to watch the moon diminish in perspective. The return trip was so uneventful that at one point we put on a special tape of sound effects we had brought along and played it back to an astounded audience in Houston. It began with the sound of a speeding diesel locomotive and continued with dogs barking and a whole range of other sound effects.

The voyage to the moon was conducted within nearly half a second of the flight plan. Of all the various midcourse corrections it was possible to make en route to and from the moon, we had used only two. The training and preparation was such that even the unfamiliar surface of the moon was very nearly as we had been led to expect. I realized I wasn't in the simulator and it was a good bit more real, but virtually nothing was unexpected. The extensive studies and preparations were that good.

On the morning of July 24, nine days after we had left the earth, we began to reenter the earth's atmosphere, once again traveling at twenty-five thousand miles an hour.

Man had once again conquered a new frontier. This, perhaps the most spectacular voyage into the unknown yet made, took man from the planet earth to the moon's surface and back again. Behind this great technological and human achievement were the efforts of thousands of people, a total of ten years of preparation, and an expenditure of some $24 billion.

The manifest beauty of all that had been done lay in its precision and the ability of man to achieve the fulfillment of his dreams. If nothing else, our voyage was a tribute to man's restless imagination and creativity.

Twelve American men have now visited the surface of the moon. If the twelve of us have any one viewpoint in common, it is that unlike most men we have a special concept of the earth. We have seen it from space as whole and bright and beautiful; we have seen it from the surface of the moon as not very large and somehow vulnerable. With all its imperfections, it is a great place to come from and an even greater place to go back to.

In subsequent years the Apollo program would be criticized and would decline in public favor. Many would say that man's traveling to the moon was not only a drain on the nation's financial resources but also useless.

Something is useless only if we do not know how to use it. If we use our moon experience wisely in the years to come, there is no doubt it will be a vital basis for greatly expanding our knowledge of the universe.

9

The two-day vacation after the world tour was spent in still another attempt to make a dent in the mounds of mail in my office. By now we had prevailed on the secretaries in the NASA mail room to open all our mail and, whenever possible, to answer it. They handled requests for photographs and the other routine mail. However, the majority of it needed a direct response and this mail was sent on to me. A few were answered, but most were stacked around my office in what looked like insurmountable piles.

I returned almost immediately to the fried-chicken circuit. Back to Chicago. I had agreed to be the guest of honor at a Masonic dinner dance called Tranquility Ball. The purpose of the evening was to raise funds to build a new crippled children's hospital. W. Clement Stone, a prominent Chicago businessman, had issued the official invitation and when I learned the extent of his involvement I accepted. Stone received national publicity a few years later when it became known he had contributed a million dollars to the campaign to reelect President Nixon. He received considerably less attention for his contribution to the children's hospital. He gave it four million.

The plan was that I would bring along a boot like the one I had worn on the lunar surface. (The real boot was still on the moon—it was excess baggage for the voyage home.) I was to put it on and step in cement which was later to be bronzed and placed in the entry of the hospital.

I call such events as these "good works," since the goal of all the activity is worthwhile. NASA agreed—they wanted me to go, in fact—and sent along Mac Herring, whom I knew slightly, as my protocol officer (their term, not mine). I called them babysitters and this would turn out to be one of my last babysitters. Joan decided to stay home.

The ball itself went off without a hitch. My contribution was relatively simple: I showed our film and added the customary narrative for it. The official function went well, but nothing else did.

After my speech there was a question and answer period. A fellow stood up and asked if I had been nauseated during weightlessness in space or training. He asked the question intelligently—he knew the training tests were called parabolas—and I felt I could answer candidly.

No, I had never been nauseated during either of my trips into space. In fact, I hadn't really been concerned that I might be. I had experienced weightlessness in training more times than I could remember, probably around a hundred. At no time had I been sick during the training for Apollo 11. In the training that preceded my Gemini flight, I had been sick only once. I threw up after violently shaking my head to test my reaction to weightlessness. It was, I told him, my considered opinion that my one experience being nauseated was not due to weightlessness but rather directly traceable to a few martinis the night before the training flight. I got a good laugh and thought nothing more of it.

I had been met at the airport by police escorts. They stayed with me until shortly after I checked into my hotel suite. There were three bottles of liquor on a table in the living room, and I offered them a drink. They declined and evidently left shortly after I did. I thought nothing of that either.

Late that evening when I returned to my room, I went to pour myself a nightcap. The liquor was gone. I ordered a couple of drinks from room service and with some bemusement wondered if fame would prove as fleeting as the liquor supply.

Mac Herring arrived with the room service waiter to announce there had been a change of plans. Instead of returning to Houston, I was to proceed to Milwaukee where I would join Mike and Neil in accepting the Père Marquette Discovery Award. Mac was immediately informed that I had no intention of going. I reminded him that, with the prior agreement with NASA, Mike and Neil were going to Marquette University in Milwaukee while I covered the function in Chicago. Neil, as I recall, hadn't especially wanted to go to Milwaukee either, while Mike had said, "Whatever you guys decide. Just let me know." The Père Marquette Discovery Award so far as I knew was just that: a discovery. No one had ever been presented with it. The whole thing smacked of a promotion for some local residents and the city of Milwaukee. The entire affair was being run by Mr. Big Brewer, a prominent local businessman whose name none of us could ever remember. Neil subsequently was informed that Mr. Big Brewer was putting pressure on his congressmen who were, in turn, putting pressure on NASA, which applied the pressure on us. When Neil accepted, everyone was placated, and I was informed that Neil would be enough and I could proceed ahead to Chicago and return to Houston.

Mr. Big Brewer wasn't going to stop until he got the works. While I was in Chicago, more pressure was applied and, without my knowledge, the powers that be were informed I'd be there.

Mac Herring knew all of this, but waited until the last minute to tell me.

"Mac, I thought a guy's protocol officer was to act on his behalf. Why didn't you tell me this was going on?"

"They told me to keep quiet until a decision had been made."

In other words, Mac was a company man. I suppose a case can be made for his point of view, but my main concern was that my protocol officer both keep me informed and act in my interest. Mac wasn't that man and he never traveled with me again. Before long, I dispensed with the protocol officer whenever possible, a move the budget-conscious NASA administrators appreciated. Mike and Neil pretty much did the same thing after similar experiences.

The next morning, still steaming, I met my police escorts for the trip to the airport to connect up with Mike and Neil. When I went to throw my luggage in the trunk of the car, imagine my amazement when the trunk popped open to reveal three bottles of liquor. I pretended I hadn't seen the bottles. It was impossible I could have missed seeing them, but under the circumstances it seemed the more diplomatic thing to do.

With a great flourish the police officer got into the car and roared into the traffic, siren blaring and lights blazing. I was in the back seat feeling like some sort of super criminal, so I asked them to stop all the racket and drive like ordinary people. Not a word was spoken on the way to the airport.

It was raining and Mike and Neil were forty minutes behind schedule. The ceremonies in Milwaukee were supposed to begin immediately upon our arrival at the airport. By the time the three of us were together, everybody was getting nervous except us. Mike and Neil were too busy ribbing me about getting roped in, and I was enjoying the tease. It took some of the edge off my anger to know they understood how I felt and agreed with me.

The Père Marquette Discovery Award ceremonies were not particularly memorable and were, in fact, a bit boring. Neil started the acceptance off with, "They managed to get the three of us to the moon and back within a half-second of our flight plan, but getting us from Houston to Milwaukee on time proved to be their undoing." That's all I remember.

After the presentation we were taken to a lounge where we were offered—what else?—a cold beer, by Mr. Big Brewer himself. I think Mike started it off, because Mike, if he wishes, can be devilish and ornery. He declined the beer, saying he never drank the stuff, but that he'd appreciate a martini on the rocks. Neil and I suppressed our grins and followed suit.

Next we were to go to the campus auditorium to speak briefly to the students. All three of us were somewhat apprehensive about this because the student protest was then in full swing. I personally have no objection to polite protest—it's a free country and I welcome argument. However, I have no wish to be the object of the protest, since I don't feel I've done anything to be protested. Nevertheless, the three of us were greeted outside the auditorium by a barrage of flying tomatoes. I felt no fear, only sadness. What, I wondered, did we represent that was so hateful? Why was it necessary to throw things at us? I had no answer. We stayed close to our hosts and no direct hits were scored.

After we spoke briefly to the more polite students inside the auditorium—referring obliquely to the events outside—the captain of the basketball team came up and presented each of us with a Marquette University warm-up suit and assured as they'd fit—he'd checked our sizes with NASA. The team had adopted our flight patch for their suits, adding to the compliment. Over the last several months we had been presented with dozens of plaques, punch bowls, and other symbols of accomplishment, but for some reason those warm-up suits stuck with all of us. Part of it, I suppose, is that one team of men takes pleasure in being accepted by another team. It also seemed they were giving us something of their own. It was not their intention to give more lavishly, but to give more personally. I've worn mine on many occasions and now it is nearly worn out. I have used and enjoyed it more than anything I have been given.

A few days after returning from Chicago I received a letter from a friend who had attended the ball in Chicago. He enclosed a local newspaper story on my visit. On it he wrote: "Did I understand you correctly?" The headline in effect said ALDRIN REVEALS LUNAR SICKNESS. The article itself was a rather inaccurate report of my response to the question I had been asked about being nauseated during weightlessness. It omitted my belief that my one incident of nausea—not on the moon, not in space, but flying a zero-gravity training flight in a KC-135—had been induced not by being weightless but by a few martinis the night before.

There had been a newspaper reporter in the audience that night and not a very good one at that. The article itself was misleading and the headline was completely wrong.

Once again I became furious with the press. It was a fury not much different than the one I felt shortly after returning from the moon, and not much different than my anger over the handling of my speech at the AFL-CIO convention.

My uncle, Bob Moon, had come to Cape Kennedy for the launch of the flight and then had gone on to Houston to stay with Joan and the kids during the mission. Bob and his wife, Audrey, live in Los Angeles and have always been close to us. At the Cape, somebody had told Bob that several scientists felt the properties of lunar rocks were such that they might burst into flame once they were inside the oxygen atmosphere of the cabin of our lunar lander or the spacecraft itself. He asked me if this was so and I told him it was something the NASA scientists scoffed at and considered highly unlikely. The very few rocks not stored in vacuum-sealed flameproof boxes and a special few sample rocks would be watched carefully as they were introduced to the oxygen in the cabin. If any change was noted in them, they would be instantly removed. Bob and I dropped the matter there.

On the plane back to Houston, Bob fell into a casual conversation with his seatmate. Bob mentioned our talk about rocks. A week or so later Bob received a newspaper clipping headlined ALDRIN FEARS LUNAR ROCKS. Bob's seatmate had been a reporter, a fact never disclosed to Bob, who by now was embarrassed as hell about the whole thing. I was also embarrassed—more for Bob than for myself—and also angry at the inaccuracy of the article and the degree of unprofessionalism the incident indicated.

When the other distortion took place over my comments in Chicago, I decided to speak out. For my forum, I selected a press conference scheduled for shortly after the lift-off of *Apollo 12*, the second lunar landing. When a flight is in progress, NASA wisely calls back all astronauts on any public tours and we all willingly cooperate. It's a precautionary matter and good sense as well. There might be something we can contribute to any decisions or trouble during the flight. Also there might be a disaster of some sort and one of us might find himself halfway across the country facing a barrage of unanswerable questions. Whoever got caught in this might not even know what had happened.

Thus, in the relative seclusion of the early days of Apollo 12, I made my move as politely as possible. I began by saying that in no way was I hitching myself onto Spiro Agnew, who in those days was attacking the press almost fulltime. I did, however, wish to make a few comments about some of the coverage we were receiving. I cited my own experience and said that others had had the same problem. I urged them to try harder to be accurate and asked that they not invent drama where no drama existed. As I concluded, I tried to inject a little humor by apologizing for the fact that we seemed so dull that invention was sometimes necessary to attract readers and listeners.

There was a moment of silence, followed by the usual questions—this time all directed to Neil and none to me. Afterward, a couple of newsmen I knew came up and apologized. I insisted an apology wasn't necessary and that, as I had just publicly stated, I felt most of our coverage was actually quite good but that the exceptions were fairly disastrous.

I would have preferred that the matter be dropped at the press conference, but it speaks well of the freedom of the press in this country that they were unafraid to publish criticism directed at them. What's more, they went to great lengths to quote me accurately.

We observed Thanksgiving 1969 out of custom, and with grief. As soon as I had a free weekend after the world tour, Joan and I drove to Galveston to see Tommy Manison, who was then three. Tommy was the son of Tom and Robin Manison, close friends we had made through the church we attended. Joan and I and the kids had all become involved in one way or another with Camp Manison, the camp Tom ran near the space center. The Manisons are robust, open, friendly, and outdoor-loving Texans with whom we shared many good times.

Tommy developed leukemia. In the early stages of the disease he developed a burning desire for a helicopter ride and when Joan learned about it, she told me. It was strictly against Air Force and NASA rules to take people for helicopter rides, but I had—as had other Air Force fathers—landed in a field one day and taken my kids for a ride, leaving Joan standing in the middle of nowhere wringing her hands. When Tommy wanted a ride, I got another pilot to come along to hold him and he was thrilled.

Tommy was not expected to be alive at the end of the world trip, but Joan nevertheless returned with a number of gifts for him. We choked back our tears as we helped the frail little boy unwrap his treasures from a world he would never know. He died Thanksgiving weekend.

Operation Giant Step came alive again for two days as we completed our world tour in Canada, where the elections were over and Prime Minister Pierre Trudeau was securely in office. We went first to Ottawa, where the weather was colder than Seoul, if that's possible; there we were received by the Canadian Parliament. The next day we were given a reception in Montreal, a city Joan and I instantly liked. Trudeau was the most informal of all the heads of state we had met and he handily accomplished the difficult chore of treating us as though he had known us all our lives. As for the three of us and our wives, one and all we fell back into the protocol touring business as though we were old hands at it. In fact, we were old hands, it just didn't occur to any of us until we went to Canada. The trip actually revived Joan and me, a rather surprising reaction considering the grueling trip that had preceded this last two-day jaunt.

The speechmaking and traveling stopped briefly for the holidays and as soon as the Christmas debris was cleaned up, we headed for Acapulco for a week-long family vacation.

Early in January 1970, I resumed traveling from one end of the country to the other making public appearances and giving speeches. The vast majority of the appearances were arranged by NASA, a few by me. Mike and Neil did pretty much the same thing. Whenever possible, logistics were co-ordinated in such a way that when I was, say, on the East Coast, a number of appearances would be set up in the East Coast area so that I could get the maximum amount of work done with a minimum of flying all over the country.

We were soon once again off for Washington to accept the National Geographic Society's Hubbard Award. It is a prestigious award and one I was particularly honored to accept. As have millions of American boys before and after me, I first discovered *National Geographic* magazine as a young man keenly scouting around for a look at bare breasts. In the course of satisfying my curiosity about female anatomy, I also discovered the wonders of the world as reported by this fine magazine. Each month I looked forward to vicarious trips to exotic places on the earth until one day I myself would share in the magazine's perfectly constructed report on man's first visit to another planet. Joan came along and had such a good time, she never again asked me to throw out the stack of old *National Geographics* we always seem to have in the garage.

From Washington we continued on to New York for an appearance on *The Today Show*. When it was over, Hugh Downs and I fell to discussing children and I found myself relating the experience at Marquette and my feelings about students and young people. Hugh, it turned out, shared my puzzlement and concern.

The experience with the students at Marquette set me to brooding. I felt students were angry because they felt excluded, that they did not share with other people the triumph we represented. They were angry because people were starving and fighting on earth, while millions were spent to send three men to the moon. If so, their anger has some justification. I disagree strongly that sending men to the moon was a waste of money, but I can share their anger that people here on earth are at war and that others are starving. And so began my involvement with young people.

That involvement received a powerful push in the spring of 1970, after the tragedies at Kent State and Jackson State. Out of all this sadness came a goal for me. I developed a plan to organize some kind of program or conference for young people. I called it "Conference on Youth Representation." I set out to recruit other adults who were interested in working with young people. I figured the first recruits ought to be Mike and Neil, but in spite of my insistence, both declined, pleading there was already too much to do. I understood, but I was disappointed anyway. I reestablished contact with Hugh Downs and he too set about recruiting. This we did by discussing our plans with just about any person of importance we met.

The final list, prepared before our first meeting, included such people as Margaret Mead, the noted anthropologist; Sargent Shriver; Congressman Robert Taft; Kingman Brewster, the respected—particularly by students—president of Yale; Roy Wilkins and James Farmer, prominent figures in the civil rights movement; John Gardner, the respected Common Cause advocate; Fran Tarkenton, a noted athlete;

and Lance Rentzel, another fine athlete whose personal tribulations were yet to come.

We gathered for a planning meeting at NBC's studios in Rockefeller Center, on the set of *The Today Show*, early in May 1970.

Our stated goal was to open a dialogue with young people, a dialogue that, if successful, the young people would continue on their own. The best medium, we decided, was public television. The goals of the program evolved into the defining of an issue by the youth group and the exposure of the issue on television. Following the television airing, further discussion would be held at local levels followed by as complete a vote or sampling of opinion as was possible. The consensus of the local meetings would then be presented to the various parties involved on the other side of the issue for their response on public television.

Together we planned our first conference, which we hoped would be a seedling for further and bigger conferences. The next meeting was scheduled for June 16, 1970, at the American Friends Service Committee Building in Washington, D.C. It struck me as an appropriate location: an organization with concern for the human condition, somewhat liberal, and not particularly establishment.

The next thing to do was to find as broad a cross-section of students, non-students and young people as possible. The major national student organizations were contacted and their representatives were invited. Several were present from the University of California at Berkeley. The NAACP and SCLC were contacted, as were the youth organizations of both the Republican and Democratic parties. I also invited a social worker from the Houston area.

Eighteen young adults accepted my invitation to Washington and I helped several of them pay for their hotel expenses. The adult sponsors paid their own expenses.

The morning of our first meeting we gathered and introduced one another. It seemed cordial and earnest, but the young people appeared guarded almost to the point of sus-piciousness.

Underlying their discussions seemed to be the questions: "Why are you doing this? What do you hope to gain from it?"

I answered as honestly as I could. I said that I personally had absolutely nothing to gain from a financial standpoint, and that the amount of prestige I might possibly gain was related more directly to what they accomplished than any-thing I might do. I said that in my travels I had learned that young people of this country—the people who ap-peared more concerned about the world situation than many adults—did not have a proper voice in either govern-ment or industry; nor were their views truly represented in the media unless there was a riot of some sort, and even then the riot was the news, not the problems that brought on the riot. I added that it was my intention to stay very much out of the way during the meetings and to participate mostly as a listener.

And that's exactly what I did. For two days I listened as young people—some of them angry, others complacent—poured out their opinions. For someone educated at West Point, whose life had been lived pretty much in the service of his government—one student called it "a pretty uptight way to live" in spite of my protests to the contrary—it was quite a revelation.

I was fascinated—and terribly frustrated—by the extreme diversity of opinions represented. What frustrated me most was that as the conference wore on, no one seemed willing to give an inch. Only infrequently would I hear words to the effect of, "I'll concede you that," and then it was a verbal concession with a strong indication that the actual conces-sion itself would be a long time coming. Nevertheless, it was stimulating.

At the end, everyone went home having expended a great

deal of energy and most everyone remained steadfast in their convictions. Most of the adult sponsors had, at various times, found themselves under heavy siege for their beliefs, with the possible exception of Margaret Mead, whom everybody appeared to worship.

I went home tired but stimulated. I was searching for some way to find a concrete point of view shared by young people, some one point of agreement. Weeks later I reluctantly admitted I had found one: they all agreed that they shared a mutual suspicion of adults, prominent adults in particular. Nevertheless, I personally considered the conference a success and set about planning another. The first thing I noticed was that the adult sponsors began to drop out or plead "other obligations." They realized better than I did at the time that if the conference had been a success, a second conference would not be arranged by the adult sponsors, but by the young people. The only useful purpose we could serve would be to kick it off and stick around to offer our opinion—if we were asked. The kick-off, as much as it stimulated me, apparently failed.

From time to time, I get out the transcripts of the meeting and casually look through them. What I find, particularly in the remarks I made, is a kind of idealism mixed with a bit of naïveté.

As I had let the initiative fall to the young people, no adult advisers were invited to the last conference, which gradually splintered and fell apart because of the lack of unity. I had set out to do something I hoped would help. If I couldn't do this, what could I do? I brooded endlessly. I am by nature a reserved man and I am not inclined to passionately argue in favor of my personal beliefs. Yet, I felt that the conference might be one place where we could all get down to what one student leader had called the "nitty-gritty." I for one was an eager pupil, but it seemed no one wanted to go to school with me.

On July 20, 1970, Mike, Neil, and I flew to Jefferson City, Missouri, for the anniversary of our landing on the moon. Jefferson City was chosen because our spacecraft was on a tour of the country and at the moment that's where it was. We each made little speeches, but by and large the event and the anniversary were not much celebrated. It was also becoming increasingly rare for the three of us to be together. Like politicians in an election year, we all seemed to be on the stump.

To look at the schedule I kept through most of 1970 and 1971 is now dizzying. I traveled most of every week, trying to make it home for the weekends. Yet when I try to remember a particular event or a particular city, my recollection becomes a blur of airports, antiseptic hotel rooms, hands to shake, autographs to sign, speeches, banquets—no one of them especially different from any other. If the schedule seems astounding in retrospect, it did not seem so at the time. I settled hard into a rut I did not particularly like but felt obligated to accomplish. It had no beginning, middle, or end.

I was off making an appearance somewhere when a little boy, about eight, ran up to me in the airport. He said that I was his hero—all the astronauts were his heroes—and that he'd like to ask me a question. He wanted to know if everyone in my home was truly happy and if my wife and I ever yelled at each other like his folks did. My first instinct—almost by training, I guess—was to say we were happy and we never argued. Instead, I told him I was sure we yelled more at our house than people did at his. He looked reassured.

Every so often I would attempt to return to the NASA routine, but it never lasted. Catching up with the rapid changes in technology was all but impossible and what was the point of trying? By now it was obvious we would never fly in space again and could never return to any sort of routine life at NASA. Both Neil and I felt sorry for Mike because he, too, was forever being hauled out for public appearances and speeches as we were—but Mike paid the dues without ever setting foot on the moon. He stayed up there and waited while we landed on the moon. Mike left NASA fairly soon after the world tour to become associated with the State Department, a switch that caused any number of complaints from editorial writers and various government officials. Before long, he left the State Department and became a director at the Smithsonian Institution, where he is today. I see him whenever I'm in Washington or he's in Los Angeles.

Shortly after we returned from the moon, Neil told me he had been offered the presidency of an important university. He later declined, evidently feeling he had insufficient experience for the job. As the traveling and speaking wore on, Neil became more and more withdrawn. He too attempted an occasional return to the astronaut business, only to realize it simply wasn't going to work. In little more than a year and a half after going to the moon, Neil held a press conference—his last, he said at the time—and announced he was leaving the space program to teach engineering and aerodynamics at the University of Cincinnati. The nature of his new job struck many people as rather disappointing, the implication being he could have had a much better job. It seemed to me that Neil was a particularly private man among men who are basically private by nature. He was always interested in teaching and he had said so on several occasions. He was also speaking the truth when he said the announcement of his resignation would be his last press conference. I think Neil has said very few words for public consumption since that day. He is only infrequently seen in public. Out of sentiment, he attended the lift-off of the last Apollo flight in December 1972. So did I. It was the first time I had seen Neil in more than a year.

I too began considering what to do—where to go—next.

I am by nature so deliberative that I did not notice when my deliberations turned to procrastination and indecision. It was all a part of what was happening to me, but I was not conscious of it. People are seldom aware of the unconscious working of their minds and I was no exception. I was slowly but surely allowing part of me to guide the rest of me into trouble.

I even made a comment on my feelings to a group of aerospace doctors. They were having a convention in St. Louis, and, through NASA, I was invited to receive an honorary membership for the three of us. Instead of spending countless hours poring over copious notes wondering what I might say—as I customarily did—this time the decision was instinctive and quick. Before my brief words of acceptance there was an award ceremony honoring doctors for various projects. I was impressed with the ceremonies—the awards were in the form of sizable checks, and the whole process seemed to be an annual rotation of patting each other on the back.

I told them that a greal deal of time and money had been spent, and rightly so, determining the effects of space travel on the human body. Medically, we were closely observed. I then pointed out that no one, not even the scientists and doctors directly involved, had made any studies of the impact of postflight activities on the emotional health of astronauts. I pointed out we were all basically pilots and scientists and, as such, were not at all accustomed to a public life style. I suggested very little was known about how space travelers might cope with the abrupt changes in their lives following their return from travel in space.

Afterward, a number of doctors approached me to say they agreed with my suggestion and were in fact surprised to learn there had been any effect on any of us.

In truth, the effect was not just on us as individuals—it could influence entire families and, by this time, it was taking its toll on the Aldrins. Mike by now was in the throes of adolescence and it was proving to be an especially difficult time for all of us. He was disdainful and remote to Jan and Andy, and openly argumentative with Joan and me. When he made a demand on either Joan or me that we found either unreasonable or wrong, we would refuse, after carefully pointing out the reasons. Mike would listen and walk away, only to develop intense headaches a short time later.

We decided to seek help. A local psychologist named Dr. Robert Prall began to work with both Joan and Mike. They had a session with him each Friday. He sometimes saw them together, but usually they went separately. Eventually, at Dr. Prall's suggestion, I started attending the Friday sessions.

Mike responded almost immediately. It soon appeared obvious that Mike had experienced a trauma when, at age five, he was separated from Joan and me because of our long hospitalization with hepatitis. We had, it seemed, been forced to leave him at a crucial time in his life. He also felt terribly guilty about all the trouble there had been while we were on our tour of the world.

Within six months Mike no longer attended, while Joan and I kept going—acutely aware of our own problems and conscious of the fact that Jan and Andy would soon be entering adolescence. Mike's attitude kept on improving, although he became rebellious from time to time. We have come to know it is Mike's nature and it isn't really rebellion: Mike is a very independent guy and for someone so young, he has great insight. There is a sign he recently made and hung in his bathroom that contains, I think, Mike's wry comment on life. It says IF YOU CAN'T DAZZLE THEM WITH BRILLIANCE, BAFFLE THEM WITH BULLSHIT.

Dr. Prall eventually dismissed Joan and zeroed in on me. He never came right out and said it, but I think he sensed my by now acute need for professional help. I remained with him until some months later when it became obvious to both of us I needed medication which he, as a psychologist, was not able to prescribe.

In August 1970 I set about organizing the family for a trip to Sweden, my grandfather's homeland, and one of my last major tours in behalf of NASA, though I'm not sure whether NASA really cared if I went or not.

Mike especially looked forward to the trip because he wanted to go to Amsterdam to visit friends. Mike had gotten interested in dogs, borzois in particular, through a family he had met in our neighborhood. Their hobby was breeding borzois and Mike was their most avid pupil. When they had moved to Amsterdam, we had told him that one day he could visit them. Mike, just fifteen, chose to precede the rest of us to Europe, leaving two nervous parents standing at the airport in Houston. He was no sooner off the ground than Joan, in tears, was saying, "My baby's gone." Her baby was by this time nearly six feet tall.

When the rest of us arrived in Amsterdam two weeks later, we were met at the airport by an ebullient Mike. He wanted to show us Maika, a female puppy who, he explained, really needed him. We dutifully met Maika but remained noncommittal about buying her.

We were in Sweden for fourteen days, some of them interesting but most of them uncomfortable. At no time did I feel I had any control over what I was doing or being asked to do, and this made me very uneasy.

The purpose of the trip was to receive the Swedish version of The Order of the Vasa, a citation presented to Swedish-Americans by the Swedish American Society. I had previously received the American version of this award.

It was not a diplomatic trip—no one had asked to make it official and, considering the state of relations between Sweden and America at the time, it was just as well. About the only favorable project America had going in Sweden at this time was Dr. Jerome H. Holland, the American ambassador. He had been an all-American football player in college and he was black. During his first few months in Sweden he had greeted everything from taunts to rotten eggs with a fresh and likable openness. By now, he was one of the more popular residents in the country. He presided over several semiofficial functions involving us and all of them were most pleasant.

I received my Order of the Vasa at a big park in Stockholm. The ceremonies were polite and friendly but once again I felt the same sort of reserve in Sweden that had bothered me in Norway nearly a year before. Of all the dignitaries present at the park and later at the official banquet, only Ambassador Holland was greeted with obvious enthusiasm.

Andy had been promised a scuba dive down to a sunken ship in the harbor and I promised to go along. He couldn't wait to go, while I had certain doubts about it. I figured the water in Stockholm harbor was probably plenty cold even in the summer and I was right. Only Andy was unaffected by the cold. The divers who were to lead us were brothers named Nahlin. They were professional divers with a most interesting sideline: they spent their spare time training blind youngsters to dive. Two blind teenagers, a boy and a girl, led Andy and I down to the sunken ship with the Nahlin brothers close behind us.

Before the dive, Andy had been told he could bring back a souvenir. The exact nature of the souvenir had never been mentioned; I suppose we all figured Andy would pick up a small chip of wood or a bolt. Not Andy. I surfaced first and was out of the water waiting with our hosts when Andy and his blind guide struggled to the surface with his memento: a six-foot-long plank about the width of a railroad tie. There was much laughter and applause as Andy proudly pulled his treasure on board the ship. We never did figure out how to ship it back to the United States and the last we saw of it was when it was taken to the embassy.

Several official functions and a few days later, we departed for Karlstad, the city of the sun. It was, of course, raining. Karlstad is the capital of Värmland, where my grandfather was born. We visited the house where he was born, a bulky, square two-story building with four bedrooms. It is now owned by a builder who, in the tradition of his trade, has restored it. I was invited to sign my name on the wall.

I signed my name a lot. The Swedes are great chroniclers of their countrymen, especially those who emigrated from Sweden. I signed a number of registers as the grandson of an emigrant blacksmith named Aldrin. I met with my cousin, Henry, his wife, and their daughter. I first met him several years before when he toured the U.S. We talked of family history and his wish to one day emigrate to the United States. Henry is a photoengraver, and the Labor Department has restricted the emigration into the United States for that profession. I have tried several times but have not succeeded in getting him a visa.

I spoke at various engineering, aeronautical, and technological institutes, and generally found the experience uncomfortable mostly because I didn't speak Swedish. The question-and-answer periods, however, were usually successful. I also toured a number of air bases and observed various activities planned for my benefit by the Swedish air force.

Victor Hasselblad was our host for a weekend of relaxation on his estate in Rao. Hasselblad designed the cameras we used to take photographs in space and we had much to talk about. He was also a charming host, particularly for the children, who by this time were officially bored with official functions. Jan cut her hand on a Swedish steel knife we had been presented. As Joan led her out of the dining room, dripping blood on the carpet, Jan asked, "Do I have to go to any more banquets, Mom?" We hunted mushrooms, fished, and on Saturday night Dr. and Mrs. Hasselblad tossed a party to celebrate Sweden's short crayfish season.

It was a large and boisterous affair. There was a great deal of drinking and mounds of crayfish. One of the guests was the opera singer Birgit Nilsson, whose bargaining tactics were at the time driving the officials of New York's Metropolitan Opera up the wall. I had read about this in the newspaper and mentioned to her that she drove a hard bargain. "Oh yes, but I am a professional and I deliver the goods," she replied. Her accent and the idiomatic expression made an unlikely combination.

After dinner and under happy protest ("Oh, but I never sing for free"), she got up and sang. It was a very memorable few minutes, almost as impressive as her talent for extracting meat from the spindly and unwieldy crayfish.

Prior to leaving for Sweden we had been informed that a tentative date had been scheduled by the State Department for an audience with King Gustaf VI.

Just before the trip started, we received a cable saying that the king had canceled the tentative date and rescheduled the meeting five days hence. I politely cabled the American embassy to explain we would no longer be in Sweden on the day of the audience. Their response was immediate and concise: "Audience mandatory for diplomatic relations. Ambassador will couple visit with presentation of lunar rock to King." So be it.

And that's how we found ourselves fishing for four days, or as Joan called it, "sitting in a rowboat in the middle of a lake in the middle of nowhere." It was relaxing but we felt a bit of a strain on the hospitality of our hosts. Every time we insisted we could do fine on our own, they became more adamant. The last day, Joan and I threw a party in the house where my grandfather was born and invited Aldrins distant and near to visit with our various hosts. It was a good party.

Ambassador Holland accompanied us to the royal palace for our audience which, he informed us, should last no longer than fifteen minutes as custom dictated. King Gustaf lives in the body of a very old man with a mind that is incredibly alert and intelligent. He appeared most impressed with the piece of moon rock from President Nixon. He began asking questions, and pretty soon the two of us were deep in conversation. His Majesty kept me talking over the customary fifteen minute limit, something I did not notice until I became aware that Ambassador Holland was getting very fidgety. His Highness kept on talking, I kept on answering, and the ambassador kept circling like a nervous diplomat. Finally, he politely interrupted and said that we must leave. The king looked at his watch, smiled ruefully, and we were off—after extending the fifteen minutes to forty-five. Ambassador Holland said I had spent more time with the king than he had in the year he'd been in Sweden.

We departed Sweden with some relief and several shopping bags full of matches. Everywhere we went there were matchbooks on the tables when we arrived and in our kids' pockets when we left. By the time we left Majorca, our next stop, the collection had grown to epic and rather dangerous proportions.

We had been invited to Majorca by Stevie and Joel Kozol, whom we had gotten to know through my involvement in a Boston cable television firm. We moved into the guest house of their villa and settled in for a rest.

Along with the Kozols and their children, we piled into a Fiat and bumped off to the bullfights. We bought one long row of seats, adults at one end, kids at the other. It started out exciting and went steadily downhill from there. We were told the bulls were bad. By the fourth bull, patrons were expressing their displeasure by throwing cushions into the ring, something the kids really enjoyed watching. The public address system announced that it was against the law to throw cushions into the ring. I scampered over and explained this to the kids. They resisted the temptation during the last bull, but when it was all over, cushions really began to fly.

Mike could resist no longer. I started to yell at him as he threw, but it was too late. He tossed one and was reaching for another when a cop noticed the tall, fair American boy in the crowd and went after him. The Kozols and Joan and I were right behind the cop. We tried to talk him out of it, but he didn't speak English. Joan by now was in tears and ready to kill to keep "my baby from going to jail."

I figured Joel Kozol, a lawyer, ought to be able to keep my firstborn out of the pokey and me out of the newspapers. Joel thought so too.

Clutching our frightened children, we followed Mike and the policeman to the bus where people were kept waiting for the trip to jail. We talked and talked until we finally found a policeman who spoke English. Joel offered to pay bail on the spot—which we figured would go into the cop's pocket.

Not so. He wanted to know if we were American servicemen. I said sort of. Was I stationed in Germany? Sort of. I didn't know whether to say yes or no.

After giving him our local telephone number, he handed over Mike. The court would call the next day to tell us the disposition of the case. The call never came.

Meanwhile, Joan and I were fighting a battle we couldn't win. We didn't want another dog around the house—there were already two dogs and two cats—but Mike was adamant. Perhaps because of my profession and the traveling I had done for so many years, my parental guilt is greater than that of most parents. Joan, because I was gone so much, admitted she tended to overcompensate with the kids.

Thus, one balmy afternoon in Majorca, Mike put the pressure on by implying we were nogoodniks—his word, not mine—and said we did more for the other kids than for him. Our defenses collapsed. We know now that Mike was crying out for love, not a dog, but he got his dog.

While we were in the clean air of Majorca, I went on a

jogging binge. I suited up each morning and ran several miles along the road by the Kozols' house. One morning, I ran past a blue Volkswagen, which soon passed me by only to be parked around the next curve. About the third pass, a man stuck his head out the window and announced he was from a local radio station and wanted a half-hour interview. I politely declined, explaining I was on vacation. My refusal must have somehow made it onto the air, because a day later I read in the newspaper that I was in Majorca refusing to talk to anyone.

The last time we had been in Majorca—some fourteen years earlier—Joan was pregnant and left with a black eye. This trip she got a toothache and remained in pain the whole time.

The morning we were scheduled to leave, Joan was up and organizing us all. Once we were packed, I called a cab. Then I noticed shopping bags full of matchboxes sitting around and instructed the kids to leave it all right there. For their part, they refused to go home without their match collection. I explained the matches were dangerous and that the airline would probably refuse to let us carry them on, but my kids would not budge. Dilemma. Resolution: keep the boxes but leave the matches. We kept the taxi waiting ten minutes and nearly missed our plane while Joan and I frantically emptied the matchboxes. We filled three wastebaskets and two dresser drawers full of matches in the Kozols' guest house. Joan and I were both so embarrassed by this that we made it up to the Kozols by inviting them to be our guests in Acapulco the following Christmas.

Maika arrived by air freight in the middle of a rainy Monday night a few days after we got home. Joan and I stood impatiently for one hour—from midnight to one—while she was processed through customs. She was throwing up when we pulled her out of her dog cage, and she was limping.

Joan took her to the vet the next morning and was told her leg was broken. For the next few weeks, Maika clumped around in her bandages and started—as do all dogs—working her way into our family and collective hearts. Unlike Slodey, Maika has never once goosed anybody. She prefers crotches. The leg healed perfectly, except that to this day, whenever she's been scolded, Maika limps a bit for sympathy. When she had her first heat, there was an audible sigh of relief heard throughout Nassau Bay as Mike decided he wasn't up to a litter of puppies.

Back in Houston we settled into a routine of school and my travel schedule while I slid into the doldrums. A NASA protocol officer had accompanied us to Sweden and we had found him not particularly helpful. While we made the various trips and speeches, he usually remained behind in Stockholm. We made partial lists of people to send our thanks and asked him to make the final list. He never did. Joan wrote to a few people and I wrote to nine. For some reason the simple fact of someone not doing his job thoroughly made me feel as though I was being deserted. Totally unaware of the unreality of such a thought, I went to bed one night and stayed there off and on for a week. When I wasn't in bed, I sat staring at the television set.

We passed it off as fatigue from a hectic summer, choosing not to notice that Joan, Mike, Jan, and Andy, all of whom had been with me nearly all the time, suffered not at all.

To get myself going again, I made a few decisions. I determined the best thing was to avoid as many public appearances as possible and to begin considering my alternatives. I flew to Washington for a meeting with the Chief of Staff of the Air Force, leaving a trail of broad hints that I was interested in returning to the service. I wasn't at all sure that was what I wanted, but it seemed a sensible option. Once I had indicated my interest I sat back to wait as the bureaucratic machinery of the air force cranked itself into motion to consider taking me back.

Back at NASA, the space shuttle program was starting up

and I went to work with a theoretical committee, one that was to determine whether or not the booster rocket was to be manned. I argued against a manned booster and was pleased to see several of the committee support me. Yet it all ended up a futile exercise when the booster design we were working from was abandoned.

Ordinarily such a change would be greeted with a shrug of the shoulders and a fast move to another planning committee. Such casualties are inherent in a fast-changing technology and had never really bothered me at all. This time was different. My mood was starting to swing from long, enthusiastic highs to long, immobilizing lows. This was a low low.

I was asked to join the governor's conference on goals for the Texas coastal zone and I accepted. I attended several planning conferences and came to look upon these meetings as a barometer of my mood. If I did well, I felt well. If I felt I did not do well, I sunk in a morass of despair.

About this time I began to make business affiliations with various enterprises. Nearly all astronauts are involved in one private enterprise or another, generally with the approval of NASA. Alan Shepard was the shrewdest businessman of us all and is now reputed to be a millionaire. Others affiliated with organizations that ended up costing them money and, on occasion, credibility. There was an investigation into the dealings of a Texas bank not long ago and an astronaut was publicly embarrassed when it became known he was on the board of directors. I'm quite certain he wasn't the culprit, but there was an inevitable bit of guilt by association. Usually astronauts lend their names and occasional presence in exchange for shares or a salary.

General Jimmy Doolittle is an old and close friend of my father's who, since his retirement, has done a great deal of work as a member of the board of directors of Mutual of Omaha Insurance Company. Through him, I served as one of the company's directors, but my present activities are essentially intracompany, in the sense that I make no endorsements in public for them. Instead, I meet with company employees only and assist them in the conduct of their business in relation to the parent company. I am paid an annual salary.

I am also associated with a cable television company in the Boston area, an activity I look upon as an investment for the future. I own shares in the company but cannot sell them because the stock has not been publicly offered.

Both activities were officially approved by NASA. Their ruling on any affiliations was that the number not exceed three and that the business in no way exploit the space program for private gain. I have always thought the arbitrary number of activities was unnecessary and that much closer attention should be paid to the nature of the business, an opinion that did not necessarily endear me to either my colleagues or our bosses.

The number of speeches I now gave was fewer than before, but still fairly frequent. Those occasions involving pilots or service organizations were the most comfortable.

At one such function, a black-tie ball, there began what would one day become a major complication in my life.

The moral code of my generation is a strict one and only recently have the contradictions been aired, brought about mostly by the admirable candor of so many young people. We were told, but never really shown, that our obligations were to wives and children first. The obligation assumed by the husband was both physical and philosophical. In brief: no messing around. Piled on top of all that conditioning was the additional business of being an astronaut. One and all we were portrayed as devoted family men, as most of us were. The fact that we traveled a great deal—and always took along our personal biological longings but not necessarily our wives—was never mentioned. The fact of the matter is, we were not all quite the way we were portrayed to be.

There were occasions when I'd find myself alone and in need of some company. For an astronaut, the opportunities for companionship were nearly endless and sometimes I think the temptations grew rapidly in proportion to the supply. Rock musicians were not the first, nor will they be the last, to have groupies. Some of us resisted temptation; many of us resisted, then gave in. I fit in the latter category.

In a great bout of guilt, I finally brought myself to discuss my sex life with our family psychologist. I spent nearly two weeks deciding, because I was certain he would rise from his desk, point a finger toward heaven, and shout, "Thou shalt not mess around ever!" Imagine my surprise when I finished and no judgment at all was made. Prall simply looked up and said, "You're no different from many other men." We spent several sessions—by now I was seeing him twice a week—discussing this, and then he asked if Joan knew.

I said that I believed Joan harbored great suspicions and had on a number of occasions attempted to bring the subject up. And what did I do? I lied. I denied any suspicion she had.

It wasn't easy, but Joan and I finally reached an accord of sorts. It took a great deal of serious discussion and explanation. I finally convinced her that whatever might happen and however I might behave, my marriage and my family came first. One night she told me she understood as well as she thought she could and that she would try to love even those parts of me made of clay. Many couples go through these moments of reckoning diminished and shaky. Others come through with a strengthened relationship and this is what happened to us.

At the ball in New York, where I was the honored guest, I met a woman named Marianne. I courted, she resisted. The more she resisted the harder I worked.

When I had conquered, I left New York with the familiar feelings of guilt mixed with pleasure. She was an attractive divorcée with long brunette hair and I intended to look her up when I was next in New York.

Which, it turned out, was about one week later. The time was early October 1970, and I was there in an official NASA capacity to greet two Russian cosmonauts and tour the country with them for ten days.

The night I arrived in New York, I had dinner with Marianne and told her how excited I was about meeting the cosmonauts. She asked me where we were going and stopped me when I said we'd be in Los Angeles the following Saturday. Marianne would be in Los Angeles too.

Almost a year later to the day, I would be in the hospital in San Antonio and would begin putting what had happened to me in perspective. It is in the nature of certain depressive mental illnesses that life can become complicated out of all reason. For me, the pile-up of complications was getting bigger.

Chalk it up to the inroads my emotional health was making on my stability or chalk it up under the son of a bitch column, but the fact is that with Marianne I disobeyed a cardinal belief of mine: I allowed a casual, infrequent relationship to grow into one of mutual needs. Needs and demands.

The next morning I was at Kennedy Airport to meet Andrian Nikolayev and Vitaly Sevastyanov. Andrian was one of the first of the Soviet cosmonauts and his wife, Valentina Tereshkova, is the only woman to have traveled in space. As had nearly everyone in the space program, I had heard she had panicked in space and was curious to know if this was true. The men were traveling without wives and I never summoned the courage to ask her cosmonaut husband.

Neither Vitaly nor Andrian spoke English, so an American interpreter was on hand as was a Russian interpreter, a suspicious little man with thick glasses who behaved as though he worked for the secret police.

The first maneuver was a political ploy. We presented them with two trip itineraries, one including a stop at Cape Kennedy and another without Cape Kennedy. We, of course, devoutly hoped they'd accept the itinerary with Cape Kennedy because that would oblige the Soviet government to take the next visiting Americans to their launch center in Tyuratam. In spite of repeated invitations, no Russian space officials had come to the Cape and in spite of repeated indications of interest, no Americans had been invited to Tyuratam.

Our Russian guests chose the itinerary that omitted Cape Kennedy, saying there probably wasn't much to see there at this time. Oh no, I countered, there are several Saturn rockets and many other activities. No luck.

Andrian, Vitaly, and I hit it off instantly. I was particularly delighted by this because the joint American-Soviet space venture was being discussed and one of the major reasons for this trip was to see just how compatible we all were. We turned out to be very compatible.

We were off to Washington to introduce the Russians to the NASA hierarchy. Everyone met at a dinner which was planned so that all the Russian vodka on hand would melt whatever ice there was. It worked. The next day our guests asked to visit the grave of John Kennedy in addition to the scheduled visits to the Washington Monument and Mount Vernon. I made certain their request was obliged.

At Marshall Space Flight Center in Huntsville, Alabama, we observed the various projects underway. The underwater training in which I originally participated was now located at Marshall, and the Russians were fascinated to learn Rusty Schweikert would be doing an underwater test the next day while we were scheduled to tour the city. After a number of hasty telephone calls I secured permission for Vitaly to suit up and join Rusty. I got myself some scuba equipment so that I could go along, while Andrian opted to watch the exercise.

The event received much coverage and the first Russian-American training maneuver was a great success. For me, it was one of the most satisfying things I had done since returning from the moon.

We were driving to the airport in Huntsville when Andrian and Vitaly began wondering out loud—through the American interpreter—what they might do to express their thanks to the people at the space flight center. I had an idea and immediately made my suggestion. No American space flight had passed above the center and therefore no photographs had been made of it from space. The Russians, however, had passed over. I suggested a Soviet photograph taken of the center from space would indeed be most welcome. Andrian and Vitaly immediately said yes through the American interpreter and just as quickly the Russian interpreter broke his silence to say that there were no such pictures. We drove on in an embarrassed silence, all of us quite aware that there were such photographs. The Russian interpreter was like a wet blanket the whole trip, but I figured if we kept wringing him out we could have a successful tour.

We went to Houston, where Vitaly demonstrated his prowess at speed boating. Dave Scott and his wife threw a cookout which nearly all the astronauts attended. Andrian and Vitaly delivered speeches at the American Institute of Aeronautics and Astronautics convention at the Astrodome and afterward we toured the dome while Andrian and Vitaly kept asking, "How much did this cost?" Capitalism intrigued them. At the manned spacecraft center we did rendezvous and lunar-landing simulations.

During a brief stop in Los Angeles we toured the jet propulsion laboratory and Disneyland, and on our free evening we all got hilariously drunk at the Cocoanut Grove. I met

Marianne for an evening and we made plans to meet again a few days later in New York.

In San Francisco, Jeannie Bassett joined us for dinner and we took our guests to look at the Golden Gate Bridge. We had not planned to cross it, but both Andrian and Vitaly wanted to cross, so off we went. Midbridge, our typically capitalistic Cadillac limousine stalled, giving rise to much good-natured joking.

In Seattle, we stepped off the NASA plane at Boeing Field and went immediately to the Boeing test 747. With the company's chief test pilot flying copilot, Andrian took the giant plane off and circled Mt. Rainier while Vitaly snapped pictures. Vitaly then put the plane through a long series of turns and stalls and I flew it back to Seattle and landed it. The 747 may look like a beached whale, but it is in fact one of the most easy to fly and highly maneuverable planes in the air. Such a plane is a pure joy to pilots and the three of us proved no exception. We then went to the mock-up of the SST, where Vitaly enthralled the Boeing engineers with a long discussion on the aerodynamics of the Soviet supersonic transport.

The morning before the trip ended in New York we went to a press conference where a reporter asked why the Russians hadn't visited Cape Kennedy. Andrian held a brief but awkward conference with the Russian translator, then said they had not been invited to the Cape. We were astonished but kept our silence. There are many things I might do under similar circumstances for my country, but I'm not about to lie.

Following lunch at the New York Stock Exchange, several officers took us out on the balcony overlooking the floor of the exchange. Can you imagine trying to explain to a Communist cosmonaut what the hell all the frantic commotion is down there? The lights on the big board stopped listing quotations and for several minutes flashed a welcome to the three of us. The cheering from the floor was long and the market dropped several points.

On our last afternoon, as promised, I was to take Andrian and Vitaly shopping. We had made arrangements to take them to Macy's, figuring it was America's most famous and most proletarian store. As we were about to leave, their interpreter stepped up to announce that I need not go along: the Soviet counsel was going to take them to places approved by their government.

When I escorted them on board their Aerflot flight to Moscow that night they were loaded down with packages wrapped in plain brown paper. Where they went I'll never know.

The trip was a great success and far exceeded expectations. Back in Houston, I was complimented a number of times on the tour and, in particular, on the training mission at Marshall. My spirits soared and I remained in a state of euphoria for the next month.

For a change, I felt some control over my future so I made my move. I went to Washington and began meeting with the various generals in charge of the Air Force and Robert Seamans, Secretary of the Air Force. Seamans was an old MIT friend of my father's, and through Dad and a number of other people, I had made it known that I was interested in returning to the Air Force.

There were two interesting possibilities and one especially appealed to me: commandant of cadets at the Air Force Academy. It was a prestigious post and it was also full of possibilities for interesting work. The other opening was as commandant of the Aerospace School at Edwards Air Force Base, the very school it had at one time been mandatory to attend if I wanted to be an astronaut. Because I had not gone through the school and had stayed at MIT for my doctorate, my first application to NASA had been turned down. The irony of commanding a school I had never attended was somewhat pleasurable, but I preferred the job at the Air Force Academy. It seemed the quickest and most effective way to become eligible for promotion to general, although the post at Edwards was considered to be a stepping-off point for promotion as well. Whichever it would be, I asked that the move not be made until the end of the school year in June 1971.

I began cleaning up loose ends. I had been postponing any decision about joining the president's council on reading. Because I felt it my duty to complete much that I started, I was more apt to postpone or procrastinate than to decline. I declined the president's council. I had also been postponing a trip to Palm Beach that NASA had proposed several times. The city's planetarium was being renamed the Aldrin Planetarium and my presence was requested. A month of so had gone by since I had first postponed the decision, and a Florida congressman began to pressure NASA.

What had finally made me agree to go to Palm Beach and give my speech was not so much congressional pressure as it was a friend in the Palm Beach area who was a horse breeder. He offered us a year-old Appaloosa mare, the answer to all of my daughter's dreams and then some. I accepted both, the horse and the horse trade, and Joan went with me. In the middle of my speech my throat went dry and I nearly choked to death, but other than that it turned out to be a fairly routine trip.

Air Force Secretary Seamans had indicated the Air Force Academy assignment would be fine with him, so Joan and I began talking about the move to Colorado and our recollections of the good times we had had living at the academy fifteen years earlier.

Whenever it was possible, I was in New York with Marianne. She began to drop hints about getting married and I kept ignoring them until we had our first fight. I left New York thinking I'd never see her again. She called me a few days later at my office to apologize and we made another date. My duplicity was causing me great guilt, but I could see no way out of it.

Sundays, I dutifully went to the Webster Presbyterian Church, where I served as an elder, and vowed never to go to New York again. Dean Woodruff, our minister, was a close family friend, but I could not bring myself to tell him of my trouble. If I did, I was afraid I might destroy his image of astronauts in general and me in particular.

As I awaited word from the Air Force, I started sliding into a depression that neither Dr. Prall, using all his psychological ploys, nor I could overcome. I only sank deeper into despair when he suggested I might need medicine he, as a psychologist, could not prescribe and recommended I see a psychiatrist.

All the time I had gone to Dr. Prall his bill was presented for "family counseling," as it had been when Joan and Mike were going to see him. I, in turn, submitted his bills to the NASA health insurance people who promptly paid them. His manner of billing kept my problems from being known officially at NASA and the Air Force, which suited me because I didn't want the treatment entered in my records. When I went to Dr. Gerald Batte, a psychiatrist with considerable experience at treating service people, I paid the bills myself so that the treatment would not be listed on my records. The expense could have been covered by my insurance policies with the government, but the repercussion psychiatric treatment tends to have on service careers has no insurance coverage of any kind. It was best to remain secretive.

I sank even further into a morass when the Air Force made its offer. No mention of the Air Force Academy was made—they offered me the post of commandant of the Aerospace School at Edwards, California. Even when I was told there was much more potential in this job than had at first been discussed, I took no great stock in the future.

It remained for Dr. Batte to later extract from me the

possibilities. One tantalizing prospect got me going again: The space shuttle program would be a joint venture between NASA and the Air Force. The major share of the Air Force experimentation and test flying would be done in the school. As commander of the school, with extensive experience as a NASA astronaut, I had a clear shot at becoming the most likely and logical candidate for the Air Force's top man working with NASA. I also had another plus going for me: I was the first astronaut to return to the service and, as such, enjoyed a certain uniqueness.

There had been talk of a reunion of our around-the-world support group on the first anniversary of the tour, but November slipped by and it wasn't until January 1971, that the party was organized. It was to be in Washington at Neil's home, and for some peculiar reason I looked forward to the party even though my memories of the tour itself were not particularly happy.

The reunion of the world tour was pleasant and uneventful. The following day, I went to Miami for the Super Bowl game and a weekend of fishing with "the boys." That, at any rate was my official explanation to Joan. I went to the game all right, but I did my fishing with Marianne.

After a long weekend I went back to Washington, where, on the dry and cold morning of Tuesday, January 14, 1971, I announced at a press conference that I was leaving the space program the following June and returning to the Air Force. I said that the post at Edwards would be a particularly good learning experience for me, because I was one of the few astronauts who had never attended the school.

I spoke with a confidence I had never before felt, a confidence bolstered by two things. One was that Dr. Gilruth, the man whose word counted at NASA, had told me that if I became in any way dissatisfied with the Air Force, I would be welcomed back in an executive capacity at NASA. Two, I was by now on medication to control the swing of my emotions. I took one Ritalin pill per day and on the day of my press conference I took two of these strong antidepressants. I looked great: forty years old, fit and tan from a Christmas week in Acapulco with my family. There was only one problem; I believed my confidence to be rooted in reality.

From January to the end of April I alternated family and work with trips to New York. If Joan was suspicious of my behavior, she said nothing. I was seeing Dr. Batte two times a week now and I was responding to treatment.

Early in June an event was scheduled that we regarded as a new beginning for us and, as such, we looked forward to it a great deal. I wanted to be at my very best.

The occasion was a big meeting of the Lancaster, California, Chamber of Commerce. Lancaster is the town adjacent to Edwards Air Force Base, where I would be stationed, and its economy in many ways is dependent on the base. For their banquet they had invited members of the Society of Experimental Test Pilots, which included all of the best pilots in the country. I was one of the guest speakers.

What intrigued me the most—I took it as a sort of indication of good things to come—was that I would not be giving a speech. Instead, Roy Neal, the NBC newscaster, would interview me in a most informal way.

Joan and I arrived the day before the banquet to check out the on-base living quarters. I had been concerned that Joan would find the quarters less commodious and comfortable than the home we had loved and were now leaving, but she expressed great pleasure with what she saw.

We had cocktails with General Bob White, the center commander, and his wife. As a commander, he appeared to be all that I hoped for: incisive, pleasant, and eager to see me through my return to the Air Force.

The afternoon of the banquet I stopped by Roy's motel room to ask if he wanted to run over any questions with me. He assured me they would be very easy to answer and that no preparation at all was necessary.

As banquets go, this was a large one. The number of important guests had grown to such proportions that a second head table—elevated and slightly to the rear of the original —had been organized at the last minute.

General and Mrs. White were escorted to the lower table and Colonel and Mrs. Aldrin were placed near the center of the higher table. The implication was that a colonel was more important than a general. General White agreed readily and there were no repercussions, but such was not likely to be the case with other Air Force generals. Rank—particularly among generals and other senior officers—is scrupulously observed.

The problem was one I encountered a number of times in the ensuing months and one I subsequently handled as best I could by either asking that the arrangements be changed or, if this was not possible, by going directly to my senior officers after I was seated—the implication being simply that I was going to my seniors. Naturally, they were also mentioned prominently in my speech.

This first occasion, however, I was at a loss about what to do, so I simply made the best of it. I began to be more and more apprehensive as the time for my interview grew near.

The first question Roy Neal asked was, "Now that almost two years have gone by, why not tell us how it really felt to be on the moon?"

If any one question was anathema to me, that was it. Roy, I suppose, felt he had no choice. Yet, it has always been almost impossible for me to answer with any sort of decent response.

My throat went dry and I became dizzy. Carefully, I picked my way through to a reply, thinking that all the test pilots in the audience would burst out in laughter.

I remember little more of the interview. When it was over I stepped down and stood before about fifty chamber of commerce members and their wives, all waiting for autographs. I signed a few and when the shaking became uncontrollable, I grabbed Joan and ran for the door.

In the privacy of an alley near the auditorium, I choked back my emotions and quietly wept. Joan stood silently by, and when I had composed myself she took me to the nearest bar.

I was inconsolable. Joan insisted that the whole evening came off much better than I was willing to admit, and added that—as usual (this was by now a theme of hers)—I was judging myself much too harshly. I got rather drunk.

We returned to Houston with a great deal to do. Joan had an accumulation of seven years to sort out and wanted me to help. At my office, there were still stacks of mail.

The correct term for what now happened to me is a quasi-medical term, "dysfunction." What it means is that I stopped. Stopped everything. I'd go to my office in the morning, determined to work a full day and then go home to more work. I'd sit down at my desk and stare out the window. A few hours would go by and I'd drive to the beach at Galveston and walk. Then I'd go home for dinner, turn on the television, and get a bottle of Scotch. Or I'd not go home at all until everyone was in bed.

The only place I went with any regularity was to the office of Dr. Batte and by the last few weeks before we were to leave I began to pull myself together. I helped Joan organize a garage sale. We made three hundred dollars and had a good time doing it.

In the course of getting ready to move, I decided to offer a number of things to the Smithsonian. Several objects I took along to the moon and some of the gifts presented on the world tour were included, and the institute quickly accepted. I also included the Omega watch I had worn on the surface of the moon. It was the only such watch, because a timer malfunction in the LM had prompted Neil to leave his watch in the LM. NASA hired special packers who inventoried and shipped the collection to Washington.

The watches used in space were ordinary store-bought Omegas, which were given to the various crews several months before the flight and, by tradition, were kept by the individual astronaut after the flight. The Smithsonian had expressed an interest in exhibiting my watch because it was unique, and I readily agreed.

When the packages arrived at the Smithsonian, the watch —along with several medals—was missing. NASA quickly launched a security investigation but could not turn up any clues. The Government Accounting Office got wind of the investigation, and in what I think was a rather narrow-minded decision, ordered that all watches be returned to NASA. When we all heard about this we figured NASA would tell the officious GAO people to mind their own business. Instead, NASA avoided any confrontation and agreed with the GAO.

The matter probably never would have become an issue had I not decided to let the Smithsonian have my watch, and I felt badly for the other astronauts, nearly all of whom were grumbling audibly. I, meanwhile, started filling out special forms about the loss of my watch—and kept filling out one form or another for the next year until the matter was dropped.

There were no special farewells, although there were a number of small dinner parties given by friends and neighbors. Joan's theater group tossed a big party which made the social pages and inspired me into a bit of silliness. The party was outdoors and our hostess was a good and trusted friend named Maggie Plumb Denike. There was a full moon shining down on the guests assembled around the swimming pool. Joan was talking to Maggie. I sauntered over, tapped Maggie on the arm, pointed to the moon, and said, "What's that?" Maggie laughed and so did Joan, but Joan's laughter smacked of enormous relief. However bad my sense of humor might be, it was coming back.

We plunged into life at Edwards with the usual logistical

snarls one encounters with three children and a menagerie the size or ours. We moved intact except for Nova, Jan's Appaloosa, who was quarantined to Texas because of an outbreak of a contagious disease. She arrived several months after we did.

The kids settled in much better than we had expected they would. Once the argument over who got what bedroom was settled (by fiat from Joan), they quickly made friends and joined in the summer activities. We too began a round of cocktail parties and dinners.

The school itself needed revitalizing and, I thought, some humanizing. I set out to get to know the students. I made it abundantly clear that in many activities I would participate as a student too. I even attended a great many of their classes and flew with them. I informalized the morning staff meetings and did everything I could to revitalize the school. I had a goal, and I typically pursued it relentlessly.

My openness about wanting to learn seemed to effectively counter any skepticism about my presence. For a number of years the school had been sort of a prep school for astronauts, and now the Air Force wanted to deemphasize astronautics and reemphasize test piloting. The ex-astronaut heading their school agreed completely.

The first and most important recruit to my way of doing things was my deputy, Ted Twinting. Ted was liked and respected by the students, and as fighter jocks go, he hardly fit the image. Ted tended to be pudgy and looked out on the world through a round, happy face. He wasn't what one would call dashing, but he was a splendid pilot and instructor. We eventually became good friends and it was Ted more than anyone else who helped to guide me around various pitfalls and kept me informed of all that was going on.

I stuck close to the base nearly all summer. Joan and I made a couple of trips to Los Angeles for a weekend, and several times the kids came along for excursions to Disneyland and a number of other attractions. I had told Marianne I was going to Edwards and would be busy nearly all summer. I planned to let our relationship simmer on the back burner throughout the summer.

The only commandant the school had ever had who was not a graduate of the school felt he was doing a good job. My feelings of insecurity—that more was expected of me because of my association with NASA—began to diminish. As this happened, I began to force a rather peculiar change in my personality. A man who had always been studious and rather introverted decided to try being an extrovert to see if it would make him more effective. It didn't. I left the humor and self-confidence to Ted, because he was good at both. As for me, I hid my own feelings of insecurity under a blitz of hard work.

When *Apollo* 15 was launched on July 26, 1971, Joan, Mike, Jan, Andy, and I were sitting on the beach in Carpenteria, California, watching a portable television set. It was the most scientific mission yet, with plenty of geological studies, areas that always interested me. Two years had passed and a great deal had changed. As for me, I felt just fine sitting there on the beach.

The students—usually about forty—were divided into two classes, with the entire course lasting eleven months. They were, by and large, an interesting and talented group. They were mostly Air Force pilots, with a smattering of navy and marines, and a group of what were called Allied students. One was Italian, one Israeli, one Swedish, one Brazilian, and there were a couple of Germans, attending as foreign guests of the school. The group of students who graduated as I arrived had become known as the Axis class because Germany, Italy, and Japan had sent students. The Japanese student was typical of his countrymen: he took copious notes, kept all the manuals, and when he got back to Japan he became head of his government's test pilot school.

My predecessor at the school had put in an official request to take a group of students to Europe to inspect various test pilot schools there. These trips used to be annual affairs but they had been canceled for the last three years because of economics. I'm sure the fact that an astronaut would be commanding the trip had a good bit to do with its approval. We were going to visit the British Empire Test Flight School, as well as test centers in Italy, Germany, and France. We were allowed a total of eleven days for the trip to learn how other countries ran their test programs and to fly as many of their aircraft as possible.

I was pleased I was going to Europe with my twelve students and relieved that Ted Twinting would be commanding in my absence.

Our schedule had no social functions on it, which pleased me no end. We arrived in Rome in the evening and I was no sooner off the plane than the U.S. Embassy air attaché handed me a memo which began: "Many demands on your time." He couldn't have been more correct. We were to be in Rome two days and three nights, and the first night was nearly over. The social schedule read roughly: dinner with chief of staff of the Italian air force and ten members of his party, cocktails for a hundred people at the home of a prominent Italian general, and an escorted tour of Roman night life.

All that, and a long day of briefings and a still longer day of flying Italian aircraft. I came to look with great pleasure upon the time spent flying. Even an unexpected invitation to fly a single-seat Italian fighter failed to give me much pause, though such a thing would never be done in the U.S. Air Force without hours and hours of concentrated instruction and training before actual flying. I even did acrobatics flying wingman for my instructor.

While the flying was a success, I felt the social schedule was decidedly not. I made it through the first two functions, but the escorted tour of Italian night life the final night in Rome was a disaster. My Italian air force colonel/guide was well-intentioned, but he underestimated the tenacity of the *paparazzi*. They followed us everywhere, nearly knocking us over in the process. The more I resisted their attempts, the harder they fought. Worried about possible adverse publicity, I called a halt to the evening. By the next morning I was seriously worried and stayed that way through our visits to Germany and France. I spent much time on the telephone trying to make sure there would be no trouble.

The trip was turning into a nightmare. We flew to the South of France where the reception was cool—Gaullism was still rampant—and the training techniques not particularly well suited to the American style of flying. Socializing was limited and what little there was of it was agreeable.

Our arrival at Fürstenfeldbruck, where Joan, Mike, and I had lived during the invasion of Hungary, was covered extensively by the press. A battery of television cameras and photographers were waiting when we got off the plane and, naturally, they wanted to speak to me. I answered their questions as briefly as possible, flinched whenever a flash went off, and stressed that I was in Germany with a group of students and not in any other capacity. The Luftwaffe officers were good hosts, and with typical German precision, something was scheduled for nearly every minute of our visit. We did little flying, and made extensive tours of various manufacturing and testing facilities.

Near the end of our visit to Germany I telephoned Rome again. Time was in my favor; no pictures had appeared and it was now unlikely they would be published. It was a great bit of luck. I dread to think how I might have reacted if they had appeared in the newspapers.

The Empire Test Flight School was the most interesting of all. The British did not have the quantity of aircraft we had, but their variety was far greater. Pilots at the school learned to fly nearly every aircraft in the fleet, including some that were no longer flown in the United States. We were all impressed with this and decided to prepare a report favoring such a theory of educational flying. An excellent British test pilot took me for a test flight in a Hawker Hunter during which we did both normal spins and the more hazardous inverted spins. The school's flight manual—in particular, its rules on spin tests—caused much favorable comment among my instructors and students.

Our last night in England we spent dining in, a tradition started by the British services and adopted by the Americans. It was a formal stag dinner, to which we all wore our mess suits, the military equivalent of tuxedos. Such evenings traditionally begin with toasts to royalty and presidents and end in chaos. Whoever speaks takes his head—and whatever else on his person he might value—in his hands. I was the speaker, and I paced my quarters one entire afternoon deciding what to say and convincing myself I could take the ribbing. I not only took it, I gave it back, which is also traditional. Once dinner and my speech were over, ties and outer attire were removed and we settled down to some serious drinking and games.

Back at Edwards, the students went to work preparing their reports on the trip and I set out to supervise the overall report, stressing the importance of the wide variety of training aircraft used by the British. We had been exposed to nearly thirty new aircraft, and each pilot had flown an average of seven European aircraft. From an educational standpoint we all felt the trip was a resounding success.

I made a couple of ineffective stabs at our report, then assigned it to someone else. I went to the office each morning and attended all the necessary meetings, all the while acutely aware I wasn't functioning anywhere near my normal levels. At home I could do nothing. Family life went on as routinely as possible, with Joan and the kids trying to ignore the fact that I was either in bed or sitting in front of the television set.

Several times I resolved to get help, but I could not believe that I was now incapable of getting myself going.

Every time I decided to get help I began to cry; the only help available was official Air Force treatment and the matter would go into my record. I was sullen and uncommunicative, and even Joan gave up trying to draw me into conversation. One night she invited some neighbors from down the street for dinner, hoping to at least get me out of bed for a few hours. In a burst of uncharacteristic candor, I told my neighbor, who was also a doctor, what was going on. He and his wife nodded wisely throughout my explanation. When it was done, they looked at one another. He urged her to tell their story. It turned out that she, too, had undergone several severe depressions, but had worked her way out of them through religion. She was now heavily involved in her church and was feeling fine. I accepted her story as encouragement, but in no way did I believe religion could get me through. Religion helps, and I am a religious man, but I know its limitations in curing mental depression.

The report and recommendations from our European trip were finally complete and I submitted them to General White and his staff, asking that they be forwarded to Washington. Essentially, the report reflected our enthusiasm and interest in the variety of training aircraft used by the British, and it pointed up their good safety record. The safety record at Edwards had not been as good as hoped, but it had been measurably improving. Our report advocated a variety of training aircraft at a time the Air Force was about to announce a drastic cutback in the number of its training craft in a move for increased safety. My staff and I were unanimous in our feeling that a good test pilot ought to have a wide variety of experience by flying many different types of airplanes. However, General White's staff had urged that the report not be submitted, since it would only cause apprehension and possibly some trouble for us all.

I didn't particularly relish the role of devil's advocate, but I nevertheless thought the British system should receive a thorough study before any decision was made. After all, their safety record was not bad at all. I still maintain the report should have been submitted, if only so it could prove we had learned something and that other requests for such trips might receive more favorable consideration.

The news of the report sent me even deeper into despair. I could see no hope, no possibility of controlling anything. I began staying up nearly all night every night with some vague fear of sleeping in the darkness. I could once again intellectually refute such a thought, but my intellect was by now separated by the jagged and dangerous wall of my emotions. The rule of my emotions was absolute and ruthless. In no way could I stop what I felt, but I hoped somehow to stop feeling anything at all. I yearned for a brightly lit oblivion—wept for it.

In depression, I went to Dr. Dick Slarve, a colonel who had, at my request, accompanied us on the trip to Europe. I had come to like Dick and felt in some way he might understand what was happening to me, might know who could help.

I no longer cared whether or not my sickness went on my record and told him so. I desperately wanted help. Dick made a telephone call to Dr. Carlos Perry at Brooks Medical Center in San Antonio. By this time I was becoming physically ill as well. My neck, which had troubled me from time to time, was now painful, and the fingers on my left hand were going numb. Dick said that Dr. Perry would be the Air Force doctor who could best make a tentative diagnosis and then decide what treatment I should receive. An appointment was made for October 26, 1971, in San Antonio.

The knowledge that help was on the way relieved me enormously. Throughout the spring and summer I had avoided any contact with my father. I felt he might not understand my dilemma. I had also avoided Joan's family, but she had maintained contact and told them things were not going particularly well. We decided to use my twentieth class reunion at West Point as an excuse to go east and tell them I would be undergoing professional help within the Air Force. On the way back we'd stop in San Antonio to meet with Dr. Perry.

We went to Joan's dad and stepmother in Ho-Ho-Kus first, and I had no intention of continuing on to my reunion. Joan, however, was intent on making me go. Mike Archer is a gentle man with the most even disposition I have ever seen. We have always got along well.

Mike and I sat up nearly all night talking and he could not believe what I said. It was inconceivable to him that a guy with my drive and my accomplishments could feel this way. The harder I tried to explain, the deeper I tunneled in. Talking by now did little more than magnify my feelings. Conversation offered no release.

He began to realize something of the extent of it the next morning when Joan gave up trying to get me up for the drive to West Point. Mike taunted and dared me out of bed.

The drive to West Point was interrupted a number of times as Joan and I parked and went on short walks, relishing the changing color of the countryside we had all but forgotten in Texas and California.

We missed the parade and arrived late for the football game. I was relieved that no one I knew was seated near us. I dreaded signing any autographs or having my picture taken. After the game Joan coaxed me to my class reception and to my vast relief it turned out to be a pleasant evening. There were a few autographs and several pictures, but I knew who was asking and could handle it.

The next day we went to New York. Through my friend Joel Kozol, our host during our vacation on Majorca, I had become involved a year earlier in a cable television operation. The board of directors was meeting the next day in New York.

Joan returned to Ho-Ho-Kus the morning of the meeting. I was informed that most of the directors were resigning and I asked Joel to explain why. As a director, I was one of the men responsible for the company, even though at this time my interest was clouded and forced. Joel affably explained that the new chairman of the board had ordered the resignations of anyone not directly involved with the company, though the directors would continue to hold their stock. The streamlining would mean a more efficient operation. I was asked to remain on the board because I had made a number of technical suggestions and because my name gave the organization a certain credibility and stability.

I laughed out loud when he said this and within minutes I was convinced they were out to get me. The company was obviously headed for financial disaster and they were going to dump it on me. I hastily left my hotel for Marianne's apartment.

Marianne, whom I hadn't seen for months, greeted me as a long-lost and much missed lover. Within minutes she began to realize her lover was also much changed. She confessed that she, too, had been deeply depressed at times. She then allowed as how—inserted almost midsentence so that it might get by unnoticed—she was thinking of getting married again and had a proposal. I reacted with pleas and half-promises. Wait, please wait. I'll get some help. I'll get a divorce, maybe, and then we can think of some future together. She smiled and said she might wait a bit, but not for long. I fled for Ho-Ho-Kus.

I sat up nearly all night talking with Mike and my dad. If Mike had trouble understanding my problem, my dad found it impossible. He still has difficulty admitting it to himself. He urged me to wait, to hold off going to the Air Force doctor in San Antonio. I was about to refuse when Joan stepped in and made it uncomfortably clear how sick I was and that she was now physically prepared to deck anybody who tried to interfere with my going to doctors.

She made it perfectly clear she didn't give a damn whether or not my sickness had any adverse effect on my career. She cared only that I got well. Mike and my dad acquiesced in the storm of Joan's determination.

Early in the morning of October 26, 1971, we flew from Newark to San Antonio and went directly to Dr. Perry's office at Brooks Medical Center.

I told him everything I could think of and answered his questions as honestly as I could. It wasn't easy, but I maintained my composure. He then turned to Joan and asked her several questions. She answered several before I turned and saw the tears streaking her cheeks. She then looked directly at me and back to the doctor. She said that for the sake of our children and herself, she had been considering a divorce. But she had thought it all over on the plane that morning and would not even consider a divorce at this time. Later, maybe, but not now. Life at home was tolerable only when I was not around, but she wanted to see what it would be like if I was around and well. She said she was not going to kick a man who was as far down as I was. On the contrary, she was going to fight to keep me at least until such time as the two of us could sit down and make some rational decision about our life together.

I said nothing at all as she spoke. I sat perfectly still and stared at my hands. I was wringing them and it was as though they weren't even my hands at all.

Dr. Perry said he'd be in touch in about a week with some recommendation. I begged him to call sooner than that.

The next thing I remember was being in the office of Dr. Dick Slarve, insisting that I receive help immediately. It was early in the morning of October 28, just two days after I had returned from San Antonio. Dick said he had been in contact with Dr. Don Flinn, the Air Force psychiatrist who had approved me for the astronaut corps. He said that Flinn had left the service and was now on the staff of the UCLA neuro-psychiatric institute. He wanted to see me.

Within an hour of the start of our meeting, Dick had made an appointment for that afternoon at UCLA. After another hour of listening to me he was ready to cancel the appointment and send me directly back to the hospital in San Antonio.

I was by this time hopelessly snarled in the logistics of how to get myself down to Los Angeles and UCLA. I was not only incapable of making a decision, I could not even complete a coherent sentence. By early afternoon Dick had made his decisions and all of my arrangements. I would see Dr. Flinn at UCLA and then catch an early evening plane to San Antonio. A staff driver would take me to UCLA and then the airport. Dr. Perry would be waiting for the plane in San Antonio.

Dick drove me home and Joan packed my suitcase while I stood in a doorway wondering what these people were doing and how it involved me.

I began thinking about Flinn. I vaguely remembered him from eight years before, but in my state of mind at the time I was certain of one thing: the guy had mixed motives. In my condition I made him look bad because he had once certified me as rock solid in the head. He's going to put me away somewhere where I'll never be heard from again. He'll probably put me in a closet with the rest of his skeletons.

He didn't, of course, and it was all in my mind. He spent barely an hour talking with me before he walked me to the government driver and told him to take me to the airport and wait until he was certain I had got on the plane.

Late that night I got off the plane in San Antonio. Dr. Perry was waiting. We drove directly to Wilford Hall, the hospital adjoining Brooks Air Force Base.

10

I was admitted to the hospital, and a few hours later, just as I was going to bed, I made the first notation in my date book in more than two months. Under Friday, October 28, I wrote, "Sleeping pill." I took the pill and gratefully fell asleep.

The next morning I awoke, and with a jolt, realized where I was. I looked at the windows to see if there were bars. There were none. I tried my door and it was unlocked. I looked down the corridor and saw nurses running about and a man on crutches slowly walking along. If this was the booby hatch, it wasn't all that bad. It looked just like a perfectly ordinary hospital.

And in fact it was. The psychiatric ward was on the fourth floor and I was in a private room on the second floor among other patients with injured neck nerves. I could receive treatment for my neck problem and I could also quietly slip upstairs to see the psychiatrists. Should anyone discover I was in the hospital, the official explanation was to be that I was being treated for a neck problem. The other problem, if at all possible, was to be kept a secret.

From some reason I felt better that first morning. I felt that somehow I had been separated from my problems. I was given a complete physical examination, and extensive X-rays of my neck were taken. I spent the afternoon taking exactly the same mental aptitude and stability tests I had taken when I was being tested for the astronaut corps. That night, helped by another sleeping pill, I slept soundly.

The following morning I was introduced to Col. John

Sparks, M.D., the chief of psychiatry and the man who would be treating me. We chatted a few minutes and he said that since it was Friday and I still had tests to take we wouldn't begin working together until Monday. He also told me the psychological testing, interestingly enough, had produced exactly the same scores as they had the first time I took them. By Friday afternoon, lulled by a totally false and remarkably fictional security, I began to be bothered by the prospect of a weekend of inactivity.

I was walking down the hall when I saw a patient go to the desk and apply for a weekend pass. Impulsively I did the same. I saw the nurse look up my name, check my room number, and fill out the pass form. Within minutes, it was handed back to me with Dr. Sparks' signature on it.

Before I left for the airport, with no special idea of where to go—just a vague notion of visiting Houston—I telephoned an old friend and former neighbor, Merv Hughes, who immediately invited me down for the weekend with his family. He also asked if I'd stop at the PX and order a bicycle for his daughter. The type he wanted was not available just then in Houston. I ordered the bicycle and caught the Braniff commuter flight to Houston.

I spent Friday and Saturday nights with the Hugheses and took my meals with several old friends. It was a weekend in my old neighborhood. Late Saturday night I told Merv Hughes what I was in the hospital for—bolstered by Scotch I felt sufficiently self-confident to throw discretion to the winds. Sunday morning, after church, I also told Dean Woodruff, our minister. By midafternoon I was back in the hospital in San Antonio and inexplicably depressed once again. When the tears began I asked for a sleeping pill and slept fitfully.

The next morning I was shaving when the commander of the hospital came into my room and began talking with me. As I responded to his questions I became aware that he had an extremely surprised look on his face. I had so many questions and I wanted so many answers that I struck him as being only slightly rational and quite confused. His reaction was a mixture of concern about my condition and doubt that I should have been permitted out of the hospital for the weekend. It turned out that the hospital, by the precautions they had taken when admitting me elsewhere than in the psychiatric ward, had produced an opportunity I instinctively seized—I was eligible for a pass and I took it. The irony was compounded by the fact that Dr. Sparks, thinking me rational and in control because of the way I had acted when I met him, had signed the pass.

Dr. Sparks and I began our work. That first day, words struggled slowly to form ideas, only to sink into the recesses of my mind before I could utter them. For several hours each day we explored my life and thoughts. With the help of tranquilizers and antidepressants, the flow steadily grew.

Dr. Sparks sat at his desk listening and making notes, tape-recording our sessions. His questions and observations were delivered in an even, considerate tone. I sat opposite him in a green padded chair, occasionally looking past him to the wall directly behind his desk where he had several diplomas and a framed photograph of Sigmund Freud, artfully altered to make him Brigadier General Sigmund Freud.

Finally I was able to state my deepest fears about my sickness, fears so strong that I had never mentioned them to anyone. My maternal grandfather, after a long period of melancholy, chose to end his life. When my mother died in May 1968 the cause of death was listed as cardiac arrest. My father, sisters, and I had asked that this be the stated cause of death. In the last years of her life she had been listless and unhappy except during family gatherings when grandchildren were around. She had taken too many sleeping pills once before, but my father had discovered it and rushed her to a hospital. At the time we figured it might have been accidental. So, for that matter, could the second—and fatal—incident have been accidental. We recognized that she no longer had a strong will to live and something within her must have welcomed release.

Grandfather. Mother. Son? Could I have inherited this dreadful melancholy? Would I one day be suicidal? Was I now?

Dr. Sparks reserved his opinion for the future and asked if I thought I was suicidal now.

"No."

"Why not?"

"I don't believe I could kill myself because I don't think I'd be able to decide how to do it."

For the first time, we both smiled. He said we would consider and investigate this concern as thoroughly as medical science permitted.

There was another deep fear that had moved around the margins of my mind, but I had never articulated it until I was in the hospital: the flashes I had observed going to and returning from the moon. The flicker-flashes were finally determined to be minute meteorlike substances which I saw when they penetrated my eyes and passed through my brain and out through my helmet. Neil had seen them too and maybe he was right in not being especially interested in talking about them. We had subsequently learned that it was believed the flashes destroyed small amounts of the billions of cells that make up our brains. Scientific studies were being conducted in a number of places which seemed to indicate the possibility of some damage on very long space flights to distant planets.

Could this have happened to me? Could some particularly important nerve cells have been disturbed? Was that what was wrong with me?

To my surprise, Dr. Sparks knew quite a bit about the flicker-flash phenomenon. He said the possibility that this could be a cause was extremely remote, but it should be investigated.

At first we met in the morning and in the afternoon.

Within two weeks, we were meeting only in the mornings. Afternoons I spent under special heat lamps or hanging from a Rube Goldberg device to take pressure off my neck.

The X-rays of my neck revealed growths that could lead to a pinched nerve, but the doctors maintained that this in no way warranted any surgery. Due to my self-pitying concern, I wanted a quick solution and felt thwarted by their opinion. It turned out the doctors were right—months later, when I was no longer depressed, I realized that there was no noticeable pain or discomfort in my neck.

Other afternoons an intriguing lesson was being taught to me by a psychologist on Dr. Sparks' staff. He taught me to relax in a most unorthodox manner. I would lie on my back in my hospital bed and he would sit on a chair beside my head, usually on my left. I would close my eyes and concentrate on his words. The first few times we did this it struck me as ludicrous. Then it began to work. He'd intone a kind of litany, addressing himself to various parts of my body until he had covered all of me.

"Think of your right thigh. See it in your mind. Now begin to concentrate on it. Feel it relax. Soothe it in your mind. Feel it become less tense."

That's pretty much how he spoke to me, or at least that's how I remember it now when I occasionally do it myself. By the time I had fairly well given myself over to this theory, we went to work on my fingers, which were perpetually busy. They took longer, but then they, too, relaxed.

The intensity of my depression began to diminish through the combination of psychiatric therapy, psychological exercises, and the drug Thioridazine.

With Dr. Sparks, I began to review my childhood and attempted to draw some sort of verbal portrait about the kind of man I had become. Usually there were just the two of us, but the psychologist occasionally attended the sessions.

It soon emerged that my life was highly structured and that there had always existed a major goal of one sort or another. I had excelled academically, being at the top of the schools and classes I had attended during my life. Finally, there had been the most important goal of all, and it had been realized—I had gone to the moon. What to do next? What possible goal could I add now? There simply wasn't one, and without a goal I was like an inert ping-pong ball being batted about by the whims and motivations of others. I was suffering from what poets have described as the melancholy of all things done.

I had grown up as the last-born and cherished only son of a father who was accustomed to the company of men but lived in a house full of women. My grandmother had lived with us for a time. So had an aunt. Then there were my mother and two sisters. In such an atmosphere, I was urged to be the bright center of a family in which I was wanted very much; I was indulged and encouraged in all that I did. As I grew older the encouragement began to be directed to certain goals. On my own I was athletic, but I was not especially interested in schoolwork. My mother and particularly my father not only encouraged my academic work, they pushed mightily for me to improve it. By the ninth grade their will was mine and from that time on my academic record was excellent.

Besides my parents, the camp I attended for seven summers gave me another strong motivation for success. It was there I learned to compete, to strive to be the best because winners ate turkey and losers ate beans. Winners received trophies, losers nothing. Winners won the esteem of their peers and their leaders, losers did not. This attitude is in the mainstream of the American life style, and I was one of the most willing participants in the competitive area.

I was introverted and rather shy in my social life. I came to believe during this look at my life that this tendency was not encouraged but it was not discouraged either. My sisters were outgoing, sociable, and fairly independent. I might have had those same traits, but they did not surface because I was the last-born and, I suspected, the most loved. My ties to my home remained exceedingly strong until I married at an age later than my contemporaries. I also married a girl who was close to her home and family, and our families lived near each other.

Throughout almost all my life I had been incapable of idle chatter or small talk. In many ways, I still am. I had the great good fortune of entering a business I truly loved and I was only too happy to talk business at any time, and I had a reputation for doing just that.

My concentration on business had, I slowly came to believe, seriously hampered my ability as a father and husband. As often as not, I was off on business halfway across the country. My time at home was spent either to relax or to engage in an intensive bout of fatherhood. My kids never knew what to expect from me, and as kids naturally do, they had become somewhat wary of me. Joan had sensed this and tried to compensate for it.

As a husband, I had not been perfectly faithful. I had also been absent at crucial times. My own image of myself as a husband and father further contrasted with what I read about myself and my family. And with what they read about themselves.

The astronauts as a group were under a special contract to *Life* magazine for the exclusive rights to our stories. Families were included in this contract. We were compensated for this, but not as excessively as many people think. Individual shares decreased as the number of astronauts increased. My share went quickly from sixteen thousand dollars the first year to three thousand dollars. Neil, Mike, and I wrote—with a more than considerable assist from two earnest *Life* writers—a book called *First on the Moon*. Royalties from this were divided equally among all the active astronauts. One by one the three of us left the space program and lost our share of royalties from the book. If the book is still earning money, the proceeds are being divided among the remaining astronauts—not the three of us.

I suppose the portrayal we received in *Life* and subsequently in nearly all the media helped the space program a great deal. Unfortunately, nearly all of it had us squarely on the side of God, Country, and Family. To read it was to believe we were the most simon-pure guys there had ever been. This simply was not so. We may have regularly gone to church, but we also celebrated some pretty wild nights.

In our family portraits and photographs of our family gatherings, we looked to be happy, open-faced, well-adjusted people with no skeletons in the closet. More than once I flew halfway across the country to pose for these pictures, and so did many others. Often, when our children were impatient and irritable—they were no different from any other children under pressure—our wives were half rigid with fear that all hell would break loose. Joan made a spontaneous remark at the end of my Gemini flight. I telephoned home expecting to be treated to a heavy dose of family worship. Instead, with an audible sigh of relief, Joan told me that our normally unpredictable brood had behaved beautifully at all of their press conferences. Appearances counted, really counted.

After the previous space flights, Joan and I had smiled knowingly at each other when we heard the men's wives express their "pride and happiness" at the success of their husbands' flights. When *Apollo 11* had gone to the moon and back, Joan held the mandatory press conference on the front lawn shortly after splashdown. When asked how she felt, she responded: "I'm thrilled, proud, and happy." Weeks after the flight, Joan was discussing the press conference one night and turned to me and said, "Buzz, I lied. I wasn't thrilled, proud, and happy. I was scared to death and enormously relieved." The expression became a cliché, a kind of emotional antonym. All of us somehow had to reconcile the image and the actuality. My kids had been forced to reconcile the media's family portraits with the reality of day-to-day living. They had to reconcile the father they saw on television with the one they saw at home. The father at home, at least in my case, was often inattentive, tired, and asleep on the den sofa by nine o'clock.

Pressure on astronaut wives was intense. Nearly all of them were service wives—a long and honorable tradition—often requiring them to fill in for a father away fighting a war. Service wives come in all varieties, but few of them were prepared by experience for this kind of public life. We were no exception. Joan in some ways was unique, since she had the local theater as her own outlet. Many wives had no such resources and struggled unsuccessfully to participate in the lives of their husbands.

There were, of course, familiar pleasures I could relish, the kind of pleasures any family man has: Andy learning to play football all Saturday afternoon and spending Sunday afternoon with me at a Houston Oilers game; Jan, growing tall and graceful, riding a horse and shouting, "Daddy, watch this"; Mike with his animals, an independent boy responding to the obvious dependence of his pets; then Joan, who went after life with such energy but who would stop everything to sit down and spend an evening talking with me. In the seventeen years we'd been married, the conversations, debates, and even the arguments have been endlessly fascinating. Joan is many things and one of them is that she is the best company around.

These were my consolations, though for most of the first several weeks after my depression began I could not be consoled. There were days I could not get out of bed. In the hospital, though, I could be ordered out of bed and orders were something I had been trained to follow. Twenty-four years had passed since I left West Point, but I could still present myself at brace—physically and emotionally. Some mornings I responded to Dr. Sparks' questions; other mornings, I ignored his questions and carried on my litany of self-doubt and self-hate. At times I felt hopelessly snarled in the tangle of my mind. We began slowly and carefully to untangle it. My wanderings were the result of short-term goals inserted for satisfaction when long-term goals were either too formidable or were giving me trouble of one sort or another. When a major goal had been accomplished, it was only a matter of time before a short-term goal would assume the achievability and desirability of a long-term goal.

Marianne. With her, I had entered a second and short-term life style. Before this my professional life had been my work. When the long-term goal was achieved I had reached for a substitute. The substitute was Marianne.

Playing off my life styles one against the other had started me on my way to a collision within myself. I had used my two life styles in the most extreme way to establish a maze through which I could travel no more. I finally became helplessly lost within myself.

The first indication was a noticeable shift in my moods. The last two and a half years of my life—from the time I left the lunar quarantine quarters until I entered Wilford Hall —were characterized by depression, which occasionally deepened, then rose to a temporary brief high of optimism, only to sink again to a new low.

There was no possible way of setting a goal that would match the goals already achieved. But it *was* possible to carefully pick over my priorities and make an adjustment to certain realities that were now beginning to appear to me.

Because I had always been so success-oriented, I set myself a goal: I would learn to live my life differently. I would put the past into perspective and look carefully at the future.

Goals. The desire to excel. Single-mindedness. Three things in my character that had gotten me into deep difficulty. One by one, with the sort of perverse logic prevailing at this time, I began to make decisions.

I wanted, more than anything else, to begin again—if at all possible. I, of course, believed it to be possible. I would leave the Air Force just as I had left NASA. They existed in the past.

My marriage. It, too, was a goal. I had been raised—trained, drilled, and otherwise completely bound in the ethic of the times—to believe that a man married and stayed married to the same woman all his life. It did not matter whether or not they were happy together; it mattered only that the marriage held fast. Neither Joan nor I could be described as completely happy—our marriage had had to withstand tremendous change and pressure—and now there seemed little left besides coping with the ravages of a fragmented life.

One morning I arrived to see Dr. Sparks with, I thought, all the right solutions. After listening patiently he said he suspected I was making a mistake, but I would not be convinced.

My compulsive drive to achieve goals had been my undoing. I wanted to begin anew. If I was leaving the Air Force, I was leaving behind a goal. A long, enduring marriage was previously an unassailable goal. No more. I would divorce Joan and make a totally new beginning. I would marry Marianne. That night I telephoned Marianne and told her of my decision. She was hesitant and confessed she was very near marrying another man. When I moved to California she had concluded it was all over between us. I asked her to wait awhile and she agreed. My spirits soared. It never once occurred to me I could be making a mistake—I was blinded by the optimistic prospect of a new life.

From time to time Dr. Sparks and I touched on my more deep-seated fears and finally we went to work on them.

One day the flicker-flashes merged with some memories of early childhood, an emotional parallel that made it very unlikely that any damage had been done to my brain. I was idly discussing books I had read as a youngster when I remembered there had been a period of fascination with science fiction. Then I remembered one story about a voyage to the moon during which a great deal of trouble was encountered and once the moon had been reached the space travelers departed for earth, returning home insane. It had given me nightmares as a youngster, and had secured an odd corner in my psychic life. Ironically, I would end up going on the first voyage to the moon and that corner of my psychic life would come right along with me, stirred to frightened life but unable to present itself in my consciousness until the insistent prodding of a psychiatrist unearthed it. After several subsequent explorations of the flicker-flash phenomenon and its effects, we dropped the concern as inconsequential.

My family history. It was remotely, very remotely, possible that my tendency to depression had been inherited. I had telephoned my sisters and, as well as we could, we reconstructed the nature of our mother's problems. What both she and I had were called depressions, but there any similarity ended. If anything, her problem came from repression while mine seemed to come from an oversupply of aggression and drive. But I could no longer agree that the probable cause of my mother's death should be kept a family secret and so informed my sisters, who did not approve for reasons of their own, that I wanted the matter revealed. Psychiatric science has made some great strides and one of them is that a depression, noticed and diagnosed in its early stages, can be successfully treated. If not, it will only grow until it becomes unmanageable, devastating, and, in some cases, fatal. It is no different from any other illness.

It is my devout wish to bring emotional depression into the open and so treat it as one does a physical infirmity. I want my children to know so that if they too become ill they will see the symptoms and seek help. It doesn't truly matter whether or not the cause is genetic or environmental. The point is that it must be treated, and the sooner the better. Wilford Hall is not the only place I have explored the subject of emotional depression in general or my own bout with it in particular. A number of experts have said they do not believe that in my case it is a genetic inheritance.

My relationship with my father was examined time and again. Even when he was away during World War II, his influence on our household, especially on me, was strong. He planted his own goals and aspirations in me. When I set a goal he encouraged me. When I conquered a goal he expressed the importance of still another, bigger one. I, in turn, strove mightily for his approval. The relationship was not unique—many fathers live vicariously through their sons. Still, my father was a very well-known and respected aviator who had skirted the fringes of fame most of his adult life. I am constantly amazed by the number of prominent people he knew—and knows. General Billy Mitchell, whom he had served as an aide in the Philippines, was a family friend. When the aging and sick general came to our home shortly before his death, much was made of the fact that he wanted to present a horse to my sister, Fay. Dad also knew General Jimmy Doolittle, probably the most important hero, to me, to emerge from World War II. General Doolittle has been a source of advice, a source of action, and a friend. Additionally, General Doolittle had been a student of Dad's. He had instructed him in engineering and aerodynamics. My father also knew other important men, among them Senator Albert Hawkes, who had secured my appointment to West Point.

There were, of course, times when I challenged my father's beliefs and theories. When he could not prevail upon me with his own thoughts and opinions, he liberally mentioned the traditions and opinions represented by his important friends. These were powerful arguments to use on anyone and I usually acceded to his ideas.

I fulfilled his dreams and then some. I followed in his footsteps, and found possibilities at the end of the path that had not existed when he was a young man. When I first applied to be an astronaut, he predicted I would not make it. I didn't. The second time I applied, he telephoned me one night to say that he had heard through a friend of his in Washington that I had not been selected. This subsequently proved untrue, but at the time it was disappointing. Could it be that it was a bit difficult for him to accept that my own goals had begun to exceed those he had set for me? Perhaps it raised thoughts in his mind about his own accomplishments and other goals he might have at one time set for himself.

When we made our flight, he was angered to learn I would not be the first man to step onto the moon. His anger accumulated when, after the flight, a commemorative stamp was issued proclaiming Neil as the first man on the moon. He has done everything he could to change this situation to "first men on the moon" and he continues to wage a one-man campaign against history.

Dr. Sparks and I talked about my father and I was able to reconcile myself to our relationship and to want to step out of his shadow. One thing was absolutely certain: my father loved me very much, and I did everything I could to keep that love. He believed what he did was the best for me. And I loved him too.

I began to wish that I could speak to him. Except for our visit just before I entered the hospital, I had virtually avoided him for a year, figuring my sickness would prove untenable for him. It was time for us to talk, and I now knew I could handle the situation. Our communication was ready to be restored.

After my sessions with Dr. Sparks, I'd eat a leisurely lunch and then go for long walks on the hospital grounds. I spent hours each day in thought.

Few men, particularly those who are motivated toward success, ever pause to reflect on their lives. They hurry forward with great energy, never pausing to look over their shoulders to see where they have been. If a man does this at all, it is usually near the end of his life, and it happens only because there is little else for him to do.

My depression forced me, at the age of forty-one, to stop and, for the first time, examine my life. The circumstances that brought about my study were extreme, but I now look upon this experience as one of the most valuable things I have done. It taught me to begin to live again, at an age when it is very possible to begin anew.

In the course of my treatment I began to realize certain priorities. I was able to say that what I really wanted was to live my life on my own. My entire adult life had been spent either in the Air Force or with NASA. It had, to a large extent, been a circumscribed and insulated life. I began to contemplate the possibility of leaving these things behind and striking out on my own as a civilian. In a few months, June 1972, I would complete twenty-one years of service. I was already eligible for retirement. The word "retirement" jolted me, since I was coming to regard it as a beginning, not a cessation. I decided to leave the nest I had occupied for so many years, the nest that had provided me with security and fame.

I was getting well. As I became more and more comfortable with myself, I became more aware of others.

There was a nurse on my floor, a slightly chubby and very pleasant woman by the name of Sharyn Farrell. When she had learned what I was actually in the hospital for, she undertook to cheer me up. She stuck a sticker on my pillow one morning—one of those round, smiling "be happy" stickers. She put another on the door of my room. She stopped by frequently to visit and see to my needs. She was determined to coax me back to good health.

When I finally began to feel better, I became considerably more aware of Sharyn as an individual. Behind that smiling exterior was, I suspected, a rather lonely woman. She allowed as how she didn't have a boyfriend at the moment, but she had hopes of having one soon. She was just beginning to recover from a romance gone sour.

In the course of the conversation one day, I asked what her big project at the moment was. She wanted to buy a new car and go on a diet. I encouraged her to do both and offered my assistance in buying the car. We pored over literature she collected from car dealers and settled on a Dodge.

A few days later, she came in looking discouraged. She had gone to look at the Dodge and discovered it cost a good bit more than she could afford.

One thing I believe I do well is haggling with car dealers. I told Dr. Sparks her story and said that I'd like to take her to a car dealer and do some dealing. He agreed. I was given a Saturday-afternoon pass.

We drove into San Antonio in her old clunker and I looked out and tried to see everything. It was a marvelous feeling to be out and around. We went directly to the Dodge dealer, and lucky for us, he recognized my name. The price came down, but not enough to suit me.

My uncle, Bob Moon, had bought a Mazda, the Japanese car with the rotary engine then just being introduced in America, and was very enthusiastic about it. I had driven it and was impressed both with its design and its economy. I dragged a disappointed Nurse Sharyn to the local Mazda dealer. The Dodge, she agreed, was still too much money. Good luck again, the Mazda man recognized my name. We drove one of his cars and were both impressed by it. I started haggling.

That afternoon we returned to the hospital in a new

Mazda, which she named Buzz. It was a minor excursion that became significant as a new beginning.

Thanksgiving was less than a week away and I recalled another Thanksgiving when, after a long hospitalization with hepatitis, I had gratefully rejoined my family. I wanted to go home, if only for a day.

Dr. Sparks, of course, pointed up the duplicity of my wanting to go home and also wanting a divorce. Nevertheless, it all seemed perfectly reasonable to me. I intended to go home for Thanksgiving with my family and then go East to my father and Marianne. I was, of course, constructing another elaborate labyrinth, but it was one that gave me great hope for the future and I proceeded with it. It, too, would fall apart, but in a most unexpected way.

I asked for and was granted ten days with certain provisos. If anything went wrong I was to return immediately. I was to spend time with my family and contact my father. Whenever I returned, I would stay in the hospital until we had examined the week in minute detail. I intended to do all that and more, and I felt certain I could handle the entire ten days easily.

We had a traditional family dinner, made plans for Christmas, and I proposed to Joan that she and I spend the week after Christmas in Acapulco without the kids this particular year. On the trip I was thinking of asking for a divorce. I fully expected she would be relieved. Had she not said during our first visit to the hospital in San Antonio that life with me was miserable? That she was thinking of a divorce, but would not make that decision until I was well? In gaining my freedom for a new beginning, I believed she would be getting hers.

While I was home I also went to my office to begin plowing through the accumulation of work from the previous month which I had once thought myself incapable of ever completing.

After five days at home, I said good-bye to my obviously

relieved wife and older son. Joan, instructed to keep my illness a secret, had finally confided in Mike, who had stood loyally by her side while I was hospitalized. She later said she had told him when she could no longer bear the burden of secrecy and uncertainty. The only indication she had of what was going on with me, since she had no communication from the doctors at the hospital, was from my telephone calls. She was trying to judge my condition by my mood, my tone of voice, and not by whether or not I said I was feeling well.

In New Jersey, my father and I talked for two days, not always agreeing, but talking nevertheless. He disagreed with my decision to retire, feeling I should stick it out and become a general. I said no, emphatically not.

What did I intend to do when I retired, he asked, reminding me I had three children to put through college. I said I was going into business by myself and my knowledge and experience would be available for a fee. I planned to enter various commercial ventures other than the three—a cable television company, a computer firm, and an insurance company—to which I was already committed. I was also contemplating writing a book. Whatever I did, I assured him, would in no way reflect adversely on my family, country, NASA, or the Air Force.

The third day with my father I intended to break the rest of the news. Madeline arrived from Philadelphia, and my other sister, Fay, flew in from Cincinnati. I told them I was not only leaving the Air Force, I was going to get a divorce and remarry. The news was met with a stunned silence and one by one they began to urge me to wait, to be absolutely certain of my health before I did anything so extreme as divorce. I became more insistent until finally I was adamant. I went to bed convinced beyond any doubt I was doing the right thing. My sisters and father, on the other hand, were so disturbed that when I got up the next morning my sisters had already gone and my father had left a note telling me to have a good time and be careful in New York.

At that moment, I pretty much decided to hell with my sisters and father and packed my bag for the short trip across the Hudson River to New York and Marianne.

Marianne, claiming indecision, refused to see me. There was also the matter of the other man who wanted to marry her in two months, early in February. The next two days passed in an odd but euphoric state. I was more certain than ever I wanted to marry her, even though friends of hers were now advising against it. A confidant of mine whom I visited frequently in New York was so adamant he said I couldn't even afford her.

Back at the hospital, I felt even better and more optimistic about the future than I had felt before. There was a week of morning therapy followed by afternoon relaxation exercises or long walks. Dr. Sparks doggedly kept at me about my decision to divorce and remarry and by now I was such a super-salesman for my ideas that I honestly believed I partially won him over to my way of thinking.

Finally, he said I could leave at the end of the week and he proceeded with my medical prognosis. As I understood it, my prognosis was not at all certain. I might possibly never have another depression. Then again, it was just as likely there would be another and that some form of treatment might be necessary. There was, he said, no way to be sure what would happen. I, for one, was certain. I had been through the fires of a personal hell and had no intention of going through them again. I could not now conceive of being in any way out of control ever again.

Dr. Sparks' final instruction was that I carefully avoid any build-up of conflict in the conduct of my life. I nodded in enthusiastic agreement.

When I was officially discharged, I said good-bye to Nurse Sharyn, who had gained a new car and lost seven pounds since we had met, and headed into the future. I

313

had been hospitalized a total of four weeks, not including a ten-day leave to test my progress. I couldn't wait to get going. My destiny was once again mine.

My euphoria was, to a large degree, false—something I had not realized until I had still another year's perspective on what was happening to me. It is in the nature of medical treatment in the services that the patient be up and out as soon as possible. Many of my major symptoms were cured, but there were still more to come.

Going back to Edwards was remarkable in that my return was studiously made to seem unremarkable. Joan and I had planned it this way and she did her part to see that family life continued in as much of a routine as possible. A number of times I noticed Mike watching me those first few days, but he, too, soon returned to his own preoccupations. Jan and Andy went on as though nothing had happened.

General White, my commanding officer, and Ted Twinting, my deputy, did whatever they could to reestablish me in the routine of the school. The transition was made considerably easier by the fact that after the first week in the hospital, I had made daily telephone calls to Ted. Joan and Pat Twinting had previously instituted a visiting program for the wives and families of the students and had kept up their visits during my absence.

General White and I were very relieved there had been no accidents in my absence. Safety is greatly emphasized in all flying schools, and in ours particularly, because of the high risk involved in flying as fledgling test pilots. There are lives to protect, and the equipment isn't exactly inexpensive. Just prior to my arrival at the school, two pilots had died in a B-57 crash.

It is in the nature of a military chain of command that losses of this sort reflect on a number of people. The theory, I now believe, is not without its inequities, but it is nevertheless followed dogmatically. For pilots fortunate enough to survive a crash, their accident is entered in their records.

It also reflects on the records of their commanders at the time. Even if a commander was away at the time of the crash, he was nevertheless held responsible. General White, to his considerable grief, already had two deaths and the loss of a relatively expensive B-57 on his record.

Bob White was fortunate; he was still in command. After two losses, a man in his position might find himself transferred to a considerably less prestigious post.

Special boards are set up to investigate each accident, their membership increasing in rank by the enormity of the misfortune. I hoped there would be no accidents of any sort during the six months I had left in the Air Force. Thus, when Ted Twinting came to me one day, concerned about a student, I listened very carefully.

An instructor had told Ted of a student who was subject to rather peculiar fits of pain which had sent him writhing to the floor one day in class. The student complained of infrequent but severe back pains. He was one of the better students and had a distinguished record of combat flying in Vietnam. Both Ted and I believed he should be kept off flying status until his back problem was diagnosed and treated. Within days, we had him sent to Brooks Hospital in San Antonio, where the Air Force treats most of its pilots. We felt certain they would discover some disorder, treat it, and return him to flying status.

Late one night, Joan and I made what we considered a crucial decision. The promotion boards would probably announce the new generals list in February and I was only certain that I would be either on the list or not. In the event I was not, my retirement would look like an enormous case of sour grapes. If I was promoted, my retirement would appear as though I was giving the Air Force the shaft. We decided to announce my retirement in January, before promotions were announced, and six months before I officially left the service. We agreed that it was the most honest and open way to handle a ticklish accident of timing.

I was virtually impervious to the anxieties that had plagued me in the past. I recovered instantly from my surprise when Ted, looking very worried, came into my office to show me the physicians' reports on the pilot with back trouble. They could find nothing wrong at all and recommended he be returned to flying status. It struck both of us as ironic that the traditionally conservative medical profession would tell a couple of traditionally unconservative pilot-instructors they were being too cautious. Our hands were tied. We had no choice but to allow the pilot to continue flying, even though we felt it a mistake.

For Christmas 1971 I presented Joan with something she had dreamed of having most of her life: a blond mink coat. I had hoped such an extravagant gift would make up for much that had gone before, and would help us through what was yet to come. The entire family was full of plans for where we would live and what we would do after my retirement and what followed.

The day after Christmas, Joan and I left for Acapulco, where we were joined by Joan's stepbrother and his wife. Three days later, on December 29, our seventeenth wedding anniversary, the four of us sat down to dinner and Joan raised her glass in a toast.

"Here's to seventeen, Buzz. Will we see eighteen?"

Stunned, I looked at my raised glass, and slowly, staring at the table, I put my glass down and said nothing. Instantly there were tears, and when I looked up I saw that Joan too was crying. She got up and left the table and I stayed long enough to finish my drink and endure the awkward silence of her stepbrother and his wife. Finally, I went to our room and Joan.

She was sitting on the end of the bed, smoking a cigarette and weeping.

"I've known something was wrong, Buzz. I've known for a long time."

"My life is unreal. It has been unreal for a couple of years now. I can't go on."

We talked for the next several hours, and it was a tearful conversation. Joan said she had sensed that my return from the hospital and my decision to leave the Air Force was mostly a decision to put all of the past behind me. She also wanted a new beginning and if it was not to be with me, then so be it. We would divorce. No mention was made of Marianne. I figured enough had been said for one night and I was now to have my divorce. And now that I was to have my freedom, I suddenly had mixed emotions about it.

The next morning I awoke with the sun and saw that Joan was sitting alone on our balcony in the bright morning, smoking a cigarette and drinking coffee. I quickly got up and went to sit with her.

It was, we both later agreed, as if somebody had just died. We sat in silence for a few minutes until she asked me where I was going now that I was to begin again alone.

I made my confession. I told her I wanted to marry Marianne even though she was contemplating marriage to someone else.

Joan listened to it all without any noticeable reaction. When I was done she sat silently for a moment, then put out her cigarette and, in tears once again, tore into me.

All decisions of the night before were now off. Had I wanted to go off alone and begin again that was one thing. She could understand that. There had been enormous events in our married life and monumental strains. She did not find separation entirely unwelcome. Her ultimate hope was that we'd go off alone for a while and then come back together. But another woman? What about our vow of openness? I said I was now being open. Well, as far as she was concerned, I was just too late. If I wanted a divorce, fine. But now she was going to fight it, strongly implying that she didn't think I was as healthy as I thought I was. She made it abundantly clear that I might eventually get a divorce, but it was going to cost plenty—it was going to cost all she could take. She also hoped Marianne would marry the other guy and leave me out in the cold on my ass.

We packed and, in silence, flew home. As we drove the hour and a half back to Edwards, nothing was said until we were nearly home. Joan then turned to me and asked that our children not be informed until I knew what was going to happen. She said they had already been through enough. I nodded in assent.

The next week we spent much like any other couple on the verge of divorce. Joan plunged into activities around the house while I stayed in the office longer than usual. At dinner there was polite but restrained conversation. At night, by an unspoken agreement, Joan preceded me to bed by an hour.

Unbeknownst to me, Joan went to a psychiatrist. She made the appointment hoping to sort out her feelings and partly because she felt she was being too selfish with her threats. She visited the psychiatrist three times, then abruptly stopped going. She later said she felt he would help her convince herself she wanted a divorce and she had learned just one thing by going to him: she didn't want a divorce—a thought that surprised her at the time. Months before, she had thought she wanted one and now that she could have it, she wanted none of it.

We had expected to go on this way for a month—by that time I hoped Marianne would be persuaded to marry me. Meanwhile, she refused my almost daily telephone calls. Finally I telephoned her daughter, who was coaxed into becoming my advocate. I telephoned our few mutual friends in search of support. Some were sympathetic, others refused to become involved. I was informed that she had bought a wedding dress and that she was getting married the next day.

And that's what she did. I telephoned my congratulations to the newlyweds and they were warmly received.

To this day I have no idea of the motivation behind all that went on with Marianne. If I was being used as a decoy for bigger game, I had no idea it was so. Perhaps she was reacting to both my illness and uncertainty, and once I made up my mind it was simply too late.

I told Joan. "This is no great victory for me," was her response. How true. I was at a new low. It was as though I had at one time been a good racehorse who was now finishing a claiming race—only, there was nobody who wanted to claim me. Even my original mate wasn't at all sure she wanted me back.

We decided to postpone any separation until after my retirement. To say that our marriage was threatened was to make a gigantic understatement. Yet we'd been through a great deal already and, characteristically, we set about assaying the damage. Both Joan and I, at first separately and then together, began to look at what we had left that was worth saving. We had endured—often prevailed—this far through so much, what would justify going on? One late night, sitting at the kitchen table, we held what has become for me a memorable conversation.

Incredibly enough, we were trying to act like Charlie Brown trying to kick the football Lucy pulls out from under him each and every year. We were considering the possibility of trying once again, hoping to God that the very foundation—about all we had left—wouldn't come out from under us.

Joan made it quite clear that our marriage, if it continued, would now be different from anything it had ever been. No longer would she treat me as though I was somebody special. In the seventeen years we had been married she had kept me on a pedestal. I was special to her and I was special to my family. No more. She had even forgiven my occasional wanderings and reinstalled me in my special place.

I was incredulous. She had really believed all that crap

she read about me—about her, about all of us? In her way she had. I sat there, shaking my head in disbelief. If I could not be real, warts and all, to my wife, to whom could I be real? Suddenly all of my life, all that I had accomplished, became tinged with a sort of crazy unreality.

We had nothing to lose and everything to gain by trying once again. I have had many opportunities in my life, but my gratitude for this particular opportunity surpasses anything I have ever known.

The second week of January 1972, I flew a T-33 across the country to Patrick Air Force Base in Florida. I had been scheduled to attend a flight managers' meeting to present the various views of the school at Edwards. It was a routine trip and in the middle of the week I went to Washington to prepare for a press conference to announce my retirement.

The Pentagon is a test for anyone's sense of direction and on the morning of Thursday, January 13, I found myself wandering tentatively, feeling vaguely lost, along the rings of the third floor looking for the office of the assistant secretary of defense for public affairs, the man arranging my press conference. I was on the wrong floor in more ways than one.

I noticed a sign on a door that said Chief of Staff United States Air Force at just about the time the door opened. Leading a constellation of more stars than I had ever seen at one time anywhere was Air Force Secretary Robert Seamans. The stars were attached to the shoulders of all of the important generals of the Air Force. Bob shook my hand and said he'd see me later. General John Ryan, the Air Force Chief of Staff and occupant of the office, also greeted me.

The next general to approach me had four stars and I had never met him before, but I was ninety percent certain he was General George Brown, commander of the Air Force Systems Command and, as such, my boss two echelons above me—boss, as in the "big boss." I faltered for a moment and nearly fell into one of the traps of the sort where I find myself sitting at a head table, ahead of a couple of generals and admirals. General Brown recognized me because my face was instantly familiar to the Air Force chain of command. They had probably seen it more times on television and in photographs than they would care to remember. On the other hand, I had never met General Brown.

"Hi, Colonel Aldrin, I'm General Brown."

"Yes, sir, I know. How are you?" Good recovery, I thought.

"Fine. Colonel, did you know your guys lost a plane at the test pilot school this morning?"

Wham, just like that. There is nothing quite like a bit of information of that sort delivered brusquely by a superior.

I inquired about the pilot, and General Brown said he thought, but wasn't sure, that the pilot, whose name he didn't know, was all right.

"The plane was an A-7, Colonel," he said over his shoulder as he continued down the hall.

I searched for a telephone and called Ted. The pilot had bailed out and suffered only minor scratches and bruises. It was the student pilot with the back problem whom the doctors had permitted to fly in spite of our misgivings.

Unnerved, I continued on through the day's appointments. The appointment with Secretary Seamans was extremely cordial, but he did not say whether or not I would be receiving a promotion and by now I didn't really care. There were several other meetings that day and there seemed nothing at all unusual about them other than the fact that my stay in the hospital in San Antonio was never once mentioned, although it was certain nearly every general I saw knew of it.

On Friday, January 14, 1972, I was at the Pentagon bright and early for the press conference at which I would announce my intention to retire. Dan Henkin, the assistant defense secretary for public affairs, was in charge of the proceedings. Before we started, he took me aside and said he had been asked by the general in charge of public affairs to suggest that I not say anything about what I would be doing during my remaining months in the Air Force. (In retrospect, this suggestion struck me as not at all ominous, just puzzling.) The press conference itself was brief and to the point. I made no mention of what I would be doing my last months in the service. Immediately afterward I went back to Los Angeles.

I had two things I wanted to do before going back up to Edwards. One, I wanted to pick up a new car I had ordered for Joan. Two, I wanted to make my first definite move toward becoming a civilian.

Through an attorney who had represented the astronauts in contract negotiations involving outside interests, I had located a lawyer in Los Angeles who would guide me through the complications—financial and otherwise—brought about by such an abrupt change. I was determined that everything go as smoothly as possible.

I returned early Sunday morning to play host to the Empire Test Flight School instructors who had been our hosts a few months before in England. My role as host was mandatory and, under the circumstances, a welcome diversion. Joan and I gave a cocktail party for our British guests, and General White and his wife, Doris, also attended. In the middle of the party Bob took me aside, and after stating his faith in my abilities, he suggested it might be best for the two of us to begin considering what I should do for the rest of my time in the service. He thought it would be easier for me—and give me more free time—if I took on some special work and relinquished command of the school. I said that I preferred to stay on to help institute the curriculum improvements and changes Ted and I had been working on with our staff. General White didn't say I was being removed from my command—he still thought I might not be—but he did believe we had better be prepared for all possibilities.

Early Monday morning, four days after the crash of the A-7, I was playing host at coffee before starting a briefing for the British instructors when a lieutenant arrived to summon me to the school operations office. I excused myself and left immediately.

As I entered the operations office, I instantly knew from the look on everyone's face that another disaster had struck. Another plane, a T-33, had crashed and the two pilots had bailed out.

I left for the base hospital and arrived just as the helicopter carrying the pilots touched down. They were only bruised and scratched. I then had them quickly telephone their families and remained at the hospital until they were released. Bob White arrived soon after me, and that evening, over a drink with Joan and me, he looked up and said, "I'm sure as hell glad we had that conversation last night and not tonight." He was relieved we had speculated on my future before this second crash, and so was I.

Ted and I immediately began to prepare for the accident investigations. I plunged into all the necessary arrangements, forms, and documents and did everything a commandant ought to do—and more than a commandant about to lose his command needs to do. I took particular comfort in the fact that I was capable of confronting two disasters of questionable cause such a short time after I had been unable to function at all in a hospital.

I took care to be especially methodical and thorough. I trusted nothing to luck, because luck was noticeable by its absence. So was fate. My feeling was that if I went down the hall to go to the bathroom, luck and fate would get together and see that I left the bathroom with both my shoes wet.

I was also terribly disappointed. I wanted to continue in my command, but it was quite obvious that wasn't going to happen. I was discouraged that we had not been allowed to submit our findings from the European trip, and disappointed that I wouldn't be around to see the dialogue and changes between the commander, instructors, and students take root. I was proud of the work I had done, particularly since leaving the hospital.

One especially bleak morning after the second accident an incident took place which gave me an enormous sense of satisfaction. One of the instructors stopped me in the hall to say I would be sorely missed. He himself had gone through the school when it was commanded by Chuck Yeager, the pilot who broke the sound barrier. He had always wanted to talk to Yeager, but the custom—the custom I had changed—dictated against it. All he had heard from his commandant was a "Hello" in the hall one day and a "Congratulations," when he graduated. He said the other instructors and students appreciated the changes I had instituted.

Both Ted and I were relieved almost to the point of optimism when we learned there had been witnesses to the first accident. We suspected the pilot had doubled up on maneuvers, thereby getting himself into trouble. The instruments rescued from the wreckage were, at best, inconclusive. The witnesses, an elderly couple driving along the desert, described what they had seen. What they had seen was quite clearly an example of pilot error. What especially relieved me was that Ted, who intended to remain in the service, might get through the hearing with no blemishes on his record. I hoped for the same also, but only because I was leaving the service and was concerned that outsiders not think I was leaving because of the crashes.

The accident board—to put it mildly—was a disappointment to both Ted and me and to the school itself. There was a general on the board, plus several other test pilots who had extensive experience in this type of aircraft. For some reason known only to themselves, the accident board dismissed the testimony of the witnesses and didn't even mention the pilot's history of disabling back problems. Ted and I, with considerable assistance from our staff and a hearing-board member who strongly disagreed with the conclusions, began preparing a strong rebuttal argument. General White agreed completely with our conclusion that pilot error and not supervisory faults were the cause.

The accident-board hearings for the A-7 crash virtually overlapped with the hearings on the T-33 crash. We were no sooner at work on our rebuttal to the first hearing than the conclusions of the second hearing were announced. They faulted supervisory personnel. According to the report, there weren't enough supervisory personnel observing during spin tests of the aircraft. Since I am now free to say so, I wish to say the hearing findings were clearly unrealistic. There was an instructor observing and that is all there need be. That was our requirement. The T-33 had been tested extensively and the students drilled endlessly in spins. They themselves said so at the hearing. What's more, once a pilot is checked out in the aircraft, according to regulations, he can go spin it anywhere without supervision of any sort. Both pilots had flown more hours than are considered necessary to check out in the aircraft. Furthermore, the students were being followed closely by a senior instructor in another aircraft and were under complete radar surveillance throughout their flight.

The hearing board did just so much nit-picking before deciding the blame had to be placed on some handy victims: supervisory personnel. There was one added irony to the conclusions: the president of the board had at one time been commandant of the school. When he was commandant, he had written the rules for spin-tests. To put it mildly, our rules were a far cry from the spin-test rules of the Empire Test Flight School we had found so impressive a few months before.

The new list of brigadier generals came out and I was not at all surprised to find my name was not included. I knew that the list was complete—and could not be changed

—in December, so I could be certain the two crashes were not considerations in my exclusion. I might have been on the list at one time, but if the stay in the hospital in San Antonio didn't do the job, my intention—known early in December—to retire would probably have decided my case. My personal theory—confirmed by others who, like me, have spent over twenty years learning the military ropes—is that my chances for promotion ended when I asked for psychiatric help.

There can, however, be triumphs built out of adversity. They even have a reasonable ratio between them. Joan and I were fighting adversity together and, in the process, growing stronger. We had a common cause bringing us together. She cried when I was not promoted, and I admitted I had entertained some small hopes and was disappointed too. Nevertheless, I accepted the decision and so did Joan. My father, meanwhile—using the retirement promotions of Charles Lindbergh and Richard Byrd as his precedents—continues to campaign for my promotion.

Reflecting back on the previous months it became clear that of the two decisions made in the hospital, one—divorce—proved to be clearly an error, and the second—to retire from the Air Force—to be absolutely correct. In the ten years I had been away I had changed a good deal and so had the Air Force. I could, in time, fit in perfectly, but the rush of time and the rapid technological changes made catching up an enormous undertaking. On the other hand, I had spent over twenty years in some sort of service to my country and I was ready for a change. After returning from the hospital I felt my performance as commandant and my relationship with staff members had been extremely good. We had done much toward revising and streamlining the curriculum based on my observations, suggestions from the staff, and our experience in visiting foreign test-pilot schools. It's unfortunate—and a source of personal regret—

327

that much of what was done was obscured by my retirement announcement and the two accidents.

I was made an offer of a job for my remaining months in the service, one which would require me to move to Los Angeles while Joan and the kids remained to finish the school year.

I had frankly had enough. Joan and I had a scheme of our own. We computed a number of things—from the date of rank to accrued leave and several other factors—and came to the conclusion I could legitimately ask that my retirement be moved back from June to March 1.

I asked General White if he could arrange for us to keep our base quarters so that the kids could finish up the school year. I was agreeable to paying rent if necessary. He said he would handle the matter, and didn't expect any problems with it. My request to retire earlier than planned was accepted.

My successor was announced in fairly short order. Colonel Joe Guthrie, a man I had never met, was the selection. When he arrived two weeks after the second crash I offered him my congratulations and assistance. I don't remember exactly how he said it, but in accepting my offer of assistance he implied quite clearly he sure as hell hoped he would have better luck than I had had. I appreciated this a good deal—it showed he understood what had happened and also knew the working of the system.

On March 1, 1972, I retired. General Jimmy Doolittle came up from Los Angeles for the brief ceremonies, and both General White and Ted Twinting were there, as were all the students and instructors. They seemed to enjoy participating in the ceremonies as one last show of support.

Joan and I packed up the kids, drove to Los Angeles, and looked for the third time at a house we liked. It is located in the western end of the San Fernando Valley in what Joan calls horse country, an apt phrase, since the community was built with horses included in the plans.

It is a big rambling ranch house with a guest house/study, swimming pool, stables, riding ring, lots of trees—we have an endless supply of oranges and tangerines—all spread over two acres of land. For what seemed like an exorbitant price (the real estate prices in Los Angeles are a great deal higher than in Houston, the last place we owned a home) we purchased the house. We spent March, April, and May in our quarters at Edwards splicing our lives together again and waiting for the kids to finish school.

Instead of retiring to my rocking chair—it was broken, anyway—I plunged into furious activity. Cartons and cartons of my lifelong files were transferred from my office to our garage, and completely filled it. There was no room for a car, and only Andy's motorcycle fit. The files needed to be culled and placed in order—an undertaking that proved much larger than I suspected. I have yet to complete it and it has evolved into a sort of ritual. I decide first to clean off my desk, which has a tendency to look as though there has been an explosion in a paper factory. By the time the desk is clean, the mail answered, the checkbooks balanced, and the filing done, it is the end of the month, and gradually it all starts over again.

There was also the business of business. I had energetically overseen every detail of the purchase of the house and the formation of my business by the lawyers.

There was a variety of activities to consider. At least a dozen invitations to speak had to be dealt with, along with a few business offers I had received for my civilian life. Among several business opportunities offered to me was one from Volkswagen of America. They were interested to know if I would be willing to appear in a commercial about their new computer diagnosis service system which they were beginning to install around the country. I responded by saying that I might be interested but that I'd need to know a good deal more about the system myself. Foremost in my mind was a concern that I not appear in any way to be endorsing products left and right. It would, I believe, be abusing my position as an ex-astronaut at the same time diluting whatever credibility I and others like me have among the general public.

The notion of using computers to service automobiles intrigued me for two reasons. Computers of the sort we had developed for use in space had proven so resourceful and dependable that I wanted to know if any general application of their abilities could be made. The second reason was more personal: like millions of other people, my family is plagued with cars whose mechanical problems are difficult to diagnose and constantly irritating.

I made a quick trip East to look over a computer diagnosis and servicing installation and was impressed with what I saw. I checked around and discovered that no American manufacturer at that time had any plans for such a program. I observed easily a dozen tests of the system, and much like the computers we used at NASA the results were quick and highly dependable.

After some thought, I decided that whatever else it was —and it was obviously an attempt to increase sales—the computer system was definitely an advantage to the customer. Volkswagen is, of course, a German product, but a great many American businessmen have prospered mightily because of it. Ideally, the system would catch on and American automotive manufacturers would be forced to develop similar systems in the search for more customers. I agreed to make the commercials with specific limitations on the amount of exposure they would receive, with the additional requirement that I appear to be endorsing not the sale of Volkswagens themselves but rather a service offered by Volkswagen.

With Joan as my coach, I rehearsed and memorized my two-page script and, to my surprise, found the actual making of the commercials rather easy. Joan, on the other hand, sat anxiously by, worrying I'd forget my lines or trip over my feet.

Neither Joan nor I noticed that by the middle of April I was beginning to turn more and more of the work over to my attorney. If anything, we were relieved to have someone to turn to.

Meanwhile, I stopped work on the garageful of files and began to go for long walks on the desert. I usually left shortly after the morning mail delivery. Opening the mail has always been a pleasant sort of ritual for me, but now it began to bother me. I worried that some person somewhere would ask something of me I could not easily provide. The smallest problem grew to enormous proportions as I contemplated it. I thought my skin had toughened, but I was devastated one day when I received a letter criticizing me for the Volkswagen computer-service commercials and accusing me of being un-American.

There was one thing I had to do that I found impossible: to admit to myself that it was beginning to happen again, that a depression was setting in. I had been warned of the possibility by Dr. Sparks; nevertheless I had had the supreme confidence to believe that once well I'd stay well. That my supreme confidence might have been sheer arrogance was inadmissible.

Joan confronted me whenever she thought I was receptive to conversation. I assured her that everything would be fine once we were in our new home, which I was now telling her we shouldn't have bought—it was too expensive and we didn't have enough money. Thoughts of the future and all of its uncertainties literally set me to shaking.

On June 3, 1972, a week before school let out, we moved. Three cars packed with animals and possessions formed the front of a caravan followed a few hours later by a big van. The only thing we left behind was the desert tortoise who had taken up residence in Mike's closet.

Within a week Joan had us installed in our new home.

There were quite a lot of things that still needed doing—the venting system for the washer and dryer was unsafe, the three toilets leaked, pipes were clogged, and a number of lights did not work, nor did the air-conditioning system. I made a great show of interest in assuming my role as ranking repairman, but it was all a show. I couldn't get going. It was all too much.

Late in June, on an unseasonably warm Friday evening, the kids were away and Joan and I were having a drink by the pool when she made her move. She pushed and wheedled at me until I admitted I needed help once again. She then told me that if I didn't get in touch with a doctor Monday morning, she was going to do it for me.

I did it myself. I telephoned Dr. Sparks in San Antonio, and after several minutes of conversation he told me that he didn't believe my depression this time was in any way as severe as the one that had hospitalized me. He suggested I get in contact with Dr. Flinn. I had last seen him the day I was on my way to San Antonio convinced he would put me in a booby hatch somewhere to cover up the fact that he had approved me for the astronaut program.

I telephoned Dr. Flinn immediately and went to see him that same day.

Over the next several days we explored my immediate problem: how to get going again and therapeutically work my way out of the depression. Once I had seen him, I felt a surge of optimism that together we could not only deal with my condition but overcome it.

My problem was aggravated by the abrupt changes brought about by leaving the service and a completely structured life. Joan and I had both been warned by a number of people that the change might prove difficult, but we dismissed the possibility. After all, before returning to the Air Force we had spent seven years at NASA which isn't at all like being in the service. Or so we thought.

All of my adult life had been lived in the shelter of the

service, as had Joan's. If NASA was different, it was only a matter of degree. NASA did not have the rather rigid structure of the service, but it was even more insular and protective. My apprehension about our impending independence was more difficult to deal with than the actual independence itself.

The last several months in the Air Force had been discouraging for me. My prominence as an ex-astronaut had made it all but impossible to disappear unnoticed back into the service and had accentuated the difficulties of my final departure. The two accidents would have been difficult for any commander anywhere. But I was made to feel expendable and my pride was deeply wounded. My depression about all of these things was natural, Dr. Flinn explained, and to be expected from any man.

What had made it especially difficult for me as an individual was the fact that I felt I was not entitled to have such emotions. My goal was command of every situation in which I might find myself, and such an aim was unattainable. When I sensed I was not in full command, there was no harsher judge of my actions than I myself.

To facilitate my treatment I began taking medication again. The pills were called Imipramine. During the first few weeks of treatment, the depression deepened, then began to lift—but along with increased dosage, reactions to the medicine began.

I was in Reno giving a speech, which I thought went very poorly, when things began going seriously wrong. Shortly after I finished the speech I began perspiring heavily and within minutes I was afraid I couldn't walk. Joan canceled our dinner with our hosts and coaxed me up, holding my arm all the way back to our hotel room. I spent the night awake, terrified by the thought of sleep. I sat on the edge of the bed, refusing to move. I felt unable to walk and afraid to crawl. Joan, by now as terrified as I was, but much more in control, canceled our plans to go to Lake Tahoe for two days and the next day, when I was considerably improved, we flew to Los Angeles. We went directly to UCLA and Dr. Flinn. He told us such side effects of the medication were not at all uncommon. My recovery was almost immediate.

The dosage from then on steadily decreased. I went from eight pills a day—four in the morning and four in the evening—to one per day within the next month. The effect of the pills is cumulative. It takes some time, usually several weeks, before their effect takes hold, and withdrawal responses also do not set in for some time. I waited anxiously to see what would happen as the dosage went steadily down. It became a kind of obsession with me because I wanted to take the least amount of medicine I could.

To my vast relief, there was virtually no onset of depression of any kind as the medicine was withdrawn. With renewed confidence, helped by weekly sessions with Dr. Flinn, I plunged into my first summer as a civilian.

There were a number of speeches scheduled, all involving some travel, but I kept my appointments to a minimum. I was also doing consultation work but it in no way consumed a great deal of time.

In July, Joan and I accepted an invitation from the Houston Chamber of Commerce to attend the city's celebration of the third anniversary of the lunar landing. It was a kind of test, really, to return to the old haunts, and I suspected Mike and possibly Neil would be attending. Neither did, but there were a number of astronauts in attendance. I wrote a short speech which, to my astonishment, was received with a standing ovation. At the end of it, I suggested there be an annual meeting of the ten—there are now twelve—of us who had been on the lunar surface.

I spent nearly all summer at home. I wanted time with my family and for once I had it. While Joan told people I was having a delayed adolescence, I grew a beard. My dad came to visit and his reaction to my beard—mostly gray—virtually severed all diplomatic relations for several days.

I stood by in fascination—and drove back and forth to our local Honda dealer more times than I can remember—as Andy spent the summer emerging as a first-class motorcycle mechanic. His interest in technical matters is exactly as mine was at his age. Of my three children, Andy is the most like me. He loves football, anything technical, and is rather shy. When I look at him, I see myself. Were it not for the obvious differences in clothing and photographic styles, our photographs at age fourteen would be identical —except, that is, for his hair, which is quite long and usually hides his eyes.

Jan is very much her mother's daughter, both in manner and appearance. She is a young woman now, but not old enough yet to be more interested in boys than in horses. She has appeared in her first play and shares Joan's interest in the theater. Of the three she is the best student. Joan feels that at school Jan is a classic overachiever and we find ourselves in the ironic situation of urging our sons to study while trying to get Jan to spend less time on her schoolwork.

Mike is nearly an adult. He has his own car and a harem —girls gravitate to Mike. He reads a good deal and, like his mother, is interested in the theater. He continues to be an extremely sensitive and perceptive young man who is rapidly maturing into a responsible adult.

As a family we became involved with VIVA, the organization supporting the prisoners of war and the missing in action in Southeast Asia, and we all wore the organization's special bracelets. Of the five POW-MIA men whose bracelets we wore, three were released by the North Vietnamese after the cease-fire, and my good friend Sam Johnson was one of them. To each we sent a plaque Joan and I designed which contained, along with a photograph of the moon, a small American flag and an *Apollo 11* patch which I had taken to the moon. At the bottom of the plaque is the POW bracelet, with the date of release engraved next to the date of capture, along with the name of the family member who wore the bracelet.

Joan and I took advantage of the summer to take a deep breath and test our new beginning. We made a number of short trips together, got to know some of our new neighbors, and, quite simply, tried to be as lazy as possible in a household as busy as ours. There is an honesty and openness to our relationship now, and perhaps more than most couples, we have a vast pool of experience—trials and tribulations mostly—to draw on to secure our future. For the first time there is a feeling of contentment with our lives. Certainly, there can be no turmoil to match what we have already known. We have survived together and now we want to prevail whenever possible. How happy I am with the way things turned out after the episode in Acapulco and all that came before and after it.

Maika chose summer to get pregnant. The suspense about who the father was was almost unbearable. We were certain it was the sheepdog across the street, although Mike insisted the father was Slodey. Mike was right. Maika produced a litter of seven beautiful borzoi puppies. They were born in our guest house, which is actually my office, and they stayed there until they began tearing up the place.

The day after they moved out, the twenty-four chicks I ordered from Sears arrived and, in their incubator, moved in. Yelping was replaced by noisy chirping. I bought them on an impulse and because we already had a chicken coop and two roosters, and we all like fresh eggs.

Throughout the summer, the animal count at our house grew. Andy and I stocked the pond near our swimming pool with lily pads and fish. Mike came home from a week of oceanographic studies at summer camp with a black kitten, which he named Raven. Raven tyrannized the entire household and particularly concentrated her efforts on Slodey, Maika, and our two adult Siamese.

Missy, our mongrel dog, who has been around for years in spite of her heart problem and still eagerly goes all the way down our driveway every morning for the paper, gave the kitten back as good as she gave. Although we got her for Joan and the kids, Missy is devoted to me. In Houston, at Edwards, and in our new home, whenever I was depressed, Missy would not leave my side. She cried whenever she was left.

The crowning touch was added to the animal population at our house this summer. Mike came back from a weekend visiting friends at Edwards with a solution to our constantly growing lawns: a black goat, which he named Annie. We had her only two days before Mike dropped the rest of the news over breakfast: Annie was pregnant. She produced three kids.

It might be said Joan and I lost the animal population control war, except that we've enjoyed the animals as much as our kids have.

I don't know if my belated attempt to be a full-time father and husband was successful, but the summer for me was an experience different from any other I have had in my lifetime. It was, among other things, very therapeutic.

Business commitments were met, but for once they were secondary. They increased noticeably as school started, but that was planned. I am far too young to really retire and I enjoy being involved in various projects. Besides, I have a family to support, reason enough for some business involvements.

For one week I immersed myself in the annual convention of the National Association for Mental Health and emerged as a director at large for the organization. My goal with this fine group of people is to act as a catalyst to open discussions about mental health among the general public.

Late in the summer I also began making notes for this book. I had thought of starting earlier, but I was unable to bring myself to say what I felt had to be said unless there was some assurance of a happy ending.

There is every assurance now. I still see Dr. Flinn and will probably continue going for some time. Our sessions are a kind of touchstone for me, since it is there that I attempt to carefully sort out my priorities and establish what it is I wish to do. My appointments are also reassuring because they provide a time to see how far I've come.

During the summer, Thomas Eagleton was briefly the Democratic vice-presidential candidate. I sat rooted to the television as news of his severe depression some years earlier came out. I read the articles in newspapers and magazines telling of depressions and how they were treated. As did millions of others, I was reassured when I read articles in which psychiatrists said that depression is an illness that is common but is generally kept secret. They encourage bringing the problem into the open and so praised Eagleton for publicly admitting his difficulties.

I participated in what will probably be remembered as the greatest technological achievement in the history of this country. I traveled to the moon, but the most significant voyage of my life began when I returned from where no man had been before.

When I began this book I had two intentions. I wanted it to be as honest as possible and to present the reality of my life and career not as mere fact but as I perceived the truth to be. The second and more important intention was that I wanted to stand up and be counted.

About the Authors

COLONEL EDWIN E. "BUZZ" ALDRIN, JR., graduated from West Point and received a doctor of science degree from MIT. After leaving the space program he served as commander of the Air Force Test Pilots School. Since his retirement he has been serving as a director or consultant to companies involved in aerospace, computers, cable television, insurance, and laser television, and as a director at large for the National Association for Mental Health. He lives with his wife, three teenagers, and a large variety of animals near Los Angeles, California.

WAYNE WARGA writes about the lively arts for the *Los Angeles Times* and is editor of the *Times* Sunday Calendar section. He was formerly assistant entertainment editor for *Life* magazine, and as a reporter covered everything from civil war in the Dominican Republic to Martin Luther King's marches to seven space flights. He, his wife, and young son live in Studio City, California.